THE FABER BOOK OF
CONTEMPORARY AUSTRALIAN
SHORT STORIES

ff

The Faber Book of
CONTEMPORARY
AUSTRALIAN
SHORT
STORIES

Edited by Murray Bail

faber and faber
LONDON · BOSTON

First published in 1988
by Faber and Faber Limited
3 Queen Square London WC1N 3AU

Photoset by Parker Typesetting Service Leicester
Printed in Great Britain by
Richard Clay Ltd Bungay Suffolk
All rights reserved

British Library Cataloguing in Publication Data

The Faber book of contemporary Australian
short stories.
1. Short stories, Australian   2. Australian
fiction – 20th century
I. Bail, Murray
823'.01'08994[FS]   PR9617.32
ISBN 0-571-14763-1
ISBN 0-571-15083-7 Pbk

Contents

Acknowledgements

The editor and publishers thank the following for permission to reproduce the stories in this volume: Angus and Robertson Publishers for 'Gretel' by Hal Porter from *Selected Stories*, 1971, 'Mother' by Judah Waten from *Alien Son*, 1952, and 'The Voice' by Peter Cowan from *The Empty Street*, 1965; Australian Literary Management for 'Five Acre Virgin' by Elizabeth Jolley from *Stories* (Fremantle Arts Centre Press, 1984), and 'Frederick the Great Returns to Fairfields', and 'Hostages' by Fay Zwicky from *Hostages* (Fremantle Arts Centre Press, 1983); Barbara Brooks for 'Summer in Sydney' from *Leaving Queensland* (Sea Cruise Books, 1983); Chatto and Windus and Curtis Brown for 'The Sun in Winter' by David Malouf from *Antipodes*, 1985; Rosemary Creswell for 'From a Bush Log Book: Going into the Heartlands with the Wrong Person at Christmas' and 'Libido and Life Lessons' by Frank Moorhouse from *Forty–Seventeen* (Penguin Books Australia, 1987); Curtis Brown (Aust) Pty Ltd for 'The Persimmon Tree' by Marjorie Barnard from *The Persimmon Tree and Other Stories* (Angus and Robertson, 1943; Virago, 1985); Fremantle Arts Centre Press for 'New Year' by Joan London from *Sister Ships*, 1986; Hale and Iremonger for 'John Gilbert's Dog' by David Brooks from *The Book of Sei and Other Stories*, 1985 (Faber and Faber Limited, 1988); Elizabeth Harrower for 'The Cost of Things'; A. M. Heath for 'The Meeting' by Shirley Hazzard from *People in Glass Houses* (Macmillan, 1967), published in the United States of America by Viking Penguin Inc., © 1964, 1966, 1967, by Shirley Hazzard by permission of McIntosh & Otis Inc.; McPhee Gribble Publishers for 'Melpo' and 'A Man in the Laundrette' by Beverley Farmer from *Milk*, 1983 and *Hometime*, 1985, 'The Life of Art' by Helen Garner from *Postcards from Surfers*, 1985, and 'Fires on the Beach' by Barry Hill from *A Rim of Blue*, 1978; Barbara Mobbs for 'Down at the

ACKNOWLEDGEMENTS

Dump' and 'Clay' by Patrick White from *The Burnt Ones*, 1964, and 'What We Say' by Helen Garner; Gerald Murnane for 'The Only Adam'; Penguin Books Australia for 'A Harmless Affair' and 'My Friend, Lafe Tilly' by Christina Stead from *Ocean of Story*, 1985; Dal Stivens for 'The Wonderfully Intelligent Sheep-Dog' from *Selected Stories* (Angus and Robertson, 1969); University of Queensland Press for 'American Dreams' and 'Do You Love Me?' by Peter Carey from *The Fat Man in History*, 1974 (Faber and Faber Limited, 1980) and *War Crimes*, 1979, 'Slow Dissolve' by Kate Grenville from *Bearded Ladies*, 1984, 'A Rat in the Building' by Olga Masters from *The Home Girls*, 1982, 'The Sybarites' and 'The Man of Slow Feeling' by Michael Wilding from *Aspects of the Dying Process*, 1972 and *The West Midland Underground*, 1975.

Introduction

Recalling her years in Manhattan, Christina Stead has described the city as Baghdad on the Hudson. 'The thing ... which is absolutely striking is that they all do tell tales. New York promotes story-telling ... every day generates new stories and cycles of stories.' Born in Sydney (1902) Christina Stead may have merely recognized a more congested, thickly textured version of her own place. The habit of story-telling has always been strong in Australia. Oral stories were a constant from the first morning of the European settlement when words must have made an especially loud noise and travelled long distances. There was so much to tell, so much emptiness to fill. There were plenty of tales of endurance, of 'characters', battlers in the yarn-spinning sense: ludicrous incidents, bush tragedies, anecdotes ('Remember old Joe?'), hard-luck stories. It would be hard to imagine another country built upon so many hard-luck stories.

The stories were not tall so much as horizontal. All-male, spoken in the flat voice, they travelled out from the small-town bars, camp fires and out-stations of the barren interior, reaching the coast, though not much farther, unhindered or uncorrected by the obstacles of subtlety, depth or world knowledge. The harshness and the emptiness of the land – which is noticeable even a few yards in from the coast – gave an immediate aura of sorrow to an otherwise ordinary incident, enough to induce a bout of droll nodding in the audience. And it was likely during the telling of stories a crow would croak out a mournful lament or a rude bird peculiar to the land interrupt with a raucous laugh.

For a long time the interior appeared to be a more unusual place than the few cities and towns hugging the coast. Out there in the bush people seemed to be more like 'characters', and were at least clearly defined. A man's actions were thrown into sharp relief against that largely vacant landscape, the landscape demanding a severe stoicism: all useful for the anecdote and the yarn, and providing a bleak comfort to the audience in the coastal cities. There were some very funny people out there.

The bush encouraged simplicities. It bequeathed to the nation a subculture of yarners, born liars, 'illywhackers', men who talk their lives away while rolling a cigarette in one hand, bush psychologists, bullshit artists, parliamentarians addicted to homilies and cracking jokes; everyone has a black-sheep uncle somewhere with a slightly wrecked face who can tell a good story. The habit was largely proletarian, often with a touch of Irish, and beneath it – blame the 'bush', its harshness – was an easy sentimentalism.

The written stories which naturally followed had little trouble finding a readership. At various times in Australia's short literary history, especially after the 1940s, the stories published have reached epidemic numbers, similar to the great rabbit plagues which chewed up vast areas of the best grazing land. To this day the variety of newspapers and serious, middle and low journals publishing stories, as well as pocket-size magazines and a tabloid consisting of nothing but short stories, the annual and special-subject anthologies, the Selected and Collected editions and so on, are out of all proportion to the population. In any given year since the 1940s the story collections in print in Australia would probably exceed those in England by British writers. Most Australian novelists, poets even, and historians too, have obeyed this urge to publish stories; and the high reputations of a number of writers, notably Henry Lawson, and some in this present anthology, rest on nothing but short stories. It is entirely logical to find Lawson's gaunt profile with walrus moustache and thirsty lips reproduced on the Australian ten-dollar note, although needless to say he was chronically short of ready cash during his own lifetime. (Placing a short-story writer on the pedestal of a banknote. Can there be another country which has – ?)

Lawson died in 1922. It may be fairly said that the landscape, largely via Lawson, exerted its power of dryness on Australian literature to well past the Second World War; and even long after that, the landscape encroached upon written stories the way in summer it leap-frogged into the towns and the suburbs of the sprawling cities. Because of the landscape's size and its dramatic emptiness the ratio in Australian stories between landscape and characters remained low – out of balance. Writers allowed the landscape to do their hard work. Remember, the very mention of the flat horizon or a few dry sticks was enough to provide that air of stoicism or impending tragedy. Whereas the tales told by Christina Stead's everyday New Yorkers would be curiosities about the interaction between people merely accepting the surroundings, demanding of the story tellers a natural depth and complexity. (In Australian poetry and painting the landscape remains to this day the dominating force. The main achievements celebrate the peculiarities of local space and emptiness, an extreme Antipodean version of the sublime.)

It was not until the 1940s and 1950s that writers began turning their attention more to the cities, where most of them had lived all along. But there in tone and subject it was still difficult to shake off the national dryness. Much of this cosmopolitan story-telling continued to obey the matter-of-fact empiricism of the bush. Keep it plain, nothing fancy, was the prevailing instinct. Marjorie Barnard's 'The Persimmon Tree' of 1943, the first story in the present anthology, offers an amazing rejection of this. Otherwise, the stories of this period were generally underwritten fictions that drew energy from the reader instead of feeding with energy. And they matched the political climate: a drought time of conservatism, conformity and censorship, the R. G. Menzies era.

Stoicism, pragmatism: the virtues which had built up this remote land seemed to have played havoc with the development of Australian literature. And the laconic speech patterns seemed to encourage a flat form of statement, little more.

In what amounted to a manifesto Patrick White, in 1958, condemned the national literature as a 'dreary dun-coloured offspring of journalistic realism' – justifiably, a much-quoted phrase – and with his novels set an alternative example, 'fresh forms out of the rocks and sticks of words', as he put it, agriculturally. His outstanding collection of stories, *The Burnt Ones*, was published in 1964. By then many writers had transported themselves or their subjects overseas, gaining, it seemed, an instant complexity. Others arrived from Europe as migrants carrying suitcases of stories made of strong material; indeed, the migrant experience continues to add that extra dimension to the Australian short story. And there were developments towards a lush ornate prose – a kind of spite-encrusted realism. At least it had the merit of passion and colour.

The labours of these rather lonely pioneers pushed back the dry tangle of conservatism. In the space cleared, characters moved to the foreground (still squinting, waving at flies), and now even remained indoors; imagination and more subtle perceptions were then demanded of both writer and reader. Technically, the stories from the 1950s on are generally far more accomplished than those pre-war.

A new generation in the 1970s could survey the progress from something like a cleared plateau. If there was some gratitude and interest there was still dissatisfaction.

For all the gains there appeared to be a gap between what they saw being published and what they themselves had experienced – and written. Connected, and almost more serious, was the curious, continuing lethargy in many of the stories. They were surrounded by quite a formidable wall of such stories, so it seemed. To penetrate, to at least offer alternatives, energized their writing. Being in the minority encouraged extremes of form. There was the feeling of having to wave to attract attention. Many in this younger generation consciously, deliberately, wrote against the residue of stolid realism. There were cases of rewriting the established classic, the avant-garde strategy of provocative revision. The new writing was helped along by the young writers themselves becoming editors, being invited to edit anthologies and so on, and an increasing critical interest.

Instead of Lawson and the bush they looked to the linguistic energy of the Americans; the *Paris Review*, *New Yorker*, *Transatlantic Review* were more likely to be found on their shelves than local literary journals. The inventions of the Latin Americans, notably Borges and Márquez, and later Calvino, had an influence. They showed what was possible. By giving realism an extra twist a story, a proposition, a state of mind could acquire an extra force. And to more than one writer such a twist seemed necessary against the wall of ordinary realism. If a view of the old landscape crept in it was often for its bottom-of-the-sea strangeness, such an extra-ordinary realism as to appear almost as a nervous 'surrealism'. It was allowed – and it was interesting – to speculate on general ideas rather than traditional character analysis: fiction where the writer's thoughts assume the signs of character.

From the 1970s on, a large percentage of stories were being written in the first person; and there was of course the danger there of confusing fiction with the art of the self. Women's fiction became prominent in this period, especially in the 1980s, accounting for much of the sharpest, most felt writing. It is distinguished – if it can be summarized – by an extreme subjectivity, a willingness, perhaps a necessity in the writer to come well forward on the page, in the process giving clear shape to herself, while mapping a position on the gap between men and women, between words and actions. It can be argued that this is a narrow area to be concentrating on, yet some of the most accomplished male fiction can seem remote by comparison.

The freshness in this recent Australian fiction is due to the writers' acceptance of place – they could forget about all that. Many stories are no longer set in Australia, or in any recogniz-able place at all. The feature is a willingness to take risks – intellectual, emotional, stylistic. And surely these can be seen as reflecting the writers' lives. These writers display a con-fidence whether in the treatment of dialogue, of sex, of the innocent abroad, or in the subject of language and the process of story-telling itself. And with it came humour, of the self-deprecating kind (often emerging when a writer did place one foot back into the bush), more experiments, some reaching towards the abstract. It spread throughout the 1970s and 1980s, this new confidence, as a kind of literary myxomatosis, reducing any remaining dun-coloured realism to a few pockets.

In retrospect – and in short – it was never 'realism' or 'naturalism' which held back Australian short fiction, but the exceptionally dry treatment of it.

MURRAY BAIL
June 1987

MARJORIE BARNARD

The Persimmon Tree

I saw the spring come once and I won't forget it. Only once. I had been ill all the winter and I was recovering. There was no more pain, no more treatments or visits to the doctor. The face that looked back at me from my old silver mirror was the face of a woman who had escaped. I had only to build up my strength. For that I wanted to be alone, an old and natural impulse. I had been out of things for quite a long time and the effort of returning was still too great. My mind was transparent and as tender as new skin. Everything that happened, even the commonest things, seemed to be happening for the first time, and had a delicate hollow ring like music played in an empty auditorium.

I took a flat in a quiet, blind street, lined with English trees. It was one large room, high ceilinged with pale walls, chaste as a cell in a honeycomb, and furnished with the passionless, standardized grace of a fashionable interior decorator. It had the afternoon sun which I prefer because I like my mornings shadowy and cool, the relaxed end of the night prolonged as far as possible. When I arrived the trees were bare and still against the lilac dusk. There was a block of flats opposite, discreet, well tended, with a wide entrance. At night it lifted its oblongs of rose and golden light far up into the sky. One of its windows was immediately opposite mine. I noticed that it was always shut against the air. The street was wide but because it was so quiet the window seemed near. I was glad to see it always shut because I spend a good deal of time at my window and it was the only one that might have overlooked me and flawed my privacy.

I liked the room from the first. It was a shell that fitted without touching me. The afternoon sun threw the shadow of a tree on my light wall and it was in the shadow that I first noticed that the bare twigs were beginning to swell with buds. A watercolour, pretty and innocuous, hung on that wall. One day I asked the silent woman who serviced me to take it down. After that the shadow of the tree had the wall to itself and I felt cleared and tranquil as if I had expelled the last fragment of grit from my mind.

I grew familiar with all the people in the street. They came and went with a surprising regularity and they all, somehow, seemed to be cut to a very correct pattern. They were part of the *mise-en-scène*, hardly real at all and I never felt the faintest desire to become acquainted with any of them. There was one woman I noticed, about my own age. She lived over the way. She had been beautiful I thought, and was still handsome with a fine tall figure. She always wore dark clothes, tailor made, and there was reserve in her every movement. Coming and going she was always alone, but you felt that that was by her own choice, that everything she did was by her own steady choice. She walked up the steps so firmly, and vanished so resolutely into the discreet muteness of the building opposite, that I felt a faint, a very faint, envy of anyone who appeared to have her life so perfectly under control.

There was a day much warmer than anything we had had, a still, warm, milky day. I saw as soon as I got up that the window opposite was open a few inches, 'Spring comes even to the careful heart,' I thought. And the next morning not only was the window open but there was a row of persimmons set out carefully and precisely on the sill, to ripen in the sun. Shaped like a young woman's breasts their deep, rich, golden-orange colour seemed just the highlight that the morning's spring tranquillity needed. It was almost a shock to me to see them there. I remembered at home when I was a child there was a grove of persimmon trees down one side of the house. In the autumn they had blazed deep red, taking your breath away. They cast a rosy light into rooms on that side of the house as if a fire were burning outside. Then the leaves fell and left the pointed dark gold fruit clinging to the bare branches. They never lost their strangeness – magical, Hesperidean trees. When I saw the *Firebird* danced my heart moved painfully because I remembered the persimmon trees in the early morning against the dark windbreak of the loquats. Why did I always think of autumn in springtime?

Persimmons belong to autumn and this was spring. I went to the window to look again. Yes, they were there, they were real. I had not imagined them, autumn fruit warming to a ripe transparency in the spring sunshine. They must have come, expensively packed in sawdust, from California or have lain all winter in storage. Fruit out of season.

It was later in the day when the sun had left the sill that I saw the window opened and a hand come out to gather the persimmons. I saw a woman's figure against the curtains. *She* lived there. It was her window opposite mine.

Often now the window was open. That in itself was like the breaking of a bud. A bowl of thick cream pottery, shaped like a boat, appeared on the sill. It was planted, I think, with bulbs. She used to water it with one of those tiny, long-spouted, hand-painted cans that you use for refilling vases, and I saw her gingerly loosening the earth with a silver table fork. She didn't look up or across the street. Not once.

Sometimes on my leisurely walks I passed her in the street. I knew her quite well now, the texture of her skin, her hands, the set of her clothes, her movements. The way you know people when you are sure you will never be put to the test of speaking to them. I could have found out her name quite easily. I had only to walk into the vestibule of her block and read it in the list of tenants, or consult the visiting card on her door. I never did.

She was a lonely woman and so was I. That was a barrier, not a link. Lonely women have something to guard. I was not exactly lonely. I had stood my life on a shelf, that was all. I could have had a dozen friends round me all day long. But there wasn't a friend I loved and trusted above all the others, no lover, secret or declared. She had, I supposed, some nutrient hinterland on which she drew.

The bulbs in her bowl were shooting. I could see the pale new-green spears standing out of the dark loam. I was quite interested in them, wondered what they would be. I expected tulips, I don't know why. Her window was open all day long now, very fine thin curtains hung in front of it and these were never parted. Sometimes they moved but it was only in the breeze.

The trees in the street showed green now, thick with budded leaves. The shadow pattern on my wall was intricate and rich. It was no longer an austere winter pattern as it had been at first. Even the movement of the branches in the wind seemed different. I used to lie looking at the shadow when I rested in the afternoon. I was always tired then and so more permeable to impressions. I'd think about the buds, how pale and tender they were, but how implacable. The way an unborn child is implacable. If man's world were in ashes the spring would still come. I watched the moving pattern and my heart stirred with it in frail, half-sweet melancholy.

One afternoon I looked out instead of in. It was growing late and the sun would soon be gone, but it was warm. There was gold dust in the air, the sunlight had thickened. The shadows of trees and buildings fell, as they sometimes do on a fortunate day, with dramatic grace. *She* was standing there just behind the curtains, in a long dark wrap, as if she had come from her bath and was going to dress, early, for the evening. She stood so long and so still, staring out – at the budding trees, I thought – that tension began to accumulate in my mind. My blood ticked like a clock. Very slowly she raised her arms and the gown fell from her. She stood there naked, behind the veil of the curtains, the scarcely distinguishable but unmistakable form of a woman whose face was in shadow.

I turned away. The shadow of the burgeoning bough was on the white wall. I thought my heart would break.

CHRISTINA STEAD

A Harmless Affair

Everything went right in this love affair from the beginning. It began just after Lydia had thought, 'It's spring and an empty spring; it's years since I felt really in love, I must be getting stupid – never looking outside my eyes, never longing for anything else.' The next day she went to a party and there met a lot of distinguished people, people who had all arrived at their destinations. Lydia hated this sort of party – to be with people who were famous made her feel that life had stopped and there was nothing more to live for, whereas she wanted to keep on living, and for that reason preferred people who had not arrived at the top, or anywhere else, but who still nourished impossible ambitions and desires. There had been some unpleasantness about the invitation, on that account. The woman invited her: she wrote and accepted the invitation and she had not known the woman was famous: she only found it out after. And then the woman had not invited Lydia's husband. Lydia was known as 'Miss Parsons' in the laboratory and so she often used the name outside. This woman was a doctor, a simple ordinary woman, and after accepting the invitation, Lydia had discovered that she was not only Dr Brown, but also Mary Cohoet, a great social light and humanitarian, and one who was so far above the battle that she believed in meeting people from all strata of society – radicals, conservatives, revolutionary artists, writers in society papers and so on. Lydia had been invited because she had done some work in bacteriology and was still a young woman, and had travelled – she had some social graces in fact, although her parents were very poor.

Lydia put on a French dress and shoes and arrived late: the studio room in the duplex apartment was nearly full, people were drinking sherry and cocktails, and yet there was a flat, round-shouldered air in the room, which revealed, at a glance, that the guest of honour had not yet arrived. He was a man who had lived in China a long time and was going to make a plea for aid for the Chinese people.

Lydia felt very much at her ease, for a wonder, that day. It was an early spring day: thin sunlight slanted through the great studio windows and made the scattered people look untidy. Lydia saw she was the best-dressed woman there – not the richest dressed, but the woman with the best cut frock. The hostess was even a little surprised at her appearance, evidently, and began to introduce her to the people there. Lydia tried to remember the names, but only seized one here and there. There was a line-up of young men more or less ill dressed standing in the sun, an accidental line-up – they had been standing in a group and the circle had opened out into a parade line when the distinguished hostess appeared. Dr Brown named them.

'Dr Lyall, my cousin, Dr West, Roy Finch, Captain Paul Charters, Herr von Wirtz . . .' and so on. After one or two more introductions they had reached the other end of the room. Lydia received a cocktail and was left to herself. Seeing no one there she knew and everyone awkward, she turned back to the group, which again opened into a parade line when she approached and going straight to a tall young man with a black thicket of hair, said, 'Did Dr Brown say Paul Charters, or Paul Charteris?' He laughed, 'Well, she says Charters, but *I* call it Charteris.'

'Then you're the journalist and soldier,' Lydia said confidently. He laughed, 'Yes. I'm the journalist and soldier.'

The other men had discreetly moved away by this.

'We have all your books at home,' said Lydia. She bubbled with uncommon good spirits.

'All,' she went on: 'so if you ever find one's missing, come and get it at our place. My husband's a great admirer of yours.' Charteris was in a good temper: for some reason, she beamed at Charteris, she felt idiotic and yet delighted. Dr Brown tore them away from each other to introduce the guest of honour, Mr Henri Lafargue. Lydia began to chat with Lafargue in an inspired fashion: she became terrified, for fear that this singular animation would leave her in the middle of a sentence and Lafargue would find her stupid. But no, Dr

Brown tore Lafargue away from her, with something of a frown; she had no right to hog the guest of honour, she knew, but she was in a very strange exhilarated state and did not wish to come back to earth.

Later in the evening, Dr Brown came back, 'I did not know you were married. How stupid you must think me not to have invited your husband too. Please forgive me.' Lydia was puzzled, then remembered she had mentioned her husband to Paul Charteris.

She was different that evening from any time in her life. She liked a lot of people immensely: she invited at least half a dozen of them to come to their apartment and meet her husband. She came away by herself and walked a long way by herself in the dark, missing several subway entrances on purpose. There was plenty of time to go home and take up the cordial connubial relations she enjoyed with her husband.

About a week later, Charteris telephoned at ten o'clock in the morning, asking if she had really meant her invitation and if he could come and see them. Suddenly the same confident exhilarated mood took her and she answered, 'Yes, of course, whenever you like,' but in a voice and mood quite unlike herself.

'Can I choose my own date?' asked Charteris.

'Of course.'

'Any time?'

'Any time.'

'Thanks,' said Charteris and rang off.

She told her husband that the famous Paul Charteris was really coming to see them. But he did not telephone again and she almost forgot him. Then a month later, he telephoned again, 'Hello Lydia,' he said coolly: 'can I come and see you today?'

'Yes, of course.'

'At three o'clock?'

'Yes.'

'Thanks,' said Charteris, and rang off.

Lydia scarcely gave a second's thought to his coming, although generally she fussed round the house, tidied herself up for hours before even the most uninteresting visitor arrived.

Charteris came at four o'clock. 'I'm sorry,' he said. 'I was with Anna Brown, getting things ready for Lafargue's lecture. How are you Lydia?'

Lydia felt herself trembling with joy. 'This is my husband, Tom Dunne,' she said. It was with a vague disappointment that she saw the two men take an immediate liking to each other.

Charteris' coat was greasy and old, his hair uncombed and his skin was bad: she could see he was not living well and that he was over-tired. Just as they sat down, and her husband had begun some question about Charteris' work in China, the telephone rang and Tom said, 'I know that's for me, that's my broker,' with the good natured parade of influence he sometimes made, and he dashed to the telephone and began chaffing the broker, calling him by his first name and putting on a wonderful variety show for the benefit of Charteris and herself. She sat down in his vacated chair and said to Charteris, 'You have been over-working, haven't you?' Charteris looked straight at her, and said,

'Oh Lydia, I never had any of the luck in life,' he hung his head and then suddenly looked again and smiled softly.

'How do you mean, Paul?' She felt towards him as towards Tom in their quieter marital moments.

'I have no luck,' he said looking at her with meaning. What meaning? She could not quite believe that he meant what he seemed to mean, that is, that she was already married. Tom had suddenly ceased his jokes and cutting-up at the telephone and was finishing his conversation in brief businesslike words.

'I didn't know you were married,' said Charteris. 'Anna Brown didn't know either.' He said it very coolly, with wide open eyes on her face and he seemed cunning to her, for it was impossible to tell whether this followed from his first words, or not.

'No,' said Lydia.

Paul smiled into her face with a look of humble affection, and yet there was a cunning in his coolness, that made her speechless. However, she was thinking very fast, weighing her chances with him, his chances with her, the outcome of love between them.

All this happened in the first five minutes. Their conversation had been carried on in a low, but natural tone, and Tom had hurried back from the telephone, as if intrigued, all the same. Thereafter Tom, of course, led the conversation on to China. Lydia had always admired Tom's brilliance and scholarship and was very surprised to see that not only was Paul equal to him in brilliance and scholarship, but seemed cooler, surer of himself, and moreover had exactly the same kind of thinking as Tom. Tom walked, talked, Paul answered him, argued with him, opulently showered him with his own ideas, and every few minutes would turn on her a golden smile, the kind of smile, Lydia had always thought up to now, that was only exchanged between lovers. And she felt herself giving him, too, those rare golden smiles: she felt very happy, at ease, as if floating on an inland brook, in midsummer in full sunlight. She had never felt at ease with a man like that in her life before, except with Tom, but in a different, more maternal way, with Tom. She had no maternal feeling towards this stranger, but no sinful nor vulgar adulterous feeling either. Only a feeling as if the love of the ages of gold existed between them and would never be disturbed.

Presently, because she could take no part in their conversation, which had become 'a feast of the intellect', she retired to her own workroom and went on with a monograph in bacteriology she was doing. This did not please Tom very much: he always liked her to be there, to listen to his brilliance, and to love and admire him; so he called her, 'Lydia! Make us some coffee.' She came out at once, as she was used to doing, and as she passed the door, Paul smiled at her and said, 'Well, if you come like that when people call you'll never get your work done. *I* wouldn't do it.'

Everything about him was natural and sweetly audacious. When she gave him the coffee, he smiled at her as if he were absolutely sure of her love. 'What a strange thing,' she thought: 'I must be seeing things! I'm just mad, that's all. He's being pleasant.' But she saw he smiled at her husband coolly, carelessly, with the faint air of an adversary, and would turn from one of those rather crisp looks, to give her one of those smiles that was slowly dissolving her out of herself, out

CHRISTINA STEAD

of her wifehood, back into her childhood, into the romantic and rapturous child she had been. She felt that Paul knew instinctively the kind of child, girl and woman she had been up till now – the kind of family life she had had, all about her, her secret thoughts were the most open things in nature to him. She was obsessed by him, but it was a kind of dream: and when the door closed on him, she rushed into Tom's arms with a quiet rapture. Standing there, thinking of Tom's goodness and their happiness, she found herself looking at the hall mirror.

'Tom,' she said slowly, 'who does Charteris remind you of?' Tom looked into the mirror too. 'Of someone,' he said thoughtfully.

'Of someone we know very well?' said Lydia, puzzled.

'Yes: someone we see often,' Tom continued.

'Tom,' Lydia continued in a low voice, 'look at me.'

'Yes,' her husband answered, after a scrutiny: 'you are right. He is so like you that you might be twins.'

She looked closer at the glass, 'All the time, I had an odd feeling that I had known him for many years. But it was only myself!' She laughed: and noticed on Tom's face a baffled expression.

It happened that soon after that Tom and Charteris began to work together on a textbook, and all their meetings were at some office in town. Lydia encouraged this and even refused to go with Tom: 'Why? I just sit there while you two gas.'

And again shortly after this, Tom got an appointment in another state, for two years. They returned to (. . .) at the end of that time, on a Sunday evening and went straight to Broadway to see a movie in the 'stinkoes' along Forty-Second Street. At the corner of Broadway, Lydia saw Paul, looking very pale and untidy, and with a young woman.

'Why, there's . . .' she began.

But Paul hastily turned right about and crossed to the Times building. Lydia said 'Tom, there's Paul, there's Paul . . .' and dragged him with her. At the bus stop Paul, with a tired and almost frightened expression was standing, with a badly dressed and tired, but pretty girl who had also a timid expression.

'Hello Lydia,' he said so awkwardly, that she knew he had

14

seen them and turned away purposely. She looked at the young woman with a friendly smile.

'This is Rosetta – Rosetta Myria,' he said.

The girl seemed glad that they were friendly.

'Let's go and have a drink,' proposed Lydia. She felt masterful, confident. She wondered why Paul had wanted to avoid them, but did not care. They went to one place after another and found them nearly all crowded. At last they found a 'tavern' that had booths and almost no one there. They sat down and looked at the gallant frescoes, ordered Wiener schnitzels and beer and Paul, very ill-at-ease, conscious of his dirty collar, untidy hair and greasy coat (the same as two years before) began cracking bad jokes. Rosetta and he had been to France since they had met, and in fact, this evening had only just got off the boat with only ten cents between them and had not even tipped the stewards. This made Tom feel very jolly and he urged them to eat and drink and lent them some money. Paul easily accepted the money, Rosetta looked relieved. Lydia invited them to come and see them and they accepted for the next Saturday. Paul put on a bold air as soon as he had eaten and told some broad jokes. He was always a frank fellow and tonight he seemed to want to appear as rollicking as they had known him before. What had happened to make him so blue?

Lydia looked at him curiously. 'This is the man I nearly lost my head over.' He certainly looked very like her, when she was looking tired and blue: his reactions were just the same, except that he was a man. When she felt 'scraggy' she tried to avoid people and then she tried to be bold, laugh it off, be vulgar. She looked at him feature by feature – he seemed miserable and ordinary, and yet very comprehensible and she was ready to defend him against the world, as one is a member of one's family. She was careful not to offend the girl Rosetta, by showing the affection she had for him. Paul sought her eye and her smile once or twice pitiably, without confidence.

She did not wait for the Saturday night and had no feeling against Rosetta. 'I don't want him,' she thought, 'and I'm glad he got someone to console him for his unhappy married life of the other year.' When Paul came, she spent the whole time talking to Rosetta. Rosetta was an agitator, conscientiously going from factory to factory where she was not blacklisted, organizing the girls. Once or twice, she looked at Paul: Paul was not so talkative, he was letting Tom talk and, rather discouraged and tired was sitting back, stretched out in the comfortable armchair, with his eyes fixed strangely and quietly on Rosetta. 'He loves her,' thought Lydia. They gave her their address: she was to come and see them. 'He was never really mine,' thought Lydia.

A fortnight later, he rang up and asked if he could come at once to see them. When he came, an hour later, Lydia craning in the darkness of the passage, at the woman behind him, saw his wife. 'I am so glad you came, Mrs Charteris.'

The woman, plain, unhappy and tempestuous, looked round the flat. 'It's very small,' she said, 'and you can see the bedroom so plain.'

'It is,' said Lydia: 'we can't do a thing here.'

'It's hard to find,' complained the woman: 'I don't know how anyone finds you.'

'Oh,' said Lydia, 'we leave the lamp in the window, and then Paul was here before.'

'Yes,' the woman gave them all a bitter look: 'he was here before of course.'

Some other people came – among them, a friend of Paul's, a journalist equally brave and famous, and with him his wife, one of the most beautiful women alive, delicate, slant-eyed, porcelain-faced. Mrs Charteris and she discussed the Spanish and Chinese wars and Lydia, who knew nothing of them, worked on an embroidered bedspread she had begun years before. She had begun it superstitiously, 'she would not marry Tom till it was finished' – but she had married Tom long before. The three men talked: when she looked up she saw Paul, stretched out as before in the very same chair, looking as bitter as old age at his wife. When they went, they all heard them begin to argue bitterly immediately outside the window and down the lane.

Their new place was in the centre of the city, near Paul's place of work. Paul dropped in several times with a manuscript he wanted Tom's advice on, and once or twice he ate there before going home to his wife. They were very poor and lived a long way out of town: he did not get home till eight in the evening. Once Paul spoke of Rosetta 'Yes, I left her and went back to my wife: it's my own fault I suppose.' Rosetta? Lydia was sure she loved him. That evening, she noticed how seedy Paul was, how a little beer paunch was developing on him, and crows' feet round his eyes, although he was not much older than herself. The hard, discouraging and dissipated life was drying him.

He began to drop in. Once she spoke of some young poet she knew and lent him the book of poems: 'This one is splendid,' she said: 'it's his finest.' He took it unwillingly, but politely. Afterwards she repeated the poem to herself: a glorious but stirring and sensual poem. She felt ashamed and yet thought, 'He will understand I meant nothing by that.'

He came in one afternoon about two o'clock to return the book. It happened that Tom was off from work early that day and he was in the apartment. She answered the door and there stood Paul, tall, wind-flushed, with his curly dark hair and a certain timidity, 'I came to return to you your books.'

'Come in, Tom is here.'

'No, no.'

'Yes, he would love to see you.'

She forgot everything that had intervened: it was as if they stood there, meeting awkwardly in a doorway in the first flush of a love affair. He entered. A journalist was there who hated Paul Charteris, a political opponent: he instantly went out, crushing on his hat, scarcely muttering 'Hullo'.

Charteris looked surprised, gained his full manhood in a moment, but merely said, 'I don't think he likes me!'

He was amiable and full of ideas after all. He went promising to come soon. He came the next day, at four o'clock. No one was there, but Lydia. She was nervous. She sat on the edge of the couch, with her whole body hidden behind an armchair, her arms and chin resting on it and began to talk. She could not stop herself talking. He listened, looked at her, in an alien way, never answered a word. She went on feverishly talking, in a high squeaky voice, as it seemed, that she detested. Suddenly, 'What is the use?' she thought and fell silent, and frowned. It was too bad of him not to answer at all. At the frown he jerked and began to talk – about himself, his brothers, his idea of writing a novel of his youth. When Tom came they were both relieved. Paul came the next day. She gave him liquor, which he liked very much. They talked about parties – she had given one which had fallen flat. 'Why?' he asked: 'give them rough liquor and beds to make love on, and no party falls flat.' He laughed tipsily. She was hurt. When Tom came home early, she was glad, and sat down in the deep armchair doing her bedspread. When he went Tom had some stories to tell. He had been talking to friends of Paul's. Paul was a heartbreaker, a Don Juan and so on: he had a new flame every five months and everyone was disgusted with him. Lydia excused him to herself, but she observed that Tom was capable of pinpricks. (And Tom had once said 'If another should love you, I'd be proud to know this lover: I would never stoop to jealousy.') A day rarely passed without Tom getting in a gentle hint about Paul's lovemaking, some little joke 'the ladykiller'. It ended by Lydia forgiving Paul entirely in her heart: 'So he is, and I love him for what he is.' She didn't know when she began speaking thus of the tender feeling she had for the erring Paul.

Paul began to drop in every day. When he went one day, she would say, 'Come tomorrow if you can, Paul: Tom will be home about five.' Paul would always come at the time mentioned and have wine or cocktails. He liked drink and Lydia always had it for him now. Tom was always there and there would be a long session of political discussion. Lydia would say nothing – just do her work and look at them both. Winter was approaching and the evenings drew in soon: in the semi-darkness Paul sat, with his legs stretched out, resting back, with a fatigued look in the deep armchair. Sometimes answering Tom and sometimes letting his inspiration flow. When he answered him, it was always pungently, with a personal philosophy. Paul had studied a long time abroad, and was an original. Lydia watched them and in these few evenings, the tender and familiar feeling she had for Paul, changed: she fell in love with him. When the lamp was lighted, he shaded his fine almond shaped eyes and listened still. At first he came two or three times a week, then every day. When they were out of liquor, she left them talking and ran out to get it. The cloak hooks stood in view of the chair he always sat in. Neither of the men made a move to go out and get the things. As she got into her things, she could look in and see Paul stretched out there: whenever he saw her he would turn and give her that melting smile of his and she would smile back from the depths of her heart, a smile that was the fulfilment of romantic love almost, something dreamed about in poetic youth. And so when she came back. Tom saw little or nothing of this, which was the only inter-change they made all day, except when she asked him a question. 'A little more port? Another glass of beer?' He never refused. One day, when she was going out, Tom asked her to go up the street and get some carbon paper too. Paul, at this, gave her a quaint tender smile, one of those he was a past master in. She was as happy as a schoolgirl to whom a professor has smiled in the street. Her heart beat fast and cheerfully going along the lane. She got into the street in a high state of mind. In the shop waiting for the boy to wrap up the carbon paper, a dark storm rushed on her, and for a few seconds, everything in the room whirled round in a glorious delirium: the dark wind rushed on, but left, where had only been a joyful excitement, the surge of adult passion. This was not like her earlier crushes with their blind rages and aches: she had been living happily with a man for a long time and she knew what happy passion was, and this that was left with her now was the night-darkened heavenly garden of love. She desired, with every sense, Paul of the tender smile and understanding heart: and joy rushed over her too, 'I thought I would never feel it again, and God be praised I am madly in love: what splendid joy.' She went back soberly, but like someone to whom glorious tidings have been announced in the street. 'I have won the lottery, yes, really,' she thought. She hastened out of her coat and hat, did not look at any of them when she came in, but began pulling corks and so on.

When she came in to give him his drink, Paul was saying, 'Yes, I'm going to China again and I'm never coming back this time: what have I to stay here for?'

No one tried to dissuade him: that was his business, and everyone felt it was his fate. He was not happy here: the recon-ciliation with his wife was a torment for both: stories were being whispered about his affairs and people were turning against him for no good reason, chiefly because of his wife's unhappiness. But it was a long way off. Lydia saw him as always to the door and asked him to come again tomorrow, 'Tom will be home at five.' 'All right,' he said, in his sweet manner.

When he came the next day, she had been through hours of desire – the first time she had ever waited for him to come, or deeply desired it. He sat there this time, in the lamplight of the early fallen day very silent, hardly saying a word, and she kept looking at him, quietly, little glances that no one could notice.

'How is it possible,' she thought 'that I am so madly in love with this man I've seen so often, and who is after all, like me, if rather handsomer and sweeter?' She began to look at him, 'Is it the mouth? Is it the eyes?' She found that each item gave her a pang and that in fact, it was each item that she had not, and then had, fallen in love with. She went out silently, unnoticed by the others and looked at herself in the mirror in the bathroom – pulling her eyes up and down, trying to get the sweet expression Paul got so easily. Her smile did not seem much like his: but in her happiness thinking about him, she caught herself looking rather like him when he smiled. This made it nearly all pure joy. She came back and stole fresh glances at him – she began to notice the parts of his body. He seemed so potent, full of manly strength that she felt like fainting: she seemed to get a little delirious although she had not drunk very much, and began to think that he was all honey, all roses, and so on. She found that she had moments of absence, when she heard nothing of what was going on, but only heard beautiful words about him, 'His limbs gather passion as the bees honey and I am the hive . . .' Her feeling this evening was so powerful that she could not believe he did not feel it, that Tom did not feel it, it seemed to have thickened and made fluid the air. He said very little, shading his eyes with his hands and looking through them, while Tom went on about Ethiopia.

When she saw him to the door that evening in the usual polite and indifferent fashion, she thought suddenly 'Oh, if I could only walk in the street with him a few minutes.' The moment of greatest joy had passed and she was already beginning to feel the pains and aches of desires, but very much more powerful than before because of her marriage, and almost uncontrollable, as convulsions or childbirth are a giant revolutionary spasm. She thought at once, 'I must not see him again.' She had to control her thought and face during the evening with Tom and have his caresses from which she had never once turned away, but all the time she was realizing with more plainness the gulf of passion and drama on which she stood. 'Another moment,' she acknowledged 'and I would have walked out into the street with him, without a hat or coat, without a penny or in my slippers: and it wouldn't have mattered how long the street was – even if it was as long as the country – that's how I felt. If he had asked me, would I have had the heart to refuse? I would follow him barefoot: I would not have the heart to refuse him.' She never had the smallest idea of leaving Tom nor of hurting him, and she loved Tom deeply and wholesomely. She then realized that she was in danger, and thought 'I must never see him again.' She began to think how she could manage this without arousing Tom's suspicions or Paul's. She could be absent, once or twice – but not more than that. 'What am I to do?' The conflict had begun: it was not a conflict between one man and another, for her relations to each of them had never changed from the beginning, she loved one because of their marriage and the chances of their coming together, but in Paul was some secret command from her own destiny, he was destiny, and they both knew it. In his wilful wayward and inconsiderate way, if he cared to ask her to do something (he would plead, with an appearance of weakness), she would do it without a second's thought: it was foretold from the earth's youth that she would meet him. She was his equal, she knew her own powers, she knew she was like him, she did not grovel before him, she knew his nature without any blindness and the things she thought of obeying him in were – following him in his many wanderings more than anything else, for as to the result of desire, she knew that he was made this way – he adored love for its own sake and if she mentioned her love to him he would love her, for the sake of love. So there was no unhappy crushed desire in her feeling, only this singular feeling of destiny which came upon her with a sure ferocity. It was the strangest and most perfect of loves. 'O, Gods,' she kept thinking 'I have known it: this is it, perfect, spotless, boundless love: how lucky I am.' To her he seemed the most imperfect of mortals, with a godlike power over her. And naturally, when she realized this, she knew she could never see him again. She feared him.

The next morning he telephoned to say that he had an immediate assignment to go to China and that once there he would never return: he would die there. These were his strange words. 'I have nothing to live for here nor there,' he said.

He could only come twice before he went, because he had so much to do. He came for one or two hurried visits then and the whole time was taken up by the journalist who was politically his opponent and who almost lived with Tom and Lydia, in the hope of gibing at Paul before he went out. They had no last moments with him at all. He went on a Monday night.

Lydia felt little that night: 'He has gone – well, fate's relieved me of him.'

The next morning she was so deeply in love with him that she could do nothing. Tom went to work and instead of starting her work herself, she pulled down the blinds and thought about her lost love, about his face, limbs and sexual beauty, his charming smile and tenderness: it was as if a smouldering fire had been poured into her flesh and she had no bones or sinews. She could do nothing, eaten up with tenderness and cruel desire. About twelve she roused herself and put on her hat to go and buy some envelopes, thinking 'Why does this happen when he's gone?' when the doorbell rang and she opened it to see Paul standing there. She took two steps forward and murmured in a low voice 'I thought you had gone.'

'It's put off till Saturday,' he said.

He came in and talked in a low, inconsequential way, almost in a low fever, of various things, but had not been there more than ten minutes when the talkative journalist, who was his political enemy, rang up and said he would be over.

'Shall I put him off?' asked Lydia, her hand over the receiver.

'He doesn't like me,' said Paul.

But she could think of no reason for putting him off: he only wanted to come over for a cup of coffee and a chat. She said, 'Paul Charteris is here.'

'Well, I won't come then' said the journalist nastily. 'You don't want me if that red is there.'

'Don't be silly, Edgar.'

'No, I won't come,' said the journalist in a pet.

'All right.'

The journalist suddenly relented: he couldn't pass up his gossip. 'Well, if you want me?'

There was no way to put him off decently. He arrived and began a sharp discussion with Paul and after that, in came Tom again, not working in the afternoon. It was really odd that, at whatever time Paul came, they could never have a minute alone. And yet she had nothing to talk to him about: she hadn't the faintest idea what she would talk to him about if she had no interruptions. She had got so used to Tom taking up every conversation and engaging everyone's attentions, that she had got out of the way of rousing herself. Perhaps Paul thought she did not care for him.

Paul came every day that week, although he was very busy – and always at different times, just when he was free, but every day that week the gossipy and touchy Edgar was there too, and every day that week also Tom was home incredibly early from work – in fact, one day he did not go at all. He liked Paul and he wanted to see him as often as he could before he went for ever.

'It's unlikely I'll ever get to China to see you,' he told Paul.

'Oh, I'll die there this year,' said Paul, rather bitterly.

'You won't.'

'Why not? Yes, I will.'

Lydia said nothing, sitting there wondering about him. Why was he going? Why did he want to die? Why did he come so often? She knew he was going and so she quietly gave herself up to contemplation of him: she would never see him again. No one noticed anything. When he came to see them for the last time, Edgar was still there. Paul said nothing the whole evening but let Edgar rail against him and his cause and the Chinese: Paul sat with his face covered with his hand

and drank everything he was given. Lydia drank a lot too: whenever she gave Paul a drink, she drank too. Tom was not much of a drinker and Edgar preferred to talk and was slow getting through his drinks. She felt herself presently very drunk, but very cool too. Paul stayed as long as he could but presently had to go home to have his last meal with his wife. Everyone offered him gifts – a pair of fur-lined gloves, socks, marching boots, a fountain pen and the like, but he turned them all down but the boots and gloves.

Edgar relented at the last moment and offered the gloves. He had always said that rat would never go off to China and now he saw him going he felt ashamed but he still said, 'He'll only sit in Hong Kong or Canton in a cosy café and send home despatches, he'll never fight.' Paul said nothing to all this. It was very strange. Lydia knew why Edgar was so biting – he was jealous that they had become so friendly with Paul: he wanted to be their bosom friend alone, himself. That was why he had been there every day that week – to be sure that she and Tom didn't get sessions alone with Paul and to find out what Paul had to say that interested them so.

Presently Paul got up to go, got his hat, and everyone said 'Goodbye and good luck.' Paul was to meet Tom on the next day to get the measurement of the boots and the gloves, but this was the last time he would call. Lydia was very jolly, took him to the door, then decided to go out to the lane with him. Paul was silent, surprised that she went to the lane with him. He was surprised that she had drunk so much. At the lane she stopped, 'Well, goodbye Paul.'

'Goodbye,' he said indifferently. She held out her hand and he took it, when suddenly she grasped his hand in both hers and pressed it hotly. He lifted his face with an expression of great surprise and smiled in delight: he searched her face and waited for what she would say:

'I'll go with you.'

'Will you?'

'I haven't got the money yet.'

'Can you get it?'

'I don't know. No.'

'No,' he said shaking his head.

'Well, goodbye, anyhow.'

24

'Goodbye,' he said smiling. He went off and she ran up the stairs.

It had only taken a minute and a murmur and no one would notice her absence. Tom was rattling away, but Edgar laughed and said, 'Here comes Lydia all excited.' Jealousy makes him say that, that's all, she thought: he's so glad Paul has gone. Heaven above, she thought, I actually said I'd go with him: I nearly walked out into the street after him. I must be careful she thought: I could never never let Tom down, never. But I forgot everything in the world beside the imperative Paul. She got their dinner ready and no one remarked anything. Paul had gone, but she was not sorry, she was inflated, ecstatic. Paul knew she loved him now. What a cool customer, she thought smiling to herself. She would have been ashamed to let any other man know she loved him, but not Paul. To Paul love was an autonomous thing with its own rule, the creator of life; he admired it for its own sake. A man able to get women from other men by sleight of hand, without struggle.

But Paul did not keep his appointment with Tom the next day. Instead he came early and to lunch. For lunch they had a visitor, a young boy who hero-worshipped Paul and who would not take their hints that they wanted to see Paul alone at the last minute. He wanted to see the famous Captain Charteris himself, especially as he was leaving for China. He stayed through lunch and after lunch: and only after a painful silence on everyone's part did he take the hint and go. It was then late, within five minutes Charteris himself was leaving. The men put on their hats to go and buy the boots and then Lydia noticed that Tom came into the passage looking rather pale (and) startled.

'He wonders if I am going to kiss Paul goodbye,' she understood by this. She was too rollicking with Paul and it was not a farewell at all. Tom stood at the door staring at them both, still with that startled look. She tried to think of something to ask him to do so that he would leave them for a moment, but she could think of nothing rational. 'Goodbye, Paul.'

'I'll try to come back for a moment later,' said Paul gently.

She was so surprised that she answered stiffly 'Oh?'

Paul was discomforted, 'I don't know if I'll have time.'

'No, no,' she said: 'no, no, you'll be busy –'

She was worried by the staring pale face of Tom, minutely observing the two of them.

'And so goodbye.'

'Goodbye.'

Paul hesitated again, worried, 'And you do my work for me.'

'I can't do that.'

'Try, Lydie.'

'Until you come back.'

'Oh, I don't think I'll come back.'

He was gone. She was so astonished by everything that she could not collect her wits. What did it mean? She saw in an instant that she had never really understood him, how clever he was.

It was a long time till Tom came back, and she thought, 'He will come back from China of course, and by then we must be out of the way: I must never see him again.' For the conflict had arisen now between the two men. The angelic, patient and deserving Tom who had been faithful to her for ten years was there, and also the undeserving but imperative Paul. Who would win? She envisaged all the consequences of going with Paul. She and Paul were too close to have any great surprises for each other – there might simply be the amusement of being with your twin for a while: after a while, Paul would have another flame – and she would get angry with him, she was sure – his dilatoriness, his flames, even his beer parties and his little paunch, which had disappeared at present, but would come back when he returned to ordinary life. Also she could sense that Paul had given up most of his ambition and hope in life: while she had not, she was still mad with it and she hoped always would be. She would make Paul laugh and Paul would seem dull to her. 'It would never work,' she thought 'and I would hurt Tom forever and for no good reason.' But she knew that if Paul said in his yearning and understanding way, 'Come to me,' she would find it hard, perhaps impossible to resist him. 'That's the end,' she said: 'if he comes back twice as large as life, I will never see him again.'

She was so resolved, that she did not miss Paul, and never thought of writing to him, although she knew other people were – Anna Brown and all the friends he had worked with in causes. Why? She and Paul understood each other: that was all there was to their friendship. It would always be so. She regretted that she had not known Paul's love, that would have been she was sure the revelation of love: and she bitterly regretted not having in her body a child of this dear and intimate man: that was what she really wanted of him, a child of him, a child like him, a child to be her perfect joy for ever, of which he would be the distant father. She wanted to love him but not live with him. She felt that she had always been married to him and lived with him for years. But with Tom, life was a constant excitement and pleasure: she felt she had only lived with Tom a few weeks, even after all this time.

Three months later, they had a telephone call late at night, telling them that Paul had been killed in action. She said nothing, a feverish activity began in her soul, she began to lament like a woman in a Greek play, in long rhythmic phrases: her heart began to slowly weave Paul's funeral dance and in her ears rang long phrases of lament. When the light was turned out, she lay in bed with Tom seeing night for the first time.

'How dark it is when the lamp is turned out,' she said. Tom listened and after a moment asked 'What do you mean by that?'

'I never noticed before.'

At that moment the church bell began to strike the hour.

'Listen to them ringing,' she said: 'Why do they ring for the hours that are gone: all the ages that are dead and they still ring the hours: it's so little – such a little sound in the night. Even the dead hour just past doesn't hear it: the people dead the past hour don't hear it and what do we care? We live tomorrow – not an hour or two, but endless days of life.'

'Lydie?' he asked in a small voice, curiously.

'Oh, Tom, let's leave here. What is there here? I don't like it.'

'Why do you say that?'

'I don't know. My heart isn't in it here.'

He was silent. She realized what he might take this to mean

and hastened to talk a lot about their circumstances. Meanwhile she was realizing what it had all meant that she had said, and that Tom perhaps guessed too – she turned away from his affectionate hands. A light from another window fell on the pillow: it was a fine pale yellow light. Among the words in her ears, she heard ones she recognized, 'Oh, Jonathan, Oh my brother Jonathan – very pleasant was thy life unto me . . .' The words went on repeating themselves. Suddenly a great sob shook her and she began to cry uncontrollably.

'Lydie, Lydie,' said the good Tom, 'Lydie what is it?'

'I never knew anyone who died before. I'm so silly, it's just new to me,' she said.

But she spent three days in uncontrollable sorrow, in tides of regrets that came and went: Tom could not help knowing that it was more than shock and he became angry on the third evening. On the third night he made love to her and she who had never refused him in her life didn't dare refuse him now.

Tom began to talk to everyone cheerfully about Paul saying 'Yes, I knew him, he was a great friend of mine,' and 'The last time I saw Paul he hardly listened to what I was saying: I guess his mind was on some girl: he was a great lover of the ladies,' and 'Oh, yes, I knew Paul intimately, I collaborated with him, but Lydie knew him even better than I did.' After a little while, this seemed very comic to Lydia, and whenever they began to talk about Paul's death and Tom said this, 'Yes, we were very close to him just before his death but Lydie knew him better than me, didn't you Lydie?' she would say 'Yes,' and begin to laugh. Everyone always looked astonished, but Tom's little gag continued to strike her as very funny. Meanwhile for quite a long time, perhaps two years or three, she knew that if the choice had been between lying in his Chinese grave with Paul or living her happy, unclouded and fertile life with Tom, she would have taken a long time to choose and what would have been the choice?

Paul had said 'Do my work for me', but no one can do another's work for him and who cares to? We only want to do our own work. She thought, though, 'I will work till I do a very fine piece of work – that will be in memory of Paul although no one will know it (and it's better that they don't, they'd laugh at both of us, the three of us) – and then I won't mind what happens.'

And whenever she went out into company, she dressed very carefully, tried her hair various ways, wondered if tonight, or next week, she would meet the other Paul that the contemporary world probably held.

My Friend, Lafe Tilly

Lafe Tilly wore his hat brim down, and his coat collar up; there were round spectacles over his hollow eyes. A little of the yellow face could be seen. He stood by the lamp, looking down. He did not take off his gloves.

'I was at a funeral last week. There was the widow and another woman, the man's brother and I myself, his only mourners. Once he had hundreds of friends, thousands perhaps. Hundreds of women loved him.'

Lafe Tilly smiled.

'He was cremated; and before that they had to embalm him and make him a new face. His was gone.'

'Gone?'

'Eva and I knew them years ago, years before any of us were married. I was a stunt pilot then: I lived in Brooklyn like everyone in our crowd; and Joe Cornaco stood out in the crowd, very political, a big talkative man, dark, thin-faced, greedy for women, spending a lot on dress, always clean shaved. He treated all the women badly. We believed in sex equality and did not think any woman had the right to complain. I married Eva, the first to marry; and soon after that Joe married Donna, a woman in our set who had been with us for years.

'She was a few months older than Joe and he talked about it. He made her a partner in his real estate business. She became his office manager. She worked hard, stayed back every night to clean up business; she looked after the staff and did his work when he was out with girls. He was out nearly every evening.

'She had been working since she was fifteen. She had never been to college. Joe had a younger brother Victor who was sent to college and became a lawyer. Donna turned out to have a good business head, better than Joe had; and she put her savings into his business, about five thousand dollars.

'Although Joe was never sentimental, always calling a spade a spade, he got into trouble several times with women. A young woman who was always dressed in black, a thin thing, committed suicide. She tried several times; no one believed her and in the end she managed it in the bath.'

He smiled most curiously. It was like a waxen face reflected in moving water, not a smiling man.

'It was after that that Donna asked him to marry her, for his own sake. He knew she was in love with him and he liked that, the quiet, loyal, patient woman to whom he complained and who understood him. They had a talk; he put his views to her: she agreed with everything he said.

'He said, "You are getting the best of the bargain, since you will be both my wife and my partner; and you are getting the man you love, whereas I do not love you." "Yes," she said. "Therefore," Joe said, "we had better have an agreement to safeguard me. You agree to look after my business and my home; you study at night to get a degree so that you will be my equal. No children. I am to have my entire liberty, as I have now, as an unmarried man." Donna agreed to everything. Between them they drew up the marriage contract and they made his brother, Victor, a lawyer by then, go over the clauses. Victor told Donna that it had no validity being contrary to public policy. She said, "If I keep to it and he keeps to it, it will be binding. We both know what we are doing." "But if he divorces you?" "He will not divorce me. He will have no reason to." "But what about you, Donna?" "I love Joe and I never expected to marry him. I know I'm not good looking. I consider I'm lucky." "Why get married?" people said to them both. But they were satisfied. A friend called Cowan and I signed the contract as witnesses. Cowan died years ago.'

He looked straight ahead, continued, 'Now Donna took into her office young girls who attracted Joe and she made friends of any other women he wanted. It was strange how they all trusted her. When, at home, he went into the backroom with a girl, she sat chatting with the others, or read a book, or did the housework till the couple came out. If they stayed there for long, she went to bed. She always said that jealousy had been left out of her nature. She didn't know how it was. All women are jealous, aren't they?' said Lafe Tilly smiling.

'Joe's brother Victor was tall, dark, fleshy, with red damp lips. He was very fond of women, too; but he went after them differently, explaining his troubles, abusing Joe, using the word love. When Joe was away for the weekend with some girl, Victor would be at the house, eating and drinking with Donna. If ever Donna complained, it was to Victor. Victor had always been jealous of Joe and he would go round spreading gossip; Donna told me this. Joe had illegitimate children, all being supported by the mothers. Donna had no children. Victor sometimes stayed the night at Donna's apartment. It was a long way to his mother's home in Queen's. "I want children," he said to Donna; "when my mother dies, I will marry. I am sorry you have no children; you would make a good mother." But Donna did not sleep with him and never had a sweetheart. She was respected and had a following among Joe's male friends.'

After a pause, Lafe said harshly, 'She was a bawd for Joe, she played on the trust the girls had in her. She was good to them as long as he wanted them and afterwards she might dry their tears for them. It depended on how they stood with Joe.'

Lafe Tilly laughed suddenly; and then became serious and reasonable as before.

'I used to see Joe on the street. He was always the same, smart, spending money on himself; and they were making money between them, a lot of money. He nicked himself once when shaving and the nick didn't heal. He went about with bits of sticking plaster on his cheek. The scratch grew and he would go about without dressing it saying the air would heal it. Later he had an operation and he kept going to the hospital for skin graftings. He went about as jaunty as ever. People began to avoid him. I did. But he didn't understand it. I know Donna tried to persuade him to stay at home; and when he insisted on going to work, she wanted him to go in the car and come straight home afterwards. They had some rows over it. He thought she was trying to keep him away from girls. He said, "Remember you signed a contract with

me; keep your word." The worse his looks, the more frantic
he was about girls and he thought everyone was standing in
his way.'

Tilly glimmered a smile.

'Naturally, I guessed. I told him to go home and stay home.
He got very angry and I didn't see him again.

'About four months ago, I had a note at the office from
Donna, which said, "Joe says please come to see him and
bring Eva with you. Come Thursday afternoon." Underneath
this was written, "I have written what Joe asked me to, but
do not bring your wife. If you want to see him you had better
come now."

'It was a new address, away out, a wooden house, on an
earth bank in a long dusty street of such houses, all three-
storey, with steps in front, downhill off a four-lane highway.
There was a funeral home a few doors down.'

Lafe showed the sharp point of his tongue as he drew in his
breath.

'I found the number which was one that Joe had always
thought a lucky number. The windows were shut, with
drapes on all the windows; it looked well cared for. The door
was opened by a good looking young girl, serious, fair type,
in a house dress. She showed me into the front room and
went away. There was complete silence for a while, then
Donna came in. She had changed very little. She had healthy
looks; her cheeks were fat and red, her black hair was braided
over her broad head and she had on some sort of aesthetic
smock, brown, with hand embroidery and unusual buttons.
She collected buttons. It was the same sort of squaw outfit
she had always worn and which she liked better than shop
clothes. It was part of their revolt against machine-made
things. She had fine eyes, but solid as stones, denser than
dogs' eyes. Otherwise, she is short, thickset and has a slow
flat voice.

'When I started to get up, she said, "Sit down, Lafe."

'She spoke in low tones, like the girl, and said Joe was
asleep. He needed all the sleep he could get; he would be in a
bad temper if not rested. She said she'd get me a drink. I said,
"Not yet, wait for Joe." She said, "You'll need it." She went
out and came back with a full bottle of Scotch whisky, which

she opened and put in front of me on the table, with one glass. She didn't want any. She asked me if I wanted some water and went away for it; but did not return.

'No one came. I thought I heard a whisper once; apart from that, the house was quiet. I poured myself a drink and had it. After a long time, the young girl came in with a jug of water and some ice. She seemed to be a servant, so I didn't offer her any; and Donna stayed away. I just sat there and drank by myself. It was hot and still. Sometimes I thought I heard a soft noise somewhere in the house or a car on the dirt road; that was all. There was nothing to do, so I just sat there on the sofa and got quite comfortable.

'The curtains were partly drawn. The sun fell on blue patches of carpet and various yellows. The place was kept very clean. On the wall were crude paintings, the sort we used to collect when naïve art was the fad. Besides these and the furniture, there were two mirrors, a long one between two windows and a big square one standing on the floor, very large, with a lacy acanthus-leaf frame, the frame about eight inches deep and with rusty gilding. It was out of place. There was a woman's handglass on the mantelpiece, some bookshelves with old intellectual bestsellers, nothing for me to read. I could see the door of the room across the hall; that was all.

'I had drunk at least half the bottle when I heard footsteps and something being dragged. There was a slow shuffle coming nearer. A door opened, there was a whisper and in answer to it, I heard a strange voice, a cawing. People were coming along the hall together. Then three people stood in the doorway. There were women behind and in front, in a dressing-gown, and slippers, wearing an eyeshade was a man. He had an immense lipless mouth, the cheeks were blown out and he wore an eyeshade. There was a paisley scarf round his neck up to the chin. They must have just fixed the scarf round his neck, because he was impatiently pulling it off as he shuffled into the room. He took no notice of me, but he approached the glass on the floor, which was at an angle so that he could see himself walking. He signalled, and they put the handglass into his hand. He dropped the scarf on the floor and took off the eyeshade. Then he began taking a careful look at himself, turning his face this way and that. He made a sound of irritation and gestured. The girl switched on the top light. The man continued to observe himself in detail. While this was going on, the girl went away and returned with a tray of coffee and other things, which she placed on the table near me. Donna stood there calmly, looking from one to the other. Presently, she said, "Lafe Tilly is here, Joe."

'The man made an irritable sound which they seemed to understand.

'The wife said in her flat commanding voice, "He's at the table by the window, if you'll look, Joe. He's been waiting."

'The man turned. I started to get up. I was drunk perhaps. I looked at him and fell back again into the soft old couch. Joe seemed to laugh. He touched his cheek, shook his head, uttered sounds and looked at me, nodding his head slowly. Donna said, "Joe says he thinks he has improved this week. It is the hot weather which does him good." The man said something. The wife said, with calm shining eyes, "Joe thinks you can understand him and that I am insulting him by interpreting. Tell him you can't, Lafe."

'I said, "Are you feeling better, Joe?"

'At further sounds from him, the girl left the room; but the wife said, "Joe, I must stay if you are going to talk to Lafe. Lafe doesn't understand a word you say." She continued to me, "Lisbeth has gone to make more coffee. Joe's is cold. Joe always drank very hot coffee, you remember; but now he never gets it. It takes so long to drink. Well, it is not our fault, Joe." There seemed to be mirth underlying her stubborn words. She continued, "Joe is not allowed to drink whisky. It would choke him. He would choke to death."

'Joe made conversation. He drew me out about politics, contradicting everything I said. He talked a lot about his health, with which he was fairly satisfied. He had improved considerably, he said, since his teeth had come out. It was a good idea of his doctor's; and it should have been done years before. He ate better and felt better. If the teeth had been taken out years before he would not have had the skin trouble. He had always had excellent teeth, always sound and white; so he had not thought of it. "Joe always had a bad skin," said the wife.

'She interpreted everything he said, being constantly interrupted by Joe. She laughed once, saying, "Joe says I am treating him like a child; he just has a speech impediment for a short time, but his speech is coming back."

'Lisbeth came with fresh coffee and poured a cup for Joe. He took a drop on his tongue from time to time and complained. Donna said. 'It is no use getting mad at us, Joe. You drink so slowly that it can't help getting cold. You take a whole hour to drink a single cup of coffee."

'Joe was sitting at the table facing the long mirror between the windows. He held out his hand and Lisbeth brought him the handglass. He continued to study his appearance with care, while he drank.

' "Ah-ah-ah," said Joe.

' "Joe wants to know why you supplied such bad paper for those new books. The ink shows through."

'I said, "We were told not to waste paper; but to use paper that the men could tear out and use in the latrines."

'Evidently Joe was laughing.

' "Ah-ah-ah."

'Joe says "Are you still with Tacker and Taylor?"

' "Yes."

'Joe says, "Is Ben Taylor still a melancholic?"

' "Just the same."

'Joe says, "He never did appeal to women. He couldn't get them."

'Joe was trying to shout with rage. In an undertone, Lisbeth said to Donna, "Let him talk."

'He wrangled with the women, equally furious if they translated or if they neglected his remarks; and at times, he rolled a drop of cold coffee round his tongue. He made enquiries after people and asked why Eva had not come.

' "She used to be one of my girls in the old days. She had a crush on me. She always had her blue eyes fixed on me." Joe laughed.

' "Donna had the crazy idea of moving out here where no one can reach me and where I can't get into town. She made a promise to me. You know that. She is not keeping that

promise. I'm a prisoner here. These women keep me in jail.
Afraid of competition, they're not getting any younger."

'He kept insulting Donna and Lisbeth. Donna translated
the insults without emotion.

' "I'll soon be back in circulation and I'll make up for lost
time. You won't cheat me!"

'He showed temper, shouted, caught sight of himself and
once more began his careful inspection.

'Presently, they helped him to get out of his chair. He
wanted to lie down; he was tired.

' "Rest is everything. Sleep rests the skin. I look much
better in the morning when I get up," he said to me.

'Donna went out to the front gate with me and I said,
"How long will it be?"

' "The doctor said it might be two months; he's starving."

' "He doesn't seem to suffer much."

' "He's drugged all the time. He's full of aspirin. And they
did some slight operation. Joe's last message to you was to
bring Eva. Don't bring her and don't tell anyone. I can't have
people."

' "Who's the girl?"

' "A girl he wanted me to engage about eighteen months
ago. I don't know whether she fell for him or she was sorry
for him. I don't know if they had an affair. What does it
matter now? It's six months since that. But he wouldn't
understand it if I sent her away. It's all he's got. It was always
the greatest thing in his life, his way with women. He would
never have gone in for politics; he didn't care for the business. This was the greatest thing. It's not his fault, is it? It's a
fault of nature."

' "And he doesn't know it's over?"

'She laughed shortly. "It's hard to believe; but he has just
bought two tickets for himself and Lisbeth to go to Lourdes.
It's only a lupus he has, he says. It's nerves. He'll be cured
there. He read about a thing like that in Zola. The girl in the
book washed her face in the fountain and the lupus at once
began to heal."

' "And you, Donna?"

' "I'll keep on looking after the business. We've done very
well. There'll be big changes round here. Victor helps me. We

37

got the land and houses cheap years ago. I'll be all right."

'A couple of days ago,' said Lafe Tilly, 'I got the funeral notice at the office. Eva knows nothing about it, so don't mention it to her.'

'No.'

'She used to admire Joe in the old days; he dazzled her. Eva never understood men. She's naïve. Joe took her sister and left her; that is why she married me. Eva and her sister were always rivals. I thought of marrying her sister, too.'

After a pause, he continued quietly, 'Lisbeth was at the funeral. Joe's brother Victor was there, assisting Donna. I think Donna expected to marry him. I went back with them to the gate. Donna said, "You'll come in, won't you, Victor?" But he jammed on his hat, said he had an appointment and hurried up the street, his big legs going fast.

'Donna did not seem to notice anything. She told Lisbeth to wait at the gate and asked me to go in. I went. She gave me a valise and a box tied with string and asked me to carry them to the girl at the gate. Donna stood on the porch and called out to the girl, 'You must go away now. You can't stay here." The girl took the bag and box, said goodbye and turned away.

' "Come in, Lafe and have a drink," said Donna. "In a minute," I said. I said to the girl, "Where are you going? Home?"

' "No, they threw me out. I'll find a place."

' "Can I get you a taxi?"

' "No. I have no money. I'll find a place."

'I went in just to see what Donna would say. "You don't mind letting the girl go like that?"

' "What has she to do with me?"

' "But you lived together for eight months."

' "I don't know her name or her address; she is nothing to me. She took my husband from me. I don't care what happens to her."

' "But Donna she has nowhere to go."

' "He never cared for her. She threw herself at him. The women are shameless these days. You can't blame Joe. I was not like the others. He married me."

' "Would you like to see Eva?"

' "No. No women any more. I don't have to now."

' "Donna, why did you go through with it?"

' "You know I signed a contract with him. You were there: you witnessed it."

' "And you stood it for that reason?"

' "Joe and I had a contract. We agreed on everything. We understood each other."

'I passed Donna today,' Lafe said. 'She looked just the same, leathery skin, with a slight moustache, a dark felt hat, a black-belted dress, her satchel. Her eyes were on the sidewalk and her brown lips muttered occasionally. I was going to meet a blonde, so I avoided her.'

He glanced sideways. 'Donna's a virgin. Imagine it.' He grinned.

'Why do you tell these stories, Lafe?'

He said nothing.

'Because you feel the pain?'

'Yes, people live in pain.'

'Would you like a drink?'

'No. Goodbye. Don't tell Eva.'

'No.'

HAL PORTER

Gretel

My mother, empty-headed as a ghost, always left everything to the last minute. She persisted faithful to this pattern of behaviour even in the matter of dying. The cablegram of omen, the invitation to her final performance, could therefore do nothing but catch me with my eyes elsewhere, and my heart nowhere. When it came, I was, in fact, at my sixth glass of Samos wine, while Ionysseus, the two-sexed drink-waiter of the tatty marble bar of the Alpha Hotel in Athens, was dealing the age-thickened cards for our nth game of agonaea. We were playing for nothing, for less than nothing: one cannot outwit boredom with boredom. Distress is, however, stimulating. Charged with emotions not to be revealed, I crumpled the cablegram, and instantly left the flaccid wine and the grimy cards. At midnight, I was buckled in my seat on a plane to Melbourne. It ripped itself away from arid and aching Greece, with me and my obligations, and my sorrow too shallow to be published. The hours passed, the extravagant exhibitions of planets and clouds, the airway transit lounges humid as Turkish baths, the ugly wreckage of civilizations, and the uglier wreckings of progress.

At my age, forty-five, one should not dream of disavowing one's personality. I had long-time been *dégagé*, and smug in being so. This sparer diet nourished me more than one spiced with convictions and passions and tolerances. I knew to a pinch how little I loved, how little I hated. The skull with its long teeth clipped together in the ultimate and only true smile not only waits at the end of life's chess-board, but is there on any and every square. Events are no more than advents. Why then exert oneself in rich antics and decorated trickery? My mother, for example, could have been side-tracked by chance into dying selfishly, while I was young and useless; she could, equally, have by-passed hazard to cumber

43

– a scatter-brained centenarian capricious and fractious as a broken umbrella. Instead, she had frolicked, entertaining and well-beloved, for nearly seventy years. Enough, surely?

I was too late, of course, for her death-bed scene. The train from Melbourne got me over the mountains, and down through the foothills, to the provincial town, an old gold-mining one, just in time for the funeral. It was suitably raining. The tree frogs were rejoicing through the canon's fruity rendition of the burial service. The cemetery, as the town was, was up hill and down dale. It seemed as vast and overgrown, no more, no less, as when I used to go there, a boy, shooting rabbits, picking wild strawberries, or pilfering from the swallows' nests under the curled-up eaves of the oven-altar that towered centrally above the graves of Chinese miners. The horizontal granite door of my father's grave had been opened to admit mother, late as ever. Above this entrance to nowhere stood my three little sisters and my brother. They were all convincingly disguised as middle-aged, middle-class, married adults. They and I stood with the unrestful earnestness of mourners. It was as though, beyond the canon's elocuting, we cocked an ear to a trite lecture from fate. How different we all were. Yet we had had the same two parents, four grandparents, eight great-grandparents, sixteen great-great-grandparents, and so on. These calculations, carried to the utmost, imply an ancestral Eden so jam-packed with billions of anthropoidal Adams and Eves that it must have been a zoo-like hell. It seems to me that these sumless matings, funnelled down to us, a mere five, should have found us more alike than we were.

When mother in her pretty box was, at last, lowered towards father, my sisters made revelations of grief of a controlled kind: mother had taught them good manners. There was also an almost animal outcry from one of the other women. Although I had not seen her for over thirty years, I knew who she was. One of mother's flapper friends of the twenties, she had lapped over into mother's matronhood and our childhoods. Not related by blood or marriage, she was nevertheless Aunt Willy to us: Wilhelmina was her name. As she sobbed too rowdily, undone by heaven-knows-what memories of mother in the days of golliwogs, tin lizzies, banjo-mandolins, and coats with collars and cuffs of monkey fur, I too was suddenly the victim of recollection. My heart, so long locked, so aseptically polished free of finger-prints, creaked with an old forgotten pain. A forgotten voice seemed to cry through the meek rain, 'I am here! I am here!' It was the voice of Aunt Willy's daughter, the girl I fell in love with when I was twelve.

At twelve, in 1929, I was at the height of my boyhood, and the family at the height of its family-hood. It seemed unthinkable that my flibbertigibbet mother and my lawyer father, who was *distrait* to the point of not being earthed, could have had the concentration to compose even one child, let alone five. Father played chess, drove his motor-car as gently as a perambulator, spoke winding sentences that drawled out of sight without reaching a full-stop, and was always mislaying a meerschaum he affected rather than, I *think*, smoked with relish and assurance. Mother, who had four Lenci dolls, and more bangles and beads than a maharanee, must have been the giddiest housekeeper this side of Jericho. Fortunately, she had authentic assistance from a tiny, toothless creature who much resembled Popeye the Sailorman, and who appeared each Friday as charwoman to amend what had been done to sully the house since her last week's visit. Little had been done by father, much by us children, but most of the domestic damage had been done by mother and the maid-of-all-work.

The house had been built in the town's boom period, before the gold fizzled out. Its solidity was late-nineteenth century, as the town's was. Surrounded by wide, tiled verandas, the house was of brick and granite, and was set in two acres of garden and orchard. Snowdrops and larkspur proliferated under the lichened fruit-trees of old-fashioned apples and pears; seedling nectarines grew cheek-by-jowl with islands of irises and tiger lilies, and uncorralled bushes of striped roses. All this was half-way down a valley slope on the edge of the town, the streets of which, like a flexible grid-iron, criss-crossed the bulges and depressions of the foothills. Each street was a tunnel of elms or oaks.

From our front veranda, we could see the hills gutted of gold, the spindly poppet-heads, and the mullock-heaps in their pelts of paspalum and chocolate lilies. Opposite us, just below the crest of the other side of the valley, was the lunatic asylum. It seemed tilted for our better viewing: we could see inside its high walls a sort of Cape Dutch Colonial barracks of beige stone scribbled on by Virginia creeper, and mathematical garden beds solid as mattresses with civic flowers like lobelia and salvia. As did the inhabitants of a medieval painting with its scrupulous perspective, minute people – loonies? – strolled, or bent to work, or merely stood like miniature scarecrows among the flower-beds.

Mother's familiar, the skivvy Mavis, was the woodman's daughter, one of nine. Her legs, knock-kneed walking sticks, suggested a being of some fragility. Not so. Mavis was strong as a nanny goat, and had untrammelled breasts, large as canteloupes, that lolloped about under her black dress, and a weighty face resembling that of Toulouse-Lautrec's Oscar Wilde, the Mae Murray lip-sticked cupid's-bow included. She and mother, busy as light-minded sorceresses, gossiped and sang as they singed batches of scones, rolled out leather pastry, and endlessly rearranged the Mary Gregories and flat-backs. In the proper season they worked with passionate incompetence to brew jams which either remained liquid for ever, or set like jasper. Their housekeeping can be summed up in the turn-of-the-screw fact that from a Sea Pie we once fished out Mavis's rolled gold brooch *and* one of mother's bridge-score pencils with a sealing-wax rosebud on the end.

Years later, Mavis was found raped and strangled under the river-bank plane trees. I was home during a university holiday, and was in the room when mother heard the news. She did not scream or break down as I expected. Before my eyes she rapidly shrivelled and abated, as though blood and frivolity had gushed to immediate waste. After a while, she uttered the thought, as women do, that lay at the back of the thought she wished to utter: 'Now I'll have no one to give my old clothes to.' She shed no tears, and remained older and dejected until the murderer, an Italian pea-picker, was hanged. On this day she treated herself to a bottle of champagne, drunk solo, and a volcanic eruption of tears from which she reappeared as though nothing had tampered with her gaiety, or spilt blood on her rose-coloured spectacles.

This excess and intensity of feeling had always to be burned away, and got mother into involvements with many a suspect charity. More often it swept her into eccentric enterprises with a number of other women whom she called, in her city accent, The Gels. These fads had, usually, one common factor – the products were *hand*-made or *hand*-painted or *hand*-stitched or *hand*-whatever. *Hand* seemed to bestow aesthetic dignity. It is impossible to recall all these bygone enthusiasms now, but their strange fruits were always turning up – lopsided cane baskets; uncircular 'pottery' ash-trays; silk flowers of quite sinister designs – royal blue chrysanthemums were the nadir; felt *boutonnières*; stuffed toys whose intention to archness was impaired by cretinous distortions or a criminal squint. Once, The Gels took to culture and play-reading. They started on Chekhov and Ibsen, but came to their senses and their own level in *The Patsy* and *The Cat and the Canary*.

Neither mother nor The Gels, thank God, made a fad or cult of their children. We were loved and smacked, fed and ordered out of the house to play, made to wash ourselves and go to bed early, learned the wisdom of seen-but-not-heard. The point was that we remained children until it was time for us to be made adults.

At the age of twelve it was too early for nature to start selling me down the river; another year, another spring, another summer, and nature would gash and tangle the strings of my voice, sprinkle hairs on me where there had been none, lubricate my eyes so that they would swivel in the direction of flesh, steam over the clear glass of my mind with the breath of lust, and tempt me to trace on this mist the first letters in the alphabet of profane love. Another spring! – but even then, already, the snake's shadow was in the cup.

From time to time, friends of mother's shingled and short-skirted maidenhood came to stay, often accompanied by their children. Sometimes there would be a more dashing, Eton-cropped, bachelor-woman who brought her own whisky. At least one night, invariably, of her stay one would hear from one's bed the Victrola playing *My Sweetie's Due at Two to Two!*, and guess that she and mother, panting and giggling, were reviving the Charleston. The most constantly recurring of these visitors was Aunt Willy who, in retrospect, seems to have been most like mother: chatterbox, rattle-pated but insolently cocksure, loving yet mocking, with a heart of gold guarded by the tongue of a wasp.

In the spring school-holidays of 1929, Aunt Willy was expected. Looking back, it is today easy to see that mother had worked out a plan. This included making Mavis take a fortnight's leave at an unusual time of the year, and bundling all of us children off to stay with honest-to-God or designated aunts. The day before this exodus, I was pig-rooted from a horse, and broke my wrist. Tears and implorings notwithstanding, I had to stay home. Mother was perfectly able to accept a broken wrist, like bee stings, cut knees, thorns in the bare soles, and fallings in the river, as among the conventional hazards of country childhood. Not for all the bangles in Bombay, however, would she let the maimed child one centimetre beyond the maternal radius. So, there I was, my arm in splints, an unnecessary rug over my knees, sitting before an unnecessary fire. The house seemed hollowly enormous, full of the ticking of clocks, and drugged with the scent from bowls of jonquils and daffodils, of which there were archipelagos in garden and orchard. Enter mother, with a plate of cracknels which, at that stage, I doted on. I was reading *A Tale of Two Cities*. Mother began plumping cushions like someone at the opening of a saucy comedy-drama.

'Aunt Willy,' she said, 'will be here in a couple of hours.'

I knew this. I was not really listening to mother who was, the years had taught me, inclined to prattle on. It is very early in life that the male learns to cast his eyes to heaven, and resignedly think, 'Women!' in a particular tone.

'She is bringing,' said mother, placing her hot hand on my cool forehead to find if it were hot, 'her little girl with her, little Gretel.'

I didn't know, neither did I care, that Aunt Willy had a daughter. If anything it was a black mark. I was not up to daughters.

'You won't be able to play with her. She's not – she's not very strong.'

I went on dropping cracknel crumbs on Miss Pross and Madame Defarge, and wishing mother in Timbuctoo. How much more satisfactory than she were the women of fiction!

'She must have absolute rest and quiet. I'm putting her in Richard's room.'

My fourteen-year-old brother Richard's room was at the back of the house, beyond the moth-eaten green baize door that vilely squawked each time it was swung, and separated the kitchen, the breakfast room, the pantry and the laundry from the front of the house. It had no fire-place, as all the other bedrooms did, and must once have been a store room. Its only window was a barred skylight.

'You must not go down there while Gretel is here. You must keep right away from the room. Never go down there. Never. Not on any account. Do you hear me, Marcus?'

Oh yes, now I heard her. Mother had gone too far. We occupy, all of us, our own five-walled tower of senses. The throne in the central chamber is the throne of intuition, so often the snoozing one. Now the slug-a-bed was as wide awake as a fish. Did I hear mother?

'Yes,' I said, pseudo-laconic. Next, choosing my time, and adopting an over-the-hills-and-far-away expression, I raised my eyes. Mother was indubitably up to something.

'What did I say, Marcus?' Mother being off-hand was patently underhand.

Not only was I more fly than mother, my intuition was less mossy. 'That I was not to disturb the little girl,' I said with perfectly pitched vagueness. For better measure in guile, 'I *love* cracknels,' I gushed, and lowered my false eyes to eighteenth-century Paris. Mother left the room with the air of one who has thrown the cover over the canary's cage.

By the time the cab arrived from the station I was well into my act of decorous invalid engrossed in good book, but my body was as open-pored as a sponge, with every pore an eye, every nerve an ear. I heard mother run along the corridor to the front door, and her high heels on the veranda tiles, on the slate of the veranda steps, on the asphalt path. I heard voices in a blurred zigzag of greetings, and attended to the last details of the indifference I was preparing to display to the apparently sacred Gretel I was now feverish to examine. Time passed. Time passed. Suddenly, I was shocked to realize that I was listening to nothing. I tried to convince myself that they were still in the garden, or that mother was pointing out the blossoming fruit trees in the orchard. This was too unlikely; plants and trees were not a thing with mother. Then, it became obvious that they were in the house without having passed my glass-panelled door. I think I gritted and ground my teeth. After ever, I heard the baize door squawking, and the female tinkle of a congested tea-tray, and a lucid – too lucid – conversation, like a rehearsed duologue, being perpetrated by mother and Aunt Willy. When they came in, the two only of them, talking and stepping as though avoiding the ears and toes of an irritable deity, it was clear that I had been – my mind mouthed the word within me – outwitted.

Aunt Willy kissed me, told me how I had grown, made the right remarks about my wrist, and fiddled with the *chou* of ninon under her chin as though it concealed a cut throat. Mother poured tea full of grouts, for she had not brought the strainer. I watched them, more through the staring eyes of the enthroned one in the innermost chamber than through my actual ones. Aunt Willy had been in tears. Her eyelashes were still moistened into spikes. She and mother bartered remarks in a way-up-yonder manner clearer than crystal, yet informed with wariness. They seemed, too, as women do when supporting a secret and painful burden, to level out their gaze, and to tilt their heads backwards with a nobility that suggested males were shell-less amateurs who, at one and the same time, were to be protected from earthy truths, and wearily despised. It was not until I had fully absorbed the nature of these social gymnastics, and had decided them deceitful, that mother handed a last-minute lie to me, 'Gretel was very, *very* tired. Aunt Willy put her straight to bed.'

The more reckless and impertinent I wished to say, 'If she were so very, *very* tired, why didn't you come down the corridor? Why didn't you come in the short and easy way, instead of the long, awkward way around by the back door?'

This, I knew, would get me nowhere, so, instead: 'I'm sorry. I hope she's soon better, Aunt Willy.'

'Oh, yes,' she said. 'Thank you, Marcus. Yes. Yes, soon.'

She put down her cup and saucer, and walked to the window. I gammoned not to see her dab at her eyes. I reached for another cracknel, and returned to Paris. Mother was too charming and honest not to tell lies. Only the careless and cruel, the inhuman and dishonest, will not lie. I had been pig-rooted from the horse, and stranded on what mother had planned as a private beach. For some reason Gretel was as forbidden as murder. This had been unmistakably borne in on me. I was, therefore, determined to see her.

I did not have a leper's chance. Did I get beyond the baize door, Aunt Willy or mother was always a sword's length away, suddenly materialized, finger on lips, with the opaque admonishing glare of a statue. Belonging, as I did, to a more civilized generation, I asked no questions and was told, therefore, none of the lies children should be told. I was compelled out of the house. I would hear mother at the telephone, and, immediately after, would be told that one of The Gels had asked me to dinner with little Johnny, or that another was sending her twins to take me for a walk. Mother's machinations, indubitably.

If I did not see the mysterious stranger, I did, at last, after four days, hear her.

It was a night of such unblemished moonlight that the air seemed volted, as though some arctic dynamo fed it with electrical fluid. On the opposite slope of the valley the lunatic asylum was more mathematically three-dimensional, more toylike and enlivened with detail than ever in daylight. At some nameless hour I was awakened by a high sweet wailing that lifted and sank, lifted and sank, with such regularity that the eye in my ear saw the sound as an undulating line of incandescence. The moon! I thought. It is the moon calling out. Yet I knew it was Gretel. I heard the thump and patter of the bare feet of the two women, the sound of doors, and fervent murmurings, and of a spoon stirring liquid in a tumbler. Presently, the line of sound faltered, thinned, faded from the air. The house pulsed and purred, seemed almost to simmer under the vibrations from the moon. Before I fell asleep to this soothing sensation, I was more determined than ever to glimpse, at least, the girl lying in the moonlight that rippled through the skylight of the last room in the secret-hidden house.

The opportunity came next afternoon. Mother telephoned the cab for Aunt Willy who was dressed more sternly than I had ever seen her. No ninon, no transparent sleeves, no vaporous dress alive with a design of smudged and outsize roses. Her silver fox furs and eye-veil did little to feminize her outfit of sombre metallic cloth and her metallic casque of hat. Even her scent had a steely sharpness. She was going 'out': I expected to be told no more, and was told no more. She walked down the path as though sleep-walking, as though drugged for some sinister assignation with High Powers in dark spectacles. I watched mother walk with her to the gate at the end of the garden, and talk with her by the cab-step while the horse tugged at the grass on the edge of the footpath. The cab drove off.

As mother was closing the gate, old Miss Stanway appeared, hobbling and hoo-hoo-ing. Miss Stanway was inescapable. Mother was trapped. I did not hesitate. With the speed of a death-adder I moved between the oak hall-chairs and serene trysts by Marcus Stone down the long passage leading to knowledge. The baize door uttered, and swung to behind me. I came to the last room. I stopped. The training of years, which forbade one to assault a privacy, disobey one's mother, or pry behind the manifest affliction of another, stayed me. Memory is more brutal than will: I remembered the moon's voice soaring through the high-ceilinged rooms of night. I saw my sinful hand float upwards, crook its knuckles, and knock. Immediately, the silence behind the painted panels changed its quality, thickened to a silence one could listen to, and which listened back at one. The hand knocked again, more loudly and sinfully.

'I am here. I am here, I am here.' It was a voice that lifted a little, and sank a little, like shallow water.

I was astounded to hear my own voice saying, 'I am here. I am Marcus. May I come in?'

'I am here,' said the voice within.

I turned the handle. The door was locked. This horrified me. Doors in the country were not locked except in the most unorthodox circumstances. Inside doors were never locked. The handle of a large iron key I had never seen before protruded from the brass-rimmed keyhole. I turned it. I opened the door. I fell in love.

Seated with upright but graceful decorum on a low armless

cedar chair was the most exquisite being I had, or have since, seen. It was a girl of my age. Her dress was of yellow velvet, the immediate yellow of a sunflower. Her long straight hair, in an era when all hair seemed clipped or cropped, curled or marcelled, was to me the miracle of the miracle. It fell like a shawl of light over her shoulders. It was the hair of Rapunzel, of all immolated princesses, of all the children lost in the snow or woods of ballads. Her hands and arms and face were whiteness without name. Above her head, on the barred skylight, lay fallen petals of almond blossom. How grey their white. On the girl's lap sat a large doll dressed as she was. It wore a necklace of white beads.

With dark eyes, behind the surface of which were extra shadows, she watched me watching her. She did not move. Then, at last, her lips moved.

'I am Gretel,' she said.

I told her again that I was Marcus.

'I am Gretel. She is Gretel.' She touched the doll's flaxen poll.

'A good idea,' I said. 'And dressed like you! But she has beads.' I remembered my manners. 'I'm sorry you've been sick. How soon will you be better?'

She did not answer, but continued to look at me, as I did at her. My love could find no words. Then inspiration came. I remembered that, among a handful of necklaces tossed to my sisters by mother, there was a white china one. 'I have a present for you,' I said. How else express love, at twelve? How else at ninety, or ever? 'I'll get it. I'll be back.' Although blinded, I was wide awake to the need for chicanery. I locked the door. If mother should escape Miss Stanway before I had decorated my idol with stolen gewgaws, the sin of disobedience would not be discovered. I ran to the front veranda. Mother was still enmeshed in Miss Stanway's tough net of scandal. I stole the white necklace. I returned to the last room.

Gretel and Gretel sat as when I had first seen them, beneath the skylight ruled across by bars, and littered with the petals of spring. I held up the necklace, and smiled and smiled like a dog.

And she smiled.

There are no words to describe how this addition of beauty to a beauty already overwhelming affected me. From that ridge higher than paradise, from that moment, began my journey down through seedy and seedier elsewheres. For a moment only I walked the dazzling tightrope. Slipping my hand from its sling, I advanced, and slid both hands under the cool streams of hair. I fumbled with the clasp. It took an eternity during which I imagined my mother's heels coming to the baize door. At last, the clasp snibbed. I stepped back. During my clumsy work the loop of the necklace had slipped behind the front of the yellow dress. For a moment longer her smile remained. Then she arched her neck to see her gift. Before I could speak, her face writhed and darkened. The doll fell as her hands rose to cover her eyes.

'It's under the dress!' I cried. 'Under the dress!'

It meant nothing. She was wailing as I had heard her wail in the night. No longer did the sound seem to me ravishing and luminous. I spoke in anguish against its inexorable regularity so much stronger than my fractured words. I backed from it. I locked the door. I hurried from the house, terrified. Mother was still at the front gate. When I had fought my public mask into place, I walked, with the right seasoning of calm, towards her. As one performing a tiresome duty, I said, 'Mother, I think that little girl wants something. She's calling out.'

Mother ran.

I stayed in the garden expecting ... expecting what? I could still hear the unfaltering wordless chant in the hollow house. I went for a long walk, mindlessly and slowly, under the trees of the switchback streets. At twilight, I returned. Several of The Gels and mother were, it was immediately apparent, merry. The Victrola was playing *The Naughty Waltz*. All the lights in the house were on.

'Where *have* you been?' cried mother in her fly-away sherry voice. 'Aunt Willy wanted to say goodbye to you.' No mention of Gretel. I walked down the corridor. The door of the final room was open; the low armless chair was empty.

Mother's funeral over, my obligations to the womb are fulfilled: the last, the very last of all obligations. I have none now, to anyone, least of all to myself. Tomorrow, I shall catch the train out of this town, these foothills, over the mountains, and down to Melbourne, down to the terminus. After the terminus, where next, Marcus? I do not know. Here, now, in the old house, my sisters' 'common sense' importunities to return in one of their cars prevent me from thinking a decision. If they and my brother Richard, the bores and the bore, do not stop trying to 'reason' with me, I shall be forced to come up with the truth rather than the facts.

'No,' I keep on saying. 'You are all terribly kind, but no. I don't want a lift. I'd rather go by train. Really. I prefer the train. Thank you, no.'

The facts are that I do prefer train travel, and that I am going by train. The truth is that my tastes are stronger than flesh and blood: I should rather be bored by my own self-sufficiency than by them. While I do not cavil, ever, at events, I can be made peevish to the point of mayhem by the after-math of events. *This* aftermath is treacherous. The brothers and sisters I parted from as young people are not the people I am with now; they usurp the names of phantoms.

Here we are in the drawing-room with its french windows open on to the tiled veranda. The horizontal granite door has closed. The rain has been removed like a device that has served its purpose.

Here we all are, the children, middle-aged, yet bickering and needling like children. Here are some of The Gels, touched by their own winters; three or four authentic uncles and aunts with the frost on them; several of those adopted aunts who were always popping skittishly in and out of our childhoods.

'Where,' I say to shut up my most persistently 'common-sense' sister, 'is Aunt Willy?'

'She's gone to see Gretel.' She says it as though saying nothing much of no one much, and sips at her brandy. 'Aunt Willy's an absurd old thing. No self-control. But she might as well grab the opportunity to see Gretel while she's here for the funeral.'

'Yes, of course,' I say, without knowing what it means. I now arrange a sentence with some care: 'Aunt Willy's seeing Gretel right now?'

'Why not? She drives up to see her every week. Done it for

years and years. She used to spend the night here with mother.'

Once again I have to think out a sentence: 'So Gretel's still here?'

'Still here. There was talk of her going to Melbourne about eight or nine years ago. But it fell through. When I was up here last time Aunt Willy was too. So I went with her to see Gretel. She must be touching fifty now . . . '

'Forty-four or forty-five,' I say.

'Perhaps. She looks eighty. Long grey hair hanging down. You can see her window from here. The top one in the tower on the right.'

She points through the french windows, across the valley, to the Cape Dutch barracks, and the sharp-cut garden beds, and the high wall, exposed like a medieval painting on the opposite slope.

My sister drains her glass. 'Get me another brandy, will you? I do wish you'd be sensible, and come down in the car with us tonight.'

'What does she look like?'

'Who look like? Oh, Gretel. Really, Marcus, you're a ghoul. Just like any loony. Sits there year after year with a grubby old doll on her lap. Quite harmless, unless they try to take the doll. Or Gretel's necklace. She keeps on stroking these white china beads, and grinning like a . . . like a . . . '

JUDAH WATEN

Mother

When I was a small boy I was often morbidly conscious of Mother's intent, searching eyes fixed on me. She would gaze for minutes on end without speaking one word. I was always disconcerted and would guiltily look down at the ground, anxiously turning over in my mind my day's activities.

But very early I knew her thoughts were far away from my petty doings; she was concerned with them only in so far as they gave her further reason to justify her hostility to the life around us. She was preoccupied with my sister and me; she was for ever concerned with our future in this new land in which she would always feel a stranger.

I gave her little comfort, for though we had been in the country for only a short while I had assumed many of the ways of those around me. I had become estranged from her. Or so it seemed to Mother, and it grieved her.

When I first knew her she had no intimate friend, nor do I think she felt the need of one with whom she could discuss her innermost thoughts and hopes. With me, though I knew she loved me very deeply, she was never on such near terms of friendship as sometimes exist between a mother and son. She emanated a kind of certainty in herself, in her view of life, that no opposition or human difficulty could shrivel or destroy. 'Be strong before people, only weep before God,' she would say and she lived up to that precept even with Father.

In our little community in the city, acquaintances spoke derisively of Mother's refusal to settle down as others had done, of what they called her propensity for highfalutin day-dreams and of the severity and unreasonableness of her opinions.

Yet her manner with people was always gentle. She spoke softly, she was measured in gesture, and frequently it seemed she was functioning automatically, her mind far away from her body. There was a grave beauty in her still, sad face, her searching, dark-brown eyes and black hair. She was thin and stooped in carriage as though a weight always lay on her shoulders.

From my earliest memory of Mother it somehow seemed quite natural to think of her as apart and other-worldly and different, not of everyday things as Father was. In those days he was a young-looking man who did not hesitate to make friends with children as soon as they were able to talk to him and laugh at his stories. Mother was older than he was. She must have been a woman of nearly forty, but she seemed even older. She changed little for a long time, showing no traces of growing older at all until, towards the end of her life, she suddenly became an old lady.

I was always curious about Mother's age. She never had birthdays like other people, nor did anyone else in our family. No candles were ever lit or cakes baked or presents given in our house. To my friends in the street who boasted of their birthday parties I self-consciously repeated my Mother's words, that such celebrations were only a foolish and eccentric form of self-worship.

'Nothing but deception,' she would say. 'As though life can be chopped into neat twelve-month parcels! It's deeds, not years, that matter.'

Although I often repeated her words and even prided myself on not having birthdays I could not restrain myself from once asking Mother when she was born.

'I was born. I'm alive as you can see, so what more do you want to know?' she replied, so sharply that I never asked her about her age again.

In so many other ways Mother was different. Whereas all the rest of the women I knew in the neighbouring houses and in other parts of the city took pride in their housewifely abilities, their odds and ends of new furniture, the neat appearance of their homes, Mother regarded all those things as of little importance. Our house always looked as if we had just moved in or were about to move out. An impermanent and impatient spirit dwelt within our walls; Father called it living on one leg like a bird.

Wherever we lived there were some cases partly unpacked, rolls of linoleum stood in a corner, only some of the windows had curtains. There were never sufficient wardrobes, so that clothes hung on hooks behind doors. And all the time Mother's things accumulated. She never parted with anything, no matter how old it was. A shabby green plush coat bequeathed to her by her own mother hung on a nail in her bedroom. Untidy heaps of tattered books, newspapers, and journals from the old country mouldered in corners of the house, while under her bed in tin trunks she kept her dearest possessions. In those trunks there were bundles of old letters, two heavily underlined books on nursing, an old Hebrew Bible, three silver spoons given her by an aunt with whom she had once lived, a diploma on yellow parchment, and her collection of favourite books.

From one or other of her trunks she would frequently pick a book and read to my sister and me. She would read in a wistful voice poems and stories of Jewish liberators from Moses until the present day, of the heroes of the 1905 Revolution and pieces by Tolstoy and Gorky and Sholom Aleichem. Never did she stop to inquire whether we understood what she was reading; she said we should understand later if not now.

I liked to hear Mother read, but always she seemed to choose a time for reading that clashed with something or other I was doing in the street or in a nearby paddock. I would be playing with the boys in the street, kicking a football or spinning a top or flying a kite, when Mother would unexpectedly appear and without even casting a glance at my companions she would ask me to come into the house, saying she wanted to read to me and my sister. Sometimes I was overcome with humiliation and I would stand listlessly with burning cheeks until she repeated her words. She never reproached me for my disobedience nor did she ever utter a reproof to the boys who taunted me as, crestfallen, I followed her into the house.

Why Mother was as she was only came to me many years later. Then I was even able to guess when she was born.

She was the last child of a frail and overworked mother and a bleakly pious father who hawked reels of cotton and other odds and ends in the villages surrounding a town in Russia. My grandfather looked with great disapproval on his off-spring, who were all girls, and he was hardly aware of my mother at all. She was left well alone by her older sisters, who with feverish impatience were waiting for their parents to make the required arrangements for their marriages.

During those early days Mother rarely looked out into the streets, for since the great pogroms few Jewish children were ever to be seen abroad. From the iron grille of the basement she saw the soles of the shoes of the passers-by and not very much more. She had never seen a tree, a flower, or a bird.

But when Mother was about fifteen her parents died and she went to live with a widowed aunt and her large family in a far-away village. Her aunt kept an inn and Mother was tucked away with her cousins in a remote part of the building, away from the prying eyes of the customers in the tap-rooms. Every evening her aunt would gaze at her with startled eyes as if surprised to find her among the family.

'What am I going to do with you?' she would say. 'I've got daughters of my own. If only your dear father of blessed name had left you just a tiny dowry it would have been such a help. Ah well! If you have no hand you can't make a fist.'

At that time Mother could neither read nor write. And as she had never had any childhood playmates or friends of any kind she hardly knew what to talk about with her cousins. She spent the days cheerlessly pottering about the kitchen or sitting for hours, her eyes fixed on the dark wall in front of her.

Some visitor to the house, observing the small, lonely girl, took pity on her and decided to give her an education. Mother was given lessons every few days and after a while she acquired a smattering of Yiddish and Russian, a little arithmetic and a great fund of Russian and Jewish stories.

New worlds gradually opened before Mother. She was seized with a passion of primers, grammars, arithmetic and story books, and soon the idea entered her head that the way out of her present dreary life lay through these books. There was another world, full of warmth and interesting things, and in it there was surely a place for her. She became obsessed with the thought that it wanted only some decisive step on her part to go beyond her aunt's house into the life she dreamed about.

Somewhere she read of a Jewish hospital which had just opened in a distant city and one winter's night she told her aunt she wanted to go to relatives who lived there. They would help her to find work in the hospital.

'You are mad!' exclaimed her aunt. 'Forsake a home for a wild fancy! Who could have put such a notion into your head? Besides, a girl of eighteen can't travel alone at this time of the year.'

It was from that moment that Mother's age became something to be manipulated as it suited her. She said to her aunt that she was not eighteen, but twenty-two. She was getting up in years and she could not continue to impose on her aunt's kindness.

'How can you be twenty-two?' her aunt replied greatly puzzled.

A long pause ensued while she tried to reckon up Mother's years. She was born in the month Tammuz according to the Jewish calendar, which corresponded to the old-style Russian calendar month of June, but in what year? She could remember being told of Mother's birth, but nothing outstanding had happened then to enable her to place the year. With all her nieces and nephews, some dead and many alive, scattered all over the vastness of the country only a genius could keep track of all their birthdays. Perhaps the girl was twenty-two, and if that were so her chance of getting a husband in the village was pretty remote; twenty-two was far too old. The thought entered her head that if she allowed Mother to go to their kinsmen in the city she would be relieved of the responsibility of finding a dowry for her, and so reluctantly she agreed.

But it was not until the spring that she finally consented to let her niece go. As the railway station was several miles from the village Mother was escorted there on foot by her aunt and cousins. With all her possessions, including photographs of her parents and a tattered Russian primer tied in a great bundle, Mother went forth into the vast world.

In the hospital she didn't find that for which she hungered; it seemed still as far away as in the village. She had dreamed of the new life where all would be noble, where men and women would dedicate their lives to bringing about a richer and happier life, just as she had read.

But she was put to scrubbing floors and washing linen every day from morning till night until she dropped exhausted into her bed in the attic. No one looked at her, no one spoke to her but to give her orders. Her one day off in the month she spent with her relatives who gave her some cast-off clothes and shoes and provided her with the books on nursing she so urgently needed. She was more than ever convinced that her deliverance would come through these books and she set about swallowing their contents with renewed zest.

As soon as she had passed all the examinations and acquired the treasured diploma she joined a medical mission that was about to proceed without a moment's delay to a distant region where a cholera epidemic raged. And then for several years she remained with the same group, moving from district to district, wherever disease flourished.

Whenever Mother looked back over her life it was those years that shone out. Then she was with people who were filled with an ardour for mankind and it seemed to her they lived happily and freely, giving and taking friendship in an atmosphere pulsating with warmth and hope.

All this had come to an end in 1905 when the medical mission was dissolved and several of Mother's colleagues were killed in the uprising. Then with a heavy heart and little choice she had returned to nursing in the city, but this time in private houses attending on well-to-do ladies.

It was at the home of one of her patients that she met Father. What an odd couple they must have been! She was taciturn, choosing her words carefully, talking mainly of her ideas and little about herself. Father bared his heart with guileless abandon. He rarely had secrets and there was no division in his mind between intimate and general matters. He could talk as freely of his feelings for Mother or of a quarrel with his father as he could of a vaudeville show or the superiority of one game of cards as against another.

Father said of himself he was like an open hand at solo and all men were his brothers. For a story, a joke, or an apt remark he would forsake his father and mother, as the saying goes. Old tales, new ones invented for the occasion, jokes rolled off his tongue in a never-ending procession. Every trifle, every incident was material for a story and he haunted music-halls and circuses, for he liked nothing better than comedians and clowns, actors and buskers.

He brought something bubbly and frivolous into Mother's life and for a while she forgot her stern precepts. In those days Father's clothes were smart and gay; he wore bright straw hats and loud socks and fancy, buttoned-up boots. Although she had always regarded any interest in clothes as foolish and a sign of an empty and frivolous nature Mother then felt proud of his fashionable appearance. He took her to his favourite resorts, to music-halls and to tea-houses where he and his cronies idled away hours, boastfully recounting stories of successes in business or merely swapping jokes. They danced nights away, though Mother was almost stupefied by the band and the bright lights and looked with distaste on the extravagant clothes of the dancers who bobbed and cavorted.

All this was in the early days of their marriage. But soon Mother was filled with misgivings. Father's world, the world of commerce and speculation, of the buying and selling of goods neither seen nor touched, was repugnant and frightening to her. It lacked stability, it was devoid of ideals, it was fraught with ruin. Father was a trader in air, as the saying went.

Mother's anxiety grew as she observed more closely his mode of life. He worked in fits and starts. If he made enough in one hour to last him a week or a month his business was at an end and he went off in search of friends and pleasure. He would return to business only when his money had just about run out. He was concerned only with one day at a time; about tomorrow he would say, clicking his fingers, his blue eyes focused mellowly on space, 'We'll see'.

But always he had plans for making great fortunes. They never came to anything but frequently they produced unexpected results. It so happened that on a number of occasions someone Father trusted acted on the plans he had talked about so freely before he even had time to leave the tea-house. Then there were fiery scenes with his faithless friends. But Father's rage passed away quickly and he would often laugh and make jokes over the table about it the very same day. He imagined everyone else forgot as quickly as he did and he was always astonished to discover that his words uttered hastily in anger had made him enemies.

'How should I know that people have such long memories for hate? I've only a cat's memory,' he would explain innocently.

'If you spit upwards, you're bound to get it back in the face,' Mother irritably upbraided him.

Gradually Mother reached the conclusion that only migration to another country would bring about any real change in their life, and with all her persistence she began to urge him to take the decisive step. She considered America, France, Palestine, and finally decided on Australia. One reason for the choice was the presence there of distant relatives who would undoubtedly help them to find their feet in that far away continent. Besides, she was sure that Australia was so different from any other country that Father was bound to acquire a new and more solid way of earning a living there.

For a long time Father paid no heed to her agitation and refused to make any move.

'Why have you picked on Australia and not Tibet, for example?' he asked ironically. 'There isn't much difference between the two lands. Both are on the other side of the moon.'

The idea of leaving his native land seemed so fantastic to him that he refused to regard it seriously. He answered Mother with jokes and tales of travellers who disappeared in balloons. He had no curiosity to explore distant countries, he hardly ever ventured beyond the three or four familiar streets of his city. And why should his wife be so anxious for him to find a new way of earning a living? Didn't he provide her with food and a roof over her head? He had never given one moment's thought to his mode of life and he could not imagine any reason for doing so. It suited him like his gay straw hats and smart suits.

Yet in the end he did what Mother wanted him to do,

though even on the journey he was tortured by doubts and he positively shouted words of indecision. But he was no sooner in Australia than he put away all thoughts of his homeland and he began to regard the new country as his permanent home. It was not so different from what he had known before. Within a few days he had met some fellow merchants and, retiring to a café, they talked about business in the new land. There were fortunes to be made here, Father very quickly concluded. There was, of course, the question of a new language but that was no great obstacle to business. You could buy and sell – it was a good land, Father said.

It was different with Mother. Before she was one day off the ship she wanted to go back.

The impressions she gained on that first day remained with her all her life. It seemed to her there was an irritatingly superior air about the people she met, the customs officials, the cab men, the agent of the new house. Their faces expressed something ironical and sympathetic, something friendly and at the same time condescending. She imagined everyone on the wharf, in the street, looked at her in the same way and she never forgave them for treating her as if she were in need of their good-natured tolerance.

Nor was she any better disposed to her relatives and the small delegation of Jews who met her at the ship. They had all been in Australia for many years and they were anxious to impress new-comers with their knowledge of the country and its customs. They spoke in a hectoring manner. This was a free country, they said, it was cultured, one used a knife and fork and not one's hands. Everyone could read and write and no one shouted at you. There were no oppressors here as in the old country.

Mother thought she understood their talk; she was quick and observant where Father was sometimes extremely guileless. While they talked Father listened with a good-natured smile and it is to be supposed he was thinking of a good story he could tell his new acquaintances. But Mother fixed them with a firm, relentless gaze and, suddenly interrupting their injunctions, said in the softest of voices, 'If there are no oppressors here, as you say, why do you frisk about like house dogs? Whom do you have to please?'

Mother never lost this hostile and ironical attitude to the new land. She would have nothing of the country; she would not even attempt to learn the language. And she only began to look with a kind of interest at the world round her when my sister and I were old enough to go to school. Then all her old feeling for books and learning was re-awakened. She handled our primers and readers as if they were sacred texts.

She set great aims for us. We were to shine in medicine, in literature, in music; our special sphere depended on her fancy at a particular time. In one of these ways we could serve humanity best, and whenever she read to us the stories of Tolstoy and Gorky she would tell us again and again of her days with the medical mission. No matter how much schooling we should get we needed ideals, and what better ideals were there than those that had guided her in the days of the medical mission? They would save us from the soulless influences of this barren land.

Father wondered why she spent so much time reading and telling us stories of her best years and occasionally he would take my side when I protested against Mother taking us away from our games.

'They're only children,' he said. 'Have pity on them. If you stuff their little heads, God alone knows how they will finish up.' Then, pointing to us, he added, 'I'll be satisfied if he is a good carpenter; and if she's a good dressmaker that will do, too.'

'At least,' Mother replied, 'you have the good sense not to suggest they go in for business. Life has taught you something at last.'

'Can I help it that I am in business?' he suddenly shouted angrily. 'I know it's a pity my father didn't teach me to be a professor.'

But he calmed down quickly, unable to stand for long Mother's steady gaze and compressed lips.

It exasperated us that Father should give in so easily so that we could never rely on him to take our side for long. Although he argued with Mother about us he secretly agreed with her. And outside the house he boasted about her, taking a peculiar pride in her culture and attainments, and repeating her words just as my sister and I did.

Mother was very concerned about how she could give us a musical education. It was out of the question that we both be taught an instrument, since Father's business was at a low ebb and he hardly knew where he would find enough money to pay the rent, so she took us to a friend's house to listen to gramophone records. They were of the old-fashioned, cylindrical kind made by Edison and they sounded far away and thin like the voice of a ventriloquist mimicking far off musical instruments. But my sister and I marvelled at them. We should have been willing to sit over the long, narrow horn for days, but Mother decided that it would only do us harm to listen to military marches and the stupid songs of the music hall.

It was then that we began to pay visits to musical emporiums. We went after school and during the holidays in the mornings. There were times when Father waited long for his lunch or evening meal, but he made no protest. He supposed Mother knew what she was doing in those shops and he told his friends of the effort Mother was making to acquaint us with music.

Our first visit to the shops were in the nature of reconnoitring sorties. In each emporium Mother looked the attendants up and down while we thumbed the books on the counters, stared at the enlarged photographs of illustrious composers, and studied the various catalogues of gramophone records. We went from shop to shop until we just about knew all there was to know about the records and sheet music and books in stock.

Then we started all over again from the first shop and this time we came to hear the records.

I was Mother's interpreter and I would ask one of the salesmen to play us a record she had chosen from one of the catalogues. Then I would ask him to play another. It might have been a piece for violin by Tchaikovsky or Beethoven or an aria sung by Caruso or Chaliapin. This would continue until Mother observed the gentleman in charge of the gramophone losing his patience and we would take our leave.

With each visit Mother became bolder and several times she asked to have whole symphonies and concertos played to us. We sat for nearly an hour cooped up in a tiny room with the salesman restlessly shuffling his feet, yawning and not knowing what to expect next. Mother pretended he hardly existed and, making herself comfortable in the cane chair, with a determined, intent expression she gazed straight ahead at the whirling disc.

We were soon known to everyone at the shops. Eyes lit up as we walked in, Mother looking neither this way nor that with two children walking in file through the passageway towards the record department. I was very conscious of the humorous glances and the discreet sniggers that followed us and I would sometimes catch hold of Mother's hand and plead with her to leave the shop. But she paid no heed and we continued to our destination. The more often we came the more uncomfortably self-conscious I became and I dreaded the laughing faces round me.

Soon we became something more than a joke. The smiles turned to scowls and the shop attendants refused to play us any more records. The first time this happened the salesman mumbled something and left us standing outside the door of the music-room.

Mother was not easily thwarted and without a trace of a smile she said we should talk to the manager. I was filled with a sense of shame and humiliation and with downcast eyes I sidled towards the entrance of the shop.

Mother caught up with me and, laying her hand upon my arm, she said, 'What are you afraid of? Your mother won't disgrace you, believe me.' Looking at me in her searching way she went on, 'Think carefully. Who is right – are they or are we? Why shouldn't they play for us? Does it cost them anything? By which other way can we ever hope to hear something good? Just because we are poor must we cease our striving?'

She continued to talk in this way until I went back with her. The three of us walked into the manager's office and I translated Mother's words.

The manager was stern, though I imagine he must have had some difficulty in keeping his serious demeanour.

'But do you ever intend to buy any records?' he said after I had spoken.

'If I were a rich woman would you ask me that question?'

Mother replied and I repeated her words in a halting voice.

'Speak up to him,' she nudged me while I could feel my face fill with hot blood.

The manager repeated his first question and Mother, impatient at my hesitant tone, plunged into a long speech on our right to music and culture and in fact the rights of all men, speaking in her own tongue as though the manager understood every word. It was in vain; he merely shook his head.

We were barred from shop after shop, and in each case Mother made a stand, arguing at length until the man in charge flatly told us not to come back until we could afford to buy records.

We met with rebuffs in other places as well.

Once as we wandered through the university, my sister and I sauntering behind while Mother opened doors, listening to lectures for brief moments, we unexpectedly found ourselves in a large room where white-coated young men and women sat on high stools in front of arrays of tubes, beakers and jars.

Mother's eyes lit up brightly and she murmured something about knowledge and science. We stood close to her and gazed round in astonishment; neither her words nor what we saw conveyed anything to us. She wanted to go round the room but a gentleman wearing a black gown came up and asked us if we were looking for someone. He was a distin-guished looking person with a florid face and a fine grey mane.

Repeating Mother's words I said, 'We are not looking for anyone; we are simply admiring this room of knowledge.'

The gentleman's face wrinkled pleasantly. With a tiny smile playing over his lips he said regretfully that we could not stay, since only students were permitted in the room.

As I interpreted his words Mother's expression changed. Her sallow face was almost red. For ten full seconds she looked the gentleman in the eyes. Then she said rapidly to me, 'Ask him why he speaks with such a condescending smile on his face.'

I said, 'My Mother asks why you talk with such a superior smile on your face?'

He coughed, shifted his feet restlessly and his face set severely. Then he glared at his watch and without another word walked away with dignified steps.

When we came out into the street a spring day was in its full beauty. Mother sighed to herself and after a moment's silence said, 'That fine professor thinks he is a liberal-minded man, but behind his smile he despises people such as us. You will have to struggle here just as hard as I had to back home. For all the fine talk it is like all other countries. But where are the people with ideals like those back home, who aspire to something better?'

She repeated those words frequently, even when I was a boy of thirteen and I knew so much more about the new country that was my home. Then I could argue with her.

I said to her that Benny who lived in our street was always reading books and papers and hurrying to meetings. Benny was not much older than I was and he had many friends whom he met in the park on Sunday. They all belonged to this country and they were interested in all the things Mother talked about.

'Benny is an exception,' she said with an impatient shrug of her shoulders, 'and his friends are only a tiny handful.' Then she added, 'And what about you? You and your companions only worship bats and balls as heathens do stone idols. Why, in the old country boys of your age took part in the fight to deliver mankind from oppression! They gave everything, their strength and health, even their lives, for that glorious ideal.'

'That's what Benny wants to do,' I said, pleased to be able to answer Mother.

'But it's so different here. Even your Benny will be swallowed up in the smug, smooth atmosphere. You wait and see.'

She spoke obstinately. It seemed impossible to change her. Her vision was too much obscured by passionate dreams of the past for her to see any hope in the present, in the new land.

But as an afterthought she added, 'Perhaps it is different for those like you and Benny. But for me I can never find my way into this life here.'

She turned away, her narrow back stooped, her gleaming black hair curled into a bun on her short, thin neck, her shoes equally down at heel on each side.

DAL STIVENS

The Wonderfully
Intelligent Sheep-Dog

By rights the wind ought to have been using my whitened ribs as a xylophone weeks ago and the crows ought to have been as fat as ticks from feeding on my unattended mob of sheep, with me tossed in as a before-dinner titbit. I was in the back of the outback, two hundred miles from anywhere, with a broken leg; but instead of having to risk a knock on the Pearly Gates everything was dodger. My leg was healing as well as it would in one of those posh city hospitals, my mob was thriving and growing pound notes right under my eyes, and the crows were too scared of Peggy, my kelpie sheep-dog, to poke their noses out of the gorge where she'd chased them.

To make things even more snitcher I was living on the fat of the land, and in a few minutes I'd sit down to a plate of roast wild duck that would have set me back ten bob at one of those flash Sydney restaurants. About an hour ago a mob of black ducks had come soaring past and settled on the billabong.

'By gosh, I'd like to sink my molars into one of those,' I said aloud to myself. I'd got into the habit long ago.

I'd hardly finished talking before Peggy, my kelpie sheep-bitch, was tugging the Cashmore out of the back of the sulky. She lugs it over to where I lay in my camp stretcher and then went off to fetch me some cartridges. I couldn't see the point of it though, because the billabong was a good quarter of a mile away and there's no shot gun made that will carry that far.

I should have trusted the kelpie. All kelpies are beautiful with sheep and as intelligent as you like. But none I ever struck were in the same paddock as Peggy. She pelted off towards that billabong and scared the blackies into the air. I expected them to head away, but Peggy knew what she was doing. There was a mirage just by my camp and, just as Peggy had worked it out, they took it for water and settled on the ground. I let them have both barrels and bagged seventeen.

If Peggy had had fingers she'd have plucked and cleaned them there and then, but she did almost everything else while I fixed the ducks up. She dragged fresh wood onto the fire, brought the pan to me, and fetched the fat tin.

I'd done my leg in six weeks ago. I went head over turkey out of the sulky when the right wheel hit a log I hadn't seen.

'Well,' I told myself then, 'you'll do a perish, mate, and no mistake. You're two hundred miles as the crow flies from anywhere.'

Talking of crows, there were millions of 'em and as soon as they saw me lying on the ground, they came and perched in the trees right over my head, cawing loudly, and sharpening their beaks on the branches, and telling themselves that supper wouldn't be long. But as it turned out they reckoned without Peggy.

I lay on the ground and thought it over. It was queer country where I was, and I could believe that no one else had ever been here except perhaps an odd swaggie like the bloke who had told me about this valley. Six months earlier the big drought had made me take to the roads with my mob of a thousand sheep. Others were in the long paddock like myself and there weren't many pickings for my mob, which were losing condition fast. Then the swaggie I'd helped out with some tobacco put me on to this spot. It was only five days' going from where I was, but it turned out to be tough. I lost a couple of hundred ewes and two or three dogs got sick and turned up their toes, leaving me only Peggy. For the last three days I had to head across country too hungry to support a cockroach. I wondered why the hell I had ever listened to that sundowner. But when we got through the valley mouth everything was dodger. The grass was thick, up to the sulky's floor in places, and there was plenty of water. Here was rich ten-pound-an-acre country in the middle of a stretch you wouldn't give tenpence an acre for – and I had it to myself. And then I had to do my leg in.

So many crows had perched in the big gums around me

that their limbs began to droop like weeping willows.

'Well, I suppose I'd better try some splints,' I said aloud to myself. The next thing Peggy is beating it off into the bush and although I yelled and whistled to her to come back, she took no notice. It wasn't like her and I put it down to the queer something or other I felt about this stretch of country. It wasn't natural, for one thing, for there to be so many crows. When I thought Peggy had cleared out I felt pretty low, I can tell you. But in less time than it takes to tell you this, Peggy is back with two bits of bark she has gnawed off, which are just the right length for splints. Before I'd quite cottoned on to what I had to do with them, Peggy has raced off again and is scrounging round the back of the sulky for an old shirt I had stowed there for me to tear into bandages.

While I'm doing that Peggy cuts loose on the crows. I've heard blokes claim the kelpies they owned were so smart they could work flies into the neck of a beer bottle, but they had nothing on Peggy. Almost before I've fixed the splints Peggy has worked those kellies into a single mob and taken the black death birds a mile up the valley where she yards them into a gorge and leaves them there, cawing madly but not game to move out. Peggy comes pelting back just as I'm saying, 'I'd have a chance now if I could get the tent fixed up. That and a good meal would help.'

The words are hardly out before Peggy is tearing around looking for poles for the tent. She had some trouble biting through the young saplings, but in the end we had enough, and we got the tent rigged between us, though Peggy had hardly enough weight for laying back on the ropes.

When the tent was up and I'd crawled into the camp stretcher I started thinking how hungry I was and was just about to tell Peggy to fetch me the hunk of corn beef; but she had other ideas. She reckoned I needed some fresh meat now that I was an invalid, and scooted away into the bush. In about ten minutes she came back with a three-quarters grown buck which I skinned and cut up. I'd barely finished the job before she was waving a bit of bark under my nose and making signs for me to put a match to it, and in no time she had built a good roasting fire.

I lived for about a month on rabbits and wild pigeons

which Peggy used to stalk and catch, and then I felt like a change of diet, particularly when I saw that mob of black ducks. Well, as I told you, Peggy worked the mirage lurk on them, and did those blackies taste good!

Peggy didn't stop at roast duck, however. I noticed that evening that she seemed upset about something. She started walking round and round in circles and every now and then she'd sigh and put a paw behind her ear.

Then suddenly she barked excitedly and beat it off into the bush and came back with Blossom, my sulky mare. While I was wondering what she was up to, she scoots off again and comes back, dragging a largish tree branch with her. She made signs to me and after a bit I cottoned on to what she wanted and hitched Blossom to the branch. As soon as that was done, Peggy chases Blossom up to the billabong and into the water. Blossom doesn't want to go in at first but Peggy isn't in a mood for any nonsense. She drives Blossom up and down and back and across that billabong. The water gets muddy and fish start choking and begin floating to the top, belly upwards. Peggy fetches in two big Murray cod and a catfish. She must have forgotten I didn't like catfish.

Afterwards, I'd only got to say I'd like some fish and Blossom would head for the bush; but, of course, she never got very far before Peggy brought her back for me to hitch to a tree branch. A couple of times Peggy varied the menu by diving into the billabong and working a couple of hundred crays into a kerosene tin she'd set on the bank. She knew I was partial to yabbies. Peggy, by the way, was well in pup by this time, but she stuck to her job.

Just about this time, I noticed something queer was happening to the sheep. I thought I was going nuts at first. The sheep were growing green wool. And Blossom was growing green hair. When I got over the shock I worked it out it must be something to do with the grass and it being spring because Peggy still kept her usual red colour. So each day for a week I nibbled a handful of the grass and sure enough my own hair and beard began to turn green. It grew so quick too that it was down to my knees in a couple of days. I knocked off eating the grass then, of course, because green wasn't a colour I'd choose myself for my hair or beard. As soon as I stopped eating the grass my hair went back to its usual brown.

The trouble with Blossom was, the green hair grew so fast that she stumbled over her mane and she could scarcely see. I had to clip her every three days and at first it was something to keep me occupied, but after a while I got fed up, particularly when I had to do it every second day.

I was worried now about the sheep because their green wool was soon about ten feet long and they couldn't move without treading on each other's fleeces and tripping each other up. They were blind as bats, too, and couldn't find their way to drink at the billabong without Peggy helping them there.

To make things worse Peggy was just about to drop her pups and this slowed her up in her work. Three of them arrived one night and before their eyes were open Peggy started training them to work the sheep. The pups made a bit of difference when they grew up a little, but I could see the job was getting worse. The fleeces were now twenty feet long and I had to clip Blossom every day. The sheep were falling over every few minutes.

'I wish there was some way of shearing the sheep,' I said to myself.

Before I could blink Peggy is heading for the billabong and barking for the three pups, all bitches, to follow her. All four kelpies dive into the water and I heard a great deal of barking and splashing going on. In about five minutes I noticed a great black and grey mass crawling over the ground. It's like a wave, about four feet high, and when it gets near I see that Peggy and her pups have hunted millions and millions of crayfish out of the billabong. Before I can tumble to what it is all about, the yabbies are crawling all over the sheep and nipping off the fleeces. You wouldn't credit how quickly those crays shore the sheep, only, of course, there were so many of them. Soon there were fleeces all over the place.

'You're a smart girl, Peggy,' I told her, 'but the fleeces ought to be gathered up.'

Peggy just barked at me as though to let me know there was nothing to worry about because she's worked out a way of fixing that, too. And she had, by golly. I hadn't noticed before, but the fleeces were getting stacked together. Peggy had her pups yarding up the bulldog and meat ants to do the job. My eyes were sticking out like organ-stops by the time the ants had finished, because they heaped all that lovely green wool into a stack as high as a six-storey building.

I was still marvelling at all this when I heard Blossom squealing her head off and saw that Peggy had sooled some of the crays on to clipping her hair. That pleased me nearly as much as all that beautiful wool that was already dyed.

It got into summer and the sheep started growing yellow wool. Almost all the ewes had lambed in the spring and the lambs grew yellow wool, too, just as fast as their mothers. Occasionally a few of the crows sneaked out of the gorge and tried to peck some of the wool out of the sheep's backs, but Peggy stopped their caper pretty smartly and hunted them back. I was able to get about now, but had to leave the work to Peggy and her pups, of course. I wouldn't have known how to start making the yabbies do their job. It was pretty hot, so Peggy sooled the crays on to the shearing every ten or twelve days. By the end of summer I had a great stack of yellow wool, a little bigger, if anything, than that of the green wool. It was as good as growing five-pound notes.

I kept tag of the days on a calendar a storekeeper had given me and one day when I was crossing off a day Peggy took a peek over my shoulder and suddenly got so excited, barking and jumping up, that I had to chase her away. What had got her worked up was the coloured picture of a Highlander in the Campbell of Breadalbane tartan on the calendar, and I put it down to her having got a kick in the ribs from a bloke in kilts at a Highland gathering on New Year's Day – or perhaps it was Peggy's Scottish blood coming out. Kelpies were bred from smooth-haired Scotch collies of the black-and-tan variety with possibly a bit of dingo, as you know, and are the most wonderfully intelligent sheep-dogs in the world.

When we started running into autumn I wondered what coloured wool the sheep would grow next. Don't ask me why, but it turned out to be blue, and by and by I had a large heap of blue wool.

I kept ticking the days off the calendar, and as winter came along the sheep began to grow black wool. About this time

Peggy and her pups ran into a spot of trouble with the crays. Most days now they took a bit of driving to their work and would try to sneak off into the bush. I can't say I blamed them, because their claws were getting worn down with all the nipping they had to do.

'We won't be able to work the poor yabbies much longer,' I said. 'We'll never be able to shear this black wool.'

Peggy just barked as though to say she thought I was a damn fool. It struck me then she had been cheeky on a number of occasions lately. But I let it pass. Peggy tore up the valley. I wasn't left long wondering what she and the pups were up to. In a few minutes there's such a cawing and croaking that it made my ears shake. Then about three million crows burst overhead in formation and went to work pecking the wool out of the sheep. If anything they were quicker than the yabbies, and I wondered then why Peggy hadn't used the kellies before. But she was right as usual. Each time they pecked the wool out during the next few weeks they pinched some of it for their nests, and the black heap, as it turned out, wasn't as tall as I had expected. All the same, it was a fair stack and I had no complaints.

'There's a fortune for me with all this wool,' I said, looking at the four heaps. 'It's a pity it couldn't be woven on the spot. It's already dyed but it needs scouring.'

Hardly had I said this before Peggy and her three pups are beating it off into the bush. They are gone about an hour and I'm wondering what they can be up to when I see a couple of hundred whirlwinds twisting and turning up the mouth of the valley. They make a roar like thunder as they pass my camp, and I have to jam my fingers in my ears. I can hardly believe what I'm seeing, but Peggy and her pups are working those willy-willies and driving them where they want them. In the next few minutes so much happens that I wonder if my eyes are letting me down. First the whirlwinds are worked into the big heaps of coloured wool and the wool is caught up and goes swirling and twisting into the air. With a roar like a thousand express trains crossing a thousand overhead bridges together the wool is whisked through the billabong and comes out scoured. With a roar like a billion stock whips all cracking together it is whirled up into the sky and spun into yarn. First, the heap of green wool, and then the others, in turn, are twirled so high and so fast your eyes can hardly follow. I've never seen any kelpies work more beautifully than Peggy and her pups did with those willy-willies.

In the next hour the sky is so full of wool being spun and then woven it is like looking at a giant maypole or about a dozen Auroras-Australis. These willy-willies went leaping and bouncing across the sky so fast I got dizzy and gave up trying to work out what they were up to, and sat back in my stretcher for a rest. They were half-way through their work before I woke up to what was happening to the wool. I was so surprised I fell out of the stretcher and got a lump on the back of my head. It's still there if you care to have a look. Those willy-willies had woven all that coloured wool into a huge piece of Campbell of Breadalbane tartan – green ground with black and blue half-inch crossings and a double yellow over-check – four miles wide and already about seven miles long, stretching up into the sky, and only half finished.

I thought it was just a fluke at first, and then I remembered how excited Peggy had been that day when she peeked over my shoulder and saw the Highlander on the calendar.

With all that tartan material I was a made man, though, it is true, I had a bit of trouble getting it out before I finished. Peggy had to rope the yabbies in to cut that great piece of Campbell tartan into lengths, and they nearly jibbed on it. They had got a bit wild while the crows had been on the job, but in the end they did what Peggy wanted.

I had to get three hundred and twenty-seven bullock teams to cart the lengths to the city. Peggy had some idea of making the crows do the job, but a bloke would have looked a bit silly following a lot of kellies along George Street, Sydney.

PATRICK WHITE

Down at the Dump

'Hi!'

He called from out of the house, and she went on chopping in the yard. Her right arm swung, firm still, muscular, though parts of her were beginning to sag. She swung with her right, and her left arm hung free. She chipped at the log, left right. She was expert with the axe.

Because you had to be. You couldn't expect all that much from a man.

'Hi!' It was Wal Whalley calling again from out of the home.

He came to the door then, in that dirty old baseball cap he had shook off the Yankee disposals. Still a fairly appetizing male, though his belly had begun to push against the belt.

'Puttin' on yer act?' he asked, easing the singlet under his armpits; easy was policy at Whalleys' place.

"Ere!' she protested. 'Waddaya make me out ter be? A lump of wood?'

Her eyes were of that blazing blue, her skin that of a brown peach. But whenever she smiled, something would happen, her mouth opening on watery sockets and the jags of brown, rotting stumps.

'A woman likes to be addressed,' she said.

No one had ever heard Wal address his wife by her first name. Nobody had ever heard her name, though it was printed in the electoral roll. It was, in fact, Isba.

'Don't know about a dress,' said Wal. 'I got a idea, though.'

His wife stood tossing her hair. It was natural at least; the sun had done it. All the kids had inherited their mother's colour, and when they stood together, golden-skinned, tossing back their unmanageable hair, you would have said a mob of taffy brumbies.

87

'What is the bloody idea?' she asked, because she couldn't go on standing there.

'Pick up a coupla cold bottles, and spend the mornun at the dump.'

'But that's the same old idea,' she grumbled.

'No, it ain't. Not our own dump. We ain't done Sarsaparilla since Christmas.'

She began to grumble her way across the yard and into the house. A smell of sink strayed out of grey, unpainted weather-board, to oppose the stench of crushed boggabri and cotton pear. Perhaps because Whalleys were in the bits-and-pieces trade their home was threatening to give in to them.

Wal Whalley did the dumps. Of course there were the other lurks besides. But no one had an eye like Wal for the things a person needs: dead batteries and musical bedsteads, a carpet you wouldn't notice was stained, wire, and again wire, clocks only waiting to jump back into the race of time. Objects of commerce and mystery littered Whalleys' back-yard. Best of all, a rusty boiler into which the twins would climb to play at cubby.

'Eh? Waddaboutut?' Wal shouted, and pushed against his wife with his side.

She almost put her foot through the hole that had come in the kitchen boards.

'Waddabout what?'

Half-suspecting, she half-sniggered. Because Wal knew how to play on her weakness.

'The fuckun *idea*!'

So that she began again to grumble. As she slopped through the house her clothes irritated her skin. The sunlight fell yellow on the grey masses of the unmade beds, turned the fluff in the corners of the rooms to gold. Something was nagging at her, something heavy continued to weigh her down.

Of course. It was the funeral.

'Why, Wal,' she said, the way she would suddenly come round, 'you could certainly of thought of a worse idea. It'll keep the kids out of mischief. Wonder if that bloody Lummy's gunna decide to honour us?'

'One day I'll knock 'is block off,' said Wal.

'He's only at the awkward age.'

She stood at the window, looking as though she might know the hell of a lot. It was the funeral made her feel solemn. Brought the goose-flesh out on her.

'Good job you thought about the dump,' she said, out-staring a red-brick property the other side of the road. 'If there's anythun gets me down, it's havin' ter watch a funeral pass.'

'Won't be from 'ere,' he consoled. 'They took 'er away same evenun. It's gunna start from Jackson's Personal Service.'

'Good job she popped off at the beginning of the week. They're not so personal at the week-end.'

She began to prepare for the journey to the dump. Pulled her frock down a bit. Slipped on a pair of shoes.

'Bet *She'll* be relieved. Wouldn't show it, though. Not about 'er sister. I bet Daise stuck in 'er fuckun guts.'

Then Mrs Whalley was compelled to return to the window. As if her instinct. And sure enough there She was. Looking inside the letter-box, as if she hadn't collected already. Bent above the brick pillar in which the letter-box had been cemented, Mrs Hogben's face wore all that people expect of the bereaved.

'Daise was all right,' said Wal.

'Daise was all right,' agreed his wife.

Suddenly she wondered: What if Wal, if Wal had ever . . .?

Mrs Whalley settled her hair. If she hadn't been all that satisfied at home – and she *was* satisfied, her recollective eyes would admit – she too might have done a line like Daise Morrow.

Over the road Mrs Hogben was calling.

'Meg?' she called. 'Marg*ret*?'

Though from pure habit, without direction. Her voice sounded thinner today.

Then Mrs Hogben went away.

'Once I got took to a funeral,' Mrs Whalley said. 'They made me look in the coffin. It was the bloke's wife. He was that cut up.'

'Did yer have a squint?'

'Pretended to.'

Wal Whalley was breathing hard in the airless room.

'How soon do yer reckon they begin ter smell?'

'Smell? They wouldn't let 'em!' his wife said very definite. 'You're the one that smells, Wal. I wonder you don't think of takin' a bath.'

But she liked his smell, for all that. It followed her out of the shadow into the strong shaft of light. Looking at each other their two bodies asserted themselves. Their faces were lit by the certainty of life.

Wal tweaked her left nipple.

'We'll slip inter the Bull on the way, and pick up those cold bottles.'

He spoke soft for him.

Mrs Hogben called another once or twice. Inside the brick entrance the cool of the house struck at her. She liked it cool, but not cold, and this was if not exactly cold, anyway, too sudden. So now she whimpered, very faintly, for everything you have to suffer, and death on top of all. Although it was her sister Daise who had died, Mrs Hogben was crying for the death which was waiting to carry her off in turn. She called: 'Me-ehg?' But no one ever came to your rescue. She stopped to loosen the soil round the roots of the aluminium plant. She always had to be doing something. It made her feel better.

Meg did not hear, of course. She was standing amongst the fuchsia bushes, looking out from their greenish shade. She was thin and freckly. She looked awful, because Mum had made her wear her uniform, because it was sort of a formal occasion, to Auntie Daise's funeral. In the circumstances she not only looked, but was thin. That Mrs Ireland who was all for sport had told her she must turn her toes out, and watch out – she might grow up knock-kneed besides.

So Meg Hogben was, and felt, altogether awful. Her skin was green, except when the war between light and shade worried her face into scraps, and the fuchsia tassels, trembling against her unknowing cheeks, infused something of their own blood, brindled her with shifting crimson. Only her eyes resisted. They were not exactly an ordinary grey.

Lorrae Jensen, who was blue, said they were the eyes of a mopey cat.

A bunch of six or seven kids from Second Grade, Lorrae, Edna, Val, Sherry, Sue Smith and Sue Goldstein, stuck together in the holidays, though Meg sometimes wondered why. The others had come around to Hogbens' Tuesday evening.

Lorrae said: 'We're going down to Barranugli pool Thursday. There's some boys Sherry knows with a couple of Gs. They've promised to take us for a run after we come out.'

Meg did not know whether she was glad or ashamed.

'I can't,' she said. 'My auntie's died.'

'Arrr!' their voices trailed.

They couldn't get away too quick, as if it had been something contagious.

But murmuring.

Meg sensed she had become temporarily important.

So now she was alone with her dead importance, in the fuchsia bushes, on the day of Auntie Daise's funeral. She had turned fourteen. She remembered the ring in plaited gold Auntie Daise had promised her. When I am gone, her aunt had said. And now it had really happened. Without rancour Meg suspected there hadn't been time to think about the ring, and Mum would grab it, to add to all the other things she had.

Then that Lummy Whalley showed up, amongst the camphor laurels opposite, tossing his head of bleached hair. She hated boys with white hair. For that matter she hated boys, or any intrusion on her privacy. She hated Lum most of all. The day he threw the dog poo at her. It made the gristle come in her neck. Ugh! Although the old poo had only skittered over her skin, too dry to really matter, she had gone in and cried because, well, there were times when she cultivated dignity.

Now Meg Hogben and Lummy Whalley did not notice each other even when they looked.

> Who wants Meg Skinny-leg?
> I'd rather take the clothes-peg . . .

Lum Whalley vibrated like a comb-and-paper over amongst the camphor laurels they lopped back every so many years for firewood. He slashed with his knife into bark. Once in a hot dusk he had carved I LOVE MEG, because that was something you did, like on lavatory walls, and in the trains, but it didn't mean anything of course. Afterwards he slashed the darkness as if it had been a train seat.

Lum Whalley pretended not to watch Meg Hogben skulking in the fuchsia bushes. Wearing her brown uniform. Stiffer, browner than for school, because it was her auntie's funeral.

'Me-ehg?' called Mrs Hogben. 'Meg!'

'Lummy! Where the devil are yer?' called his mum.

She was calling all around, in the woodshed, behind the dunny. Let her!

'Lum? Lummy, for Chris*sake*!' she called.

He hated that. Like some bloody kid. At school he had got them to call him Bill, halfway between, not so shameful as Lum, nor yet as awful as William.

Mrs Whalley came round the corner.

'Shoutin' me bloody lungs up!' she said. 'When your dad's got a nice idea. We're goin' down to Sarsaparilla dump.'

'Arr!' he said.

But didn't spit.

'What gets inter you?' she asked.

Even at their most inaccessible Mrs Whalley liked to finger her children. Touch often assisted thought. But she liked the feel of them as well. She was glad she hadn't had girls. Boys turned into men, and you couldn't do without men, even when they took you for a mug, or got shickered, or bashed you up.

So she put her hand on Lummy, tried to get through to him. He was dressed, but might not have been. Lummy's kind was never ever born for clothes. At fourteen he looked more.

'Well,' she said, sourer than she felt, 'I'm not gunna cry over any sulky boy. Suit yourself.'

She moved off.

As Dad had got out the old rattle-bones by now, Lum began to clamber up. The back of the ute was at least private, though it wasn't no Customline.

The fact that Whalleys ran a Customline as well puzzled

more unreasonable minds. Drawn up amongst the paspalum in front of Whalley's shack, it looked stolen, and almost was – the third payment overdue. But would slither with ease a little longer to Barranugli, and snooze outside the Northern Hotel. Lum could have stood all day to admire their own two-tone car. Or would stretch out inside, his fingers at work on plastic flesh.

Now it was the ute for business. The bones of his buttocks bit into the boards. His father's meaty arm stuck out at the window, disgusting him. And soon the twins were squeezing from the rusty boiler. The taffy Gary – or was it Barry? had fallen down and barked his knee.

'For Chrissake!' Mrs Whalley shrieked, and tossed her identical taffy hair.

Mrs Hogben watched those Whalleys leave.

'In a brick area, I wouldn't of thought,' she remarked to her husband once again.

'All in good time, Myrtle,' Councillor Hogben replied as before.

'Of course,' she said, 'if there are *reasons*.'

Because councillors, she knew, did have reasons.

'But that home! And a Customline!'

The saliva of bitterness came in her mouth.

It was Daise who had said: I'm going to enjoy the good things of life – and died in that pokey little hutch, with only a cotton frock to her back. While Myrtle had the liver-coloured brick home – not a single dampmark on the ceilings – she had the washing machine, the septic, the TV, and the cream Holden Special, not to forget her husband. Les Hogben, the councillor. A builder into the bargain.

Now Myrtle stood amongst her things, and would have continued to regret the Ford the Whalleys hadn't paid for, if she hadn't been regretting Daise. It was not so much her sister's death as her life Mrs Hogben deplored. Still, everybody knew, and there was nothing you could do about it.

'Do you think anybody will come?' Mrs Hogben asked.

'What do you take me for?' her husband replied. 'One of these cleervoyants?'

Mrs Hogben did not hear.

After giving the matter consideration she had advertised the death in the *Herald*:

> MORROW, Daisy (Mrs), *suddenly, at her*
> *residence, Showground Road, Sarsaparilla.*

There was nothing more you could put. It wasn't fair on Les, a public servant, to rake up relationships. And the *Mrs* – well, everyone had got into the habit when Daise started going with Cunningham. It seemed sort of natural as things dragged on and on. Don't work yourself up, Myrt, Daise used to say; Jack will when his wife dies. But it was Jack Cunningham who died first. Daise said: It's the way it happened, that's all.

'Do you think Ossie will come?' Councillor Hogben asked his wife slower than she liked.

'I hadn't thought about it,' she said.

Which meant she had. She had, in fact, woken in the night, and lain there cold and stiff, as her mind's eye focused on Ossie's runny nose.

Mrs Hogben rushed at a drawer which somebody – never herself – had left hanging out. She was a thin woman, but wiry.

'Meg?' she called. 'Did you polish your shoes?'

Les Hogben laughed behind his closed mouth. He always did when he thought of Daise's parting folly: to take up with that old scabby deadbeat Ossie from down at the showground. But who cared?

No one, unless her family.

Mrs Hogben dreaded the possibility of Ossie, a Roman Catholic for extra value, standing beside Daise's grave, even if nobody, even if only Mr Brickle saw.

Whenever the thought of Ossie Coogan crossed Councillor Hogben's mind he would twist the knife in his sister-in-law. Perhaps, now, he was glad she had died. A small woman, smaller than his wife, Daise Morrow was large by nature. Whenever she dropped in she was all around the place. Yarn her head off if she got the chance. It got so as Les Hogben could not stand hearing her laugh. Pressed against her in the hall once. He had forgotten that, or almost. How Daise laughed then. I'm not so short of men I'd pick me own

94

brother-in-law. Had he pressed? Not all that much, not inten-
tional, anyway. So the incident had been allowed to fade,
dim as the brown-linoleum hall, in Councillor Hogben's
mind.

'There's the phone, Leslie.'

It was his wife.

'I'm too upset,' she said, 'to answer.'

And began to cry.

Easing his crutch Councillor Hogben went into the hall.

It was good old Horrie Last.

'Yairs . . . yairs . . .' said Mr Hogben, speaking into the
telephone which his wife kept swabbed with Breath-o'-Pine.
'Yairs . . . Eleven, Horrie . . . from Barranugli . . . from Jackson's Personal . . . Yairs, that's decent of you, Horrie.'

'Horrie Last,' Councillor Hogben reported to his wife, 'is
gunna put in an appearance.'

If no one else, a second councillor for Daise. Myrtle Hogben was consoled.

What could you do? Horrie Last put down the phone. He and
Les had stuck together. Teamed up to catch the more pro-
gressive vote. Hogben and Last had developed the shire. Les
had built Horrie's home, Lasts had sold Hogbens theirs. If
certain people were spreading the rumour that Last and Hogben had caused a contraction of the Green Belt, then certain
people failed to realize the term itself implied flexibility.

'What did you tell them?' asked Mrs Last.

'Said I'd go,' her husband said, doing things to the change
in his pocket.

He was a short man, given to standing with his legs apart.

Georgina Last withheld her reply. Formally of interest, her
shape suggested she had been made out of several scones
joined together in the baking.

'Daise Morrow,' said Horrie Last, 'wasn't such a bad sort.'

Mrs Last did not answer.

So he stirred the money in his pocket harder, hoping perhaps it would emulsify. He wasn't irritated, mind you, by his
wife – who had brought him a parcel of property, as well as a
flair for real estate – but had often felt he might have done a
dash with Daise Morrow on the side. Wouldn't have minded

betting old Les Hogben had tinkered a bit with his wife's sister. Helped her buy her home, they said. Always lights on at Daise's place after dark. Postman left her mail on the veranda instead of in the box. In summer, when the men went round to read the meters, she'd ask them in for a glass of beer. Daise knew how to get service.

Georgina Last cleared her throat.

'Funerals are not for women,' she declared, and took up a cardigan she was knitting for a cousin.

'You didn't do your shoes!' Mrs Hogben protested.

'I did,' said Meg. 'It's the dust. Don't know why we bother to clean shoes at all. They always get dirty again.'

She stood there looking awful in the school uniform. Her cheeks were hollow from what she read could only be despair.

'A person must keep to her principles,' Mrs Hogben said, and added: 'Dadda is bringing round the car. Where's your hat, dear? We'll be ready to leave in two minutes.'

'Arr, Mum! The hat?'

That old school hat. It had shrunk already a year ago, but had to see her through.

'You wear it to church, don't you?'

'But this isn't church!'

'It's as good as. Besides, you owe it to your aunt,' Mrs Hogben said, to win.

Meg went and got her hat. They were going out through the fuchsia bushes, past the plaster pixies, which Mrs Hogben had trained her child to cover with plastic at the first drops of rain. Meg Hogben hated the sight of those corny old pixies, even after the plastic cones had snuffed them out.

It was sad in the car, dreamier. As she sat looking out through the window, the tight panama perched on her head lost its power to humiliate. Her always persistent, grey eyes, under the line of dark fringe, had taken up the search again: she had never yet looked enough. Along the road they passed the house in which her aunt, they told her, had died. The small, pink, tilted house, standing amongst the carnation plants, had certainly lost some of its life. Or the glare had drained the colour from it. How the mornings used to sparkle in which Aunt Daise went up and down between the rows, her gown dragging heavy with dew, binding with bast the fuzzy flowers by handfuls and handfuls. Auntie's voice clear as morning. No one, she called, could argue they look stiff when they're bunched tight eh Meg what would you say they remind you of? But you never knew the answers to the sort of things people asked. Frozen fireworks, Daise suggested. Meg loved the idea of it, she loved Daise. Not so frozen either, she dared. The sun getting at the wet flowers broke them up and made them spin.

And the clovey scent rose up in the stale-smelling car, and smote Meg Hogben, out of the reeling heads of flowers, their cold stalks dusted with blue. Then she knew she would write a poem about Aunt Daise and the carnations. She wondered she hadn't thought of it before.

At that point the passengers were used most brutally as the car entered on a chain of potholes. For once Mrs Hogben failed to invoke the Main Roads Board. She was asking herself whether Ossie could be hiding in there behind the blinds. Or whether, whether. She fished for her second handkerchief. Prudence had induced her to bring two – the good one with the lace insertion for use beside the grave.

'The weeds will grow like one thing,' her voice blared, 'now that they'll have their way.'

Then she began to unfold the less important of her handkerchiefs.

Myrtle Morrow had always been the sensitive one. Myrtle had understood the Bible. Her needlework, her crochet doilys had taken prizes at country shows. No one had fiddled such pathos out of the pianola. It was Daise who loved flowers, though. It's a moss-rose, Daise had said, sort of rolling it round on her tongue, while she was still a little thing.

When she had had her cry, Mrs Hogben remarked: 'Girls don't know they're happy until it's too late.'

Thus addressed, the other occupants of the car did not answer. They knew they were not expected to.

Councillor Hogben drove in the direction of Barranugli. He had arranged his hat before leaving. He removed a smile the mirror reminded him was there. Although he no longer took any risks in a re-election photograph by venturing out of the past, he often succeeded in the fleshy present. But now, in difficult circumstances, he was exercising his sense of duty. He drove, he drove, past the retinosperas, heavy with their own gold, past the lagerstroemias, their pink sugar running into mildew.

Down at the dump Whalleys were having an argument about whether the beer was to be drunk on arrival or after they had developed a thirst.

'Keep it, then!' Mum Whalley turned her back. 'What was the point of buyin' it cold if you gotta wait till it hots up? Anyways,' she said, 'I thought the beer was an excuse for comin'.'

'Arr, stuff it!' says Wal. 'A dump's business, ain't it? With or without beer. Ain't it? Any day of the week.'

He saw she had begun to sulk. He saw her rather long breasts floating around inside her dress. Silly cow! He laughed. But cracked a bottle.

Barry said he wanted a drink.

You could hear the sound of angry suction as his mum's lips called off a swig.

'I'm not gunna stand by and watch any kid of mine,' said the wet lips, 'turn 'isself into a bloody dipso!'

Her eyes were at their blazing bluest. Perhaps it was because Wal Whalley admired his wife that he continued to desire her.

But Lummy pushed off on his own. When his mum went crook, and swore, he was too aware of the stumps of teeth, the rotting brown of nastiness. It was different, of course, if you swore yourself. Sometimes it was unavoidable.

Now he avoided by slipping away, between the old mattresses, and boots the sun had buckled up. Pitfalls abounded: the rusty traps of open tins lay in wait for guiltless ankles, the necks of broken bottles might have been prepared to gash a face. So he went thoughtfully, his feet scuffing the leaves of stained asbestos, crunching the torso of a celluloid doll. Here and there it appeared as though trash might win. The onslaught of metal was pushing the scrub into the gully. But in many secret, steamy pockets, a rout was in progress: seeds had been sown in the lumps of grey, disintegrating kapok and the laps of burst chairs, the coils of spring, locked in the spirals of wirier vines, had surrendered to superior resilience. Somewhere on the edge of the whole shambles a human ally, before retiring, had lit a fire, which by now the green had almost choked, leaving a stench of smoke to compete with the sicklier one of slow corruption.

Lum Whalley walked with a grace of which he himself had never been aware. He had had about enough of this rubbish jazz. He would have liked to know how to live neat. Like Darkie Black. Everything in its place in the cabin of Darkie's trailer. Suddenly his throat yearned for Darkie's company. Darkie's hands, twisting the wheel, appeared to control the whole world.

A couple of strands of barbed wire separated Sarsaparilla dump from Sarsaparilla cemetery. The denominations were separated too, but there you had to tell by the names, or by the angels and things the RIPs went in for. Over in what must have been the Church of England Alf Herbert was finishing Mrs Morrow's grave. He had reached the clay, and the going was heavy. The clods fell resentfully.

If what they said about Mrs Morrow was true, then she had lived it up all right. Lum Whalley wondered what, supposing he had met her walking towards him down a bush track, smiling. His skin tingled. Lummy had never done a girl, although he pretended he had, so as to hold his own with the kids. He wondered if a girl, if that sourpuss Meg Hogben. Would of bitten as likely as not. Lummy felt a bit afraid, and returned to thinking of Darkie Black, who never talked about things like that.

Presently he moved away. Alf Herbert, leaning on his shovel, could have been in need of a yarn. Lummy was not prepared to yarn. He turned back into the speckled bush, into the pretences of a shade. He lay down under a banksia, and opened his fly to look at himself. But pretty soon got sick of it.

The procession from Barranugli back to Sarsaparilla was hardly what you would have called a procession: the Reverend Brickle, the Hogben's Holden, Horrie's Holden, following the smaller of Jackson's hearses. In the circumstances they were doing things cheap – there was no reason for splashing it around. At Sarsaparilla Mr Gill joined in, sitting high in that old Chev. It would have been practical, Councillor Hogben sighed, to join the hearse at Sarsaparilla. Old Gill was only there on account of Daise being his customer for years. A grocer lacking in enterprise, Daise had stuck to him, she said, because she liked him. Well, if that was what you put first, but where did it get you?

At the last dip before the cemetery a disembowelled mattress from the dump had begun to writhe across the road. It looked like a kind of monster from out of the depths of somebody's mind, the part a decent person ignored.

'Ah, dear! At the cemetery too!' Mrs Hogben protested. 'I wonder the Council,' she added, in spite of her husband.

'All right, Myrtle,' he said between his teeth. 'I made a mental note.'

Councillor Hogben was good at that.

'And the Whalleys on your own doorstep,' Mrs Hogben moaned.

The things she had seen on hot days, in front of their kiddies too.

The hearse had entered the cemetery gate. They had reached the bumpy stage toppling over the paspalum clumps, before the thinner, bush grass. All around, the leaves of the trees presented so many grey blades. Not even a magpie to put heart into a Christian. But Alf Herbert came forward, his hands dusted with yellow clay, to guide the hearse between the Methoes and the Presbyterians, onto Church of England ground.

Jolting had shaken Mrs Hogben's grief up to the surface again. Mr Brickle was impressed. He spoke for a moment of the near and dear. His hands were kind and professional in helping her out.

But Meg jumped. And landed. It was a shock to hear a stick crack so loud. Perhaps it was what Mum would have called irreverent. At the same time her banana-coloured panama fell off her head into the tussocks.

It was really a bit confusing at the grave. Some of the men helped with the coffin, and Councillor Last was far too short.

Then Mrs Hogben saw, she saw, from out of the lace

handkerchief, it was that Ossie Coogan she saw, standing the other side of the grave. Had old Gill given him a lift? Ossie, only indifferently buttoned, stood snivelling behind the mound of yellow clay.

Nothing would have stopped his nose. Daise used to say: You don't want to be frightened, Ossie, not when I'm here, see? But she wasn't any longer. So now he was afraid. Excepting Daise, Protestants had always frightened him. Well, I'm nothing, she used to say, nothing that you could pigeonhole, but love what we are given to love.

Myrtle Hogben was ropeable, if only because of what Councillor Last must think. She would have liked to express her feelings in words, if she could have done so without giving offence to God. Then the ants ran up her legs, for she was standing on a nest, and her body cringed before the teeming injustices.

Daise, she had protested the day it all began, whatever has come over you? The sight of her sister had made her run out leaving the white sauce to burn. Wherever will you take him? He's sick, said Daise. *But you can't*, Myrtle Hogben cried. For there was her sister Daise pushing some old deadbeat in a barrow. All along Showground Road people had come out of homes to look. Daise appeared smaller pushing the wheelbarrow down the hollow and up the hill. Her hair was half uncoiled. *You can't! You can't!* Myrtle called. But Daise could, and did.

When all the few people were assembled at the graveside in their good clothes, Mr Brickle opened the book, though his voice soon suggested he needn't have.

'*I am the resurrection and the life,*' he said.

And Ossie cried. Because he didn't believe it, not when it came to the real thing.

He looked down at the coffin, which was what remained of what he knew. He remembered eating a baked apple, very slowly, the toffee on it. And again the dark of the horse-stall swallowed him up, where he lay hopeless amongst the shit, and her coming at him with the barrow. What do you want? he asked straight out. I came down to the showground, she said, for a bit of honest-to-God manure, I've had those fertilizers, she said, and what are you, are you sick? I live 'ere, he said. And began to cry, and rub the snot from his snivelly nose. After a bit Daise said: We're going back to my place, What's-yer-Name – Ossie. The way she spoke he knew it was true. All the way up the hill in the barrow the wind was giving his eyes gyp, and blowing his thin hair apart. Over the years he had come across one or two lice in his hair, but thought, or hoped he had got rid of them by the time Daise took him up. As she pushed and struggled with the barrow, sometimes she would lean forward, and he felt her warmth, her firm diddies pressed against his back.

'*Lord, let me know mine end, and the number of my days: that I may be certified how long I have to live,*' Mr Brickle read.

Certified was the word, decided Councillor Hogben looking at that old Ossie.

Who stood there mumbling a few Aspirations, very quiet, on the strength of what they had taught him as a boy.

When all this was under way, all these words of which, she knew, her Auntie Daise would not have approved, Meg Hogben went and got beneath the strands of wire separating the cemetery from the dump. She had never been to the dump before, and her heart was lively in her side. She walked shyly through the bush. She came across an old suspender-belt. She stumbled over a blackened primus.

She saw Lummy Whalley then. He was standing under a banksia, twisting at one of its dead heads.

Suddenly they knew there was something neither of them could continue to avoid.

'I came here to the funeral,' she said.

She sounded, well, almost relieved.

'Do you come here often?' she asked.

'Nah,' he answered, hoarse. 'Not here. To dumps, yes.'

But her intrusion had destroyed the predetermined ceremony of his life, and caused a trembling in his hand.

'Is there anything to see?' she said.

'Junk,' he said. 'Same old junk.'

'Have you ever looked at a dead person?'

Because she noticed the trembling of his hand.

'No,' he said. 'Have you?'

She hadn't. Nor did it seem probable that she would have to

now. Not as they began breathing evenly again.

'What do you do with yourself?' he asked.

Then, even though she would have liked to stop herself, she could not. She said: 'I write poems. I'm going to write one about my Aunt Daise, like she was, gathering carnations in the dew.'

'What'll you get out of that?'

'Nothing,' she said, 'I suppose.'

But it did not matter.

'What other sorts of pomes do you write?' he asked, twisting at last the dead head of the banksia off.

'I wrote one,' she said, 'about the things in a cupboard. I wrote about a dream I had. And the smell of rain. That was a bit too short.'

He began to look at her then. He had never looked into the eyes of a girl. They were grey and cool, unlike the hot, or burnt-out eyes of a woman.

'What are you going to be?' she asked.

'I dunno.'

'You're not a white-collar type.'

'Eh?'

'I mean you're not for figures, and books, and banks and offices,' she said.

He was too disgusted to agree.

'I'm gunna have me own truck. Like Mr Black. Darkie's got a trailer.'

'What?'

'Well,' he said, 'a semi-trailer.'

'Oh,' she said, more diffident.

'Darkie took me on a trip to Maryborough. It was pretty tough goin'. Sometimes we drove right through the night. Sometimes we slept on the road. Or in places where you get rooms. Gee, it was good though, shootin' through the country towns at night.'

She saw it. She saw the people standing at their doors, frozen in the blocks of yellow light. The rushing of the night made the figures for ever still. All around she could feel the furry darkness, as the semi-trailer roared and bucked, its skeleton of coloured lights. While in the cabin, in which they sat, all was stability and order. If she glanced sideways she could see how his taffy hair shone when raked by the bursts of electric light. They had brought cases with tooth-brushes, combs, one or two things – the pad on which she would write the poem somewhere when they stopped in the smell of sunlight dust ants. But his hands had acquired such mastery over the wheel, it appeared this might never happen. Nor did she care.

'This Mr Black,' she said, her mouth getting thinner, 'does he take you with him often?'

'Only once interstate,' said Lummy, pitching the banksia head away. 'Once in a while short trips.'

As they drove they rocked together. He had never been closer to anyone than when bumping against Darkie's ribs. He waited to experience again the little spasm of gratitude and pleasure. He would have liked to wear, and would in time, a striped sweat-shirt like Darkie wore.

'I'd like to go in with Darkie,' he said, 'when I get a trailer of me own. Darkie's the best friend I got.'

With a drawnout shiver of distrust she saw the darker hands, the little black hairs on the backs of the fingers.

'Oh, well,' she said, withdrawn, 'praps you will in the end,' she said.

On the surrounding graves the brown flowers stood in their jars of browner water. The more top-heavy, plastic bunches had been slapped down by a westerly, but had not come to worse grief than to lie strewn in pale disorder on the uncharitable granite chips.

The heat made Councillor Last yawn. He began to read the carved names, those within sight at least, some of which he had just about forgot. He almost laughed once. If the dead could have sat up in their graves there would have been an argument or two.

'*In the midst of life we are in death*,' said the parson bloke.

JACK CUNNINGHAM
BELOVED HUSBAND OF FLORENCE MARY,

read Horrie Last.

Who would have thought Cunningham, straight as a silky-oak, would fall going up the path to Daise Morrow's place.

Horrie used to watch them together, sitting a while on the veranda before going in to their tea. They made no bones about it, because everybody knew. Good teeth Cunningham had. Always a white, well-ironed shirt. Wonder which of the ladies did the laundry. Florence Mary was an invalid, they said. Daise Morrow liked to laugh with men, but for Jack Cunningham she had a silence, promising intimacies at which Horrie Last could only guess, whose own private life had been lived in almost total darkness.

Good Christ, and then there was Ossie. The woman could only have been at heart a perv of a kind you hadn't heard about.

'Forasmuch as it hath pleased Almighty God of his great mercy to take unto himself the soul . . .' read Mr Brickle.

As it was doubtful who should cast the earth, Mr Gill the grocer did. They heard the handful rattle on the coffin.

Then the tears truly ran out of Ossie's scaly eyes. Out of darkness. Out of darkness Daise had called: What's up, Ossie, you don't wanta cry. I got the cramps, he answered. They were twisting him. The cramps? she said drowsily. Or do you imagine? If it isn't the cramps it's something else. Could have been. He'd take Daise's word for it. He was never all that bright since he had the meningitis. Tell you what, Daise said, you come in here, into my bed, I'll warm you, Os, in a jiffy. He listened in the dark to his own snivelling. Arr, Daise, I couldn't, he said, I couldn't get a stand, not if you was to give me the jackpot, he said. She sounded very still then. He lay and counted the throbbing of the darkness. Not like that, she said – she didn't laugh at him as he had half expected – besides, she said, it only ever really comes to you once. That way. And at once he was parting the darkness, bumping and shambling, to get to her. He had never known it so gentle. Because Daise wasn't afraid. She ran her hands through his hair, on and on like water flowing. She soothed the cramps out of his legs. Until in the end they were breathing in time. Dozing. Then the lad Ossie Coogan rode again down from the mountain, the sound of the snaffle in the blue air, the smell of sweat from under the saddle-cloth, towards the great, flowing river. He rocked and flowed with the motion of the strong, never-ending river, burying his mouth in brown cool water, to drown would have been worth it.

Once during the night Ossie had woken, afraid the distance might have come between them. But Daise was still holding him against her breast. If he had been different, say. Ossie's throat had begun to wobble. Only then, Daise, Daise might have turned different. So he nuzzled against the warm darkness, and was again received.

'If you want to enough, you can do what you want,' Meg Hogben insisted.

She had read it in a book, and wasn't altogether convinced, but theories sometimes come to the rescue.

'If you want,' she said, kicking a hole in the stony ground.

'Not everything you can't.'

'You can!' she said. 'But you can!'

She who had never looked at a boy, not right into one, was looking at him as never before.

'That's a lot of crap,' he said.

'Well,' she admitted, 'there are limits.'

It made him frown. He was again suspicious. She was acting clever. All those pomes.

But to reach understanding she would have surrendered her cleverness. She was no longer proud of it.

'And what'll happen if you get married? Riding around the country in a truck. How'll your wife like it? Stuck at home with a lot of kids.'

'Some of 'em take the wife along. Darkie takes his missus and kids. Not always, like. But now and again. On short runs.'

'You didn't tell me Mr Black was married.'

'Can't tell you everything, can I? Not at once.'

The women who sat in the drivers' cabins of the semi-trailers he saw as predominantly thin and dark. They seldom returned glances, but wiped their hands on Kleenex, and peered into little mirrors, waiting for their men to show up again. Which in time they had to. So he walked across from the service station, to take possession of his property. Sauntering, frowning slightly, touching the yellow stubble on his chin, he did not bother to look. Glanced sideways perhaps. She was the thinnest, the darkest he knew, the coolest of all the women who sat looking out from the cabin windows of the semi-trailers.

In the meantime they strolled a bit, amongst the rusty tins at Sarsaparilla dump. He broke a few sticks and threw away the pieces. She tore off a narrow leaf and smelled it. She would have liked to smell Lummy's hair.

'Gee, you're fair,' she had to say.

'Some are born fair,' he admitted.

He began pelting a rock with stones. He was strong, she saw. So many discoveries in a short while were making her tremble at the knees.

And as they rushed through the brilliant light, roaring and lurching, the cabin filled with fair-skinned, taffy children, the youngest of whom she was protecting by holding the palm of her hand behind his neck, as she had noticed women do. Occupied in this way, she almost forgot Lum at times, who would pull up, and she would climb down, to rinse the nappies in tepid water, and hang them on a bush to dry.

'All these pomes and things,' he said, 'I never knew a clever person before.'

'But clever isn't any different,' she begged, afraid he might not accept her peculiarity and power.

She would go with a desperate wariness from now. She sensed that, if not in years, she was older than Lum, but this was the secret he must never guess: that for all his strength, all his beauty, she was, and must remain the stronger.

'What's that?' he asked, and touched.

But drew back his hand in self-protection.

'A scar,' she said. 'I cut my wrist opening a tin of condensed milk.'

For once she was glad of the paler seam in her freckled skin, hoping that it might heal a breach.

And he looked at her out of his hard blue Whalley eyes. He liked her. Although she was ugly, and clever, and a girl.

'Condensed milk on bread,' he said, 'that's something I could eat till I bust.'

'Oh, yes!' she agreed.

She did honestly believe, although she had never thought of it before.

Flies clustered in irregular jet embroideries on the backs of best suits. Nobody bothered any longer to shrug them off. As Alf Herbert grunted against the shovelfuls, dust clogged increasingly, promises settled thicker. Although they had been told they might expect Christ to redeem, it would have been no less incongruous if He had appeared out of the scrub to perform on altars of burning sandstone a sacrifice for which nobody had prepared them. In any case, the mourners waited – they had been taught to accept whatever might be imposed – while the heat stupefied the remnants of their minds, and inflated their Australian fingers into foreign-looking sausages.

Myrtle Hogben was the first to protest. She broke down – into the wrong handkerchief. *Who shall change our vile body?* The words were more than her decency could bear.

'Easy on it,' her husband whispered, putting a finger under her elbow.

She submitted to his sympathy, just as in their life together she had submitted to his darker wishes. Never wanting more than peace, and one or two perquisites.

A thin woman, Mrs Hogben continued to cry for all the wrongs that had been done her. For Daise had only made things viler. While understanding, yes, at moments. It was girls who really understood, not even women – sisters, sisters. Before events whirled them apart. So Myrtle Morrow was again walking through the orchard, and Daise Morrow twined her arm around her sister; confession filled the air, together with a scent of crushed, fermenting apples. Myrtle said: Daise, there's something I'd like to do, I'd like to chuck a lemon into a Salvation Army tuba. Daise giggled. You're a nut, Myrt, she said. But never *vile*. So Myrtle Hogben cried. Once, only once she had thought how she'd like to push someone off a cliff, and watch their expression as it happened. But Myrtle had not confessed that.

So Mrs Hogben cried, for those things she was unable to confess, for anything she might not be able to control.

As the blander words had begun falling, *Our Father*, that she knew by heart, *our daily bread*, she should have felt comforted. She should of. Should of.

Where was Meg, though?

Mrs Hogben separated herself from the others. Walking stiffy. If any of the men noticed, they took it for granted she had been overcome, or wanted to relieve herself.

She would have liked to relieve herself by calling: 'Margaret Meg wherever don't you hear me Me-ehg?' drawing it out thin in anger. But could not cut across a clergyman's words. So she stalked. She was not unlike a guinea-hen, its spotted silk catching on a strand of barbed-wire.

When they had walked a little farther, round and about, anywhere, they overheard voices.

'What's that?' asked Meg.

'Me mum and dad,' Lummy said. 'Rousin' about somethun or other.'

Mum Whalley had just found two bottles of unopened beer. Down at the dump. Waddayaknow. Must be something screwy somewhere.

'Could of put poison in it,' her husband warned.

'Poison? My arse!' she shouted. 'That's because *I* found it!'

'Whoever found it,' he said, 'who's gunna drink a coupla bottlesa hot beer?'

'I am!' she said.

'When what we brought was good an' cold?'

He too was shouting a bit. She behaved unreasonable at times.

'Who wanted ter keep what we brought? Till it got good an' hot!' she shrieked.

Sweat was running down both the Whalleys.

Suddenly Lum felt he wanted to lead this girl out of earshot. He had just about had the drunken sods. He would have liked to find himself walking with his girl over mown lawn, like at the Botanical Gardens, a green turf giving beneath their leisured feet. Statues pointed a way through the glare, to where they finally sat, under enormous shiny leaves, looking out at boats on water. They unpacked their cut lunch from its layers of fresh tissue-paper.

'They're rough as bags,' Lummy explained.

'I don't care,' Meg Hogben assured.

Nothing on earth could make her care – was it more, or was it less?

She walked giddily behind him, past a rusted fuel-stove, over a field of deathly feltex. Or ran, or slid, to keep up. Flowers would have wilted in her hands, if she hadn't crushed them brutally, to keep her balance. Somewhere in their private labyrinth Meg Hogben had lost her hat.

When they were farther from the scene of anger, and a silence of heat had descended again, he took her little finger, because it seemed natural to do so, after all they had experienced. They swung hands for a while according to some special law of motion.

Till Lum Whalley frowned, and threw the girl's hand away.

If she accepted his behaviour it was because she no longer believed in what he did, only in what she knew he felt. That might have been the trouble. She was so horribly sure, he would have to resist to the last moment of all. As a bird, singing in the prickly tree under which they found themselves standing, seemed to cling to the air. Then his fingers took control. She was amazed at the hardness of his boy's body. The tremors of her flinty skin, the membrane of the white sky appalled him. Before fright and expectation melted their mouths. And they took little grateful sips of each other. Holding up their throats in between. Like birds drinking.

Ossie could no longer see Alf Herbert's shovel working at the earth.

'Never knew a man cry at a funeral,' Councillor Hogben complained, very low, although he was ripe enough to burst.

If you could count Ossie as a man, Councillor Last suggested in a couple of noises.

But Ossie could not see or hear, only Daise, still lying on that upheaval of a bed. Seemed she must have burst a button, for her breasts stood out from her. He would never forget how they laboured against the heavy yellow morning light. In the early light, the flesh turned yellow, sluggish. What's gunna happen to me, Daisy? It'll be decided, Os, she said, like it is for any of us. I ought to know, she said, to tell you, but give me time to rest a bit, to get me breath. Then he got down on his painful knees. He put his mouth to Daise's neck. Her skin tasted terrible bitter. The great glistening river, to which the lad Ossie Coogan had ridden jingling down from the mountain, was slowing into thick, yellow mud. Himself an old, scabby man attempting to refresh his forehead in the last pothole.

Mr Brickle said: *'We give thee hearty thanks for that it hath pleased thee to deliver this our sister out of the miseries of this sinful world.'*

'No! No!' Ossie protested, so choked nobody heard, though it was vehement enough in its intention.

As far as he could understand, nobody wanted to be delivered. Not him, not Daise, anyways. When you could sit together by the fire on winter nights baking potatoes under the ashes.

It took Mrs Hogben some little while to free her *crêpe de Chine* from the wire. It was her nerves, not to mention Meg on her mind. In the circumstances she tore herself worse and looked up to see her child, just over there, without shame, in a rubbish tip, kissing with the Whalley boy. What if Meg was another of Daise? It was in the blood, you couldn't deny.

Mrs Hogben did not exactly call, but released some kind of noise from her extended throat. Her mouth was too full of tongue to find room for words as well.

Then Meg looked. She was smiling.

She said: 'Yes, Mother.'

She came and got through the wire, tearing herself also a little.

Mrs Hogben said, and her teeth clicked: 'You chose the likeliest time. Your aunt hardly in her grave. Though, of course, it is only your aunt, if anyone, to blame.'

The accusations were falling fast. Meg could not answer. Since joy had laid her open, she had forgotten how to defend herself.

'If you were a little bit younger' – Mrs Hogben lowered her voice because they had begun to approach the parson – 'I'd break a stick on you, my girl.'

Meg tried to close her face, so that nobody would see inside.

'What will they say?' Mrs Hogben moaned. 'What ever will happen to us?'

'What, Mother?' Meg asked.

'You're the only one can answer that. And someone else.'

Then Meg looked over her shoulder and recognized the hate which, for a while she had forgotten existed. And at once her face closed up tight, like a fist. She was ready to protect whatever justly needed her protection.

Even if their rage, grief, contempt, boredom, apathy, and sense of injustice had not occupied the mourners, it is doubtful whether they would have realized the dead woman was standing amongst them. The risen dead – that was something which happened, or didn't happen, in the Bible. Fanfares of light did not blare for a loose woman in floral cotton. Those who had known her remembered her by now only fitfully in some of the wooden attitudes of life. How could they have heard, let alone believed in, her affirmation? Yet Daise Morrow continued to proclaim.

Listen, all of you, I'm not leaving, except those who want to be left, and even those aren't so sure – they might be parting with a bit of themselves. Listen to me, all you successful no-hopers, all you who wake in the night, jittery because something may be escaping you, or terrified to think there may never have been anything to find. Come to me, you sour women, public servants, anxious children, and old scabby, desperate men . . .

Physically small, words had seemed too big for her. She would push back her hair in exasperation. And take refuge in acts. Because her feet had been planted in the earth, she would have been the last to resent its pressure now, while her always rather hoarse voice continued to exhort in borrowed syllables of dust.

Truly, we needn't experience tortures, unless we build chambers in our minds to house instruments of hatred in. Don't you know, my darling creatures, that death isn't death, unless it's the death of love? Love should be the greatest explosion it is reasonable to expect. Which sends us whirling, spinning, creating millions of other worlds. Never destroying.

From the fresh mound which they had formed unimaginatively in the shape of her earthly body, she persisted in appealing to them.

I will comfort you. If you will let me. Do you understand?

But nobody did, as they were only human.

For ever and ever. And ever.

Leaves quivered lifted in the first suggestion of a breeze.

So the aspirations of Daise Morrow were laid alongside her small-boned wrists, smooth thighs and pretty ankles. She surrendered at last to the formal crumbling which, it was hoped, would make an honest woman of her.

But had not altogether died.

Meg Hogben had never exactly succeeded in interpreting her aunt's messages, nor could she have witnessed the last moments of the burial, because the sun was dazzling her. She did experience, however, along with a shiver of recollected joy, the down laid against her cheek, a little breeze trickling through the moist roots of her hair, as she got inside the car, and waited for whatever next.

Well, they had dumped Daise.

Somewhere the other side of the wire there was the sound of smashed glass and discussion.

Councillor Hogben went across to the parson and said the right kind of things. Half-turning his back he took a note or two from his wallet, and immediately felt disengaged. If Horrie Last had been there Les Hogben would have gone back at this point and put an arm around his mate's shoulder, to feel whether he was forgiven for unorthodox behaviour in a certain individual – no relation, mind you, but. In any case Horrie had driven away.

Horrie drove, or flew, across the dip in which the dump joined the cemetery. For a second Ossie Coogan's back flickered inside a spiral of dust.

Ought to give the coot a lift, Councillor Last suspected, and wondered, as he drove on, whether a man's better intentions were worth, say, half a mark in the event of their remaining unfulfilled. For by now it was far too late to stop, and there was that Ossie, in the mirror, turning off the road towards the dump, where, after all, the bugger belonged.

All along the road, stones, dust, and leaves, were settling back into normally unemotional focus. Seated in his high Chev, Gill the grocer, a slow man, who carried his change in a little, soiled canvas bag, looked ahead through thick lenses. He was relieved to realize he would reach home almost on the dot of three-thirty, and his wife pour him his cup of tea. Whatever he understood was punctual, decent, docketed.

As he drove, prudently, he avoided the mattress the dump had spewed, from under the wire, half across the road. Strange things had happened at the dump on and off, the grocer recollected. Screaming girls, their long tight pants ripped to tatters. An arm in a sugar-bag, and not a sign of the body that went with it. Yet some found peace amongst the refuse: elderly derelict men, whose pale, dead, fish eyes never divulged anything of what they had lived, and women with blue, metho skins, hanging around the doors of shacks put together from sheets of bark and rusty iron. Once an old downandout had crawled amongst the rubbish apparently to rot, and did, before they sent for the constable, to examine what seemed at first a bundle of stinking rags.

Mr Gill accelerated judiciously.

They were driving. They were driving.

Alone in the back of the ute, Lum Whalley sat forward on the empty crate, locking his hands between his knees, as he forgot having seen Darkie do. He was completely independent now. His face had been reshaped by the wind. He liked that. It felt good. He no longer resented the junk they were dragging home, the rust flaking off at his feet, the roll of mouldy feltex trying to fur his nostrils up. Nor his family – discussing, or quarrelling, you could never tell – behind him in the cabin.

The Whalleys were in fact singing. One of their own versions. They always sang their own versions, the two little boys joining in.

> Show me the way to go home,
> I'm not too tired for bed.
> I had a little drink about an hour ago,
> And it put ideas in me head . . .

Suddenly Mum Whalley began belting into young Gary – or was it Barry?

'Wadda *you* know, eh? Wadda *you*?'

'What's bitten yer?' her husband shouted. 'Can't touch a drop without yer turn nasty!'

She didn't answer. He could tell a grouse was coming, though. The little boy had started to cry, but only as a formality.

'It's that bloody Lummy,' Mrs Whalley complained.

'Why pick on Lum?'

'Give a kid all the love and affection, and waddayaget?'

Wal grunted. Abstractions always embarrassed him.

Mum Whalley spat out of the window, and the spit came back at her.

'Arrrr!' she protested.

And fell silenter. It was not strictly Lum, not if you was honest. It was nothing. Or everything. The grog. You was never ever gunna touch it no more. Until you did. And that bloody Lummy, what with the caesar and all, you was never ever going again with a man.

'That's somethink a man don't understand.'

'What?' asked Wal.

'A caesar.'

'Eh?'

You just couldn't discuss with a man. So you had to get into bed with him. Grogged up half the time. That was how she copped the twins, after she had said never ever.

'Stop cryun, for Chrissake!' Mum Whalley coaxed, touching the little boy's blowing hair.

Everything was sad.

'Wonder how often they bury someone alive,' she said.

Taking a corner in his cream Holden Councillor Hogben felt quite rakish, but would restrain himself at the critical moment from skidding the wrong side of the law.

They were driving and driving, in long, lovely bursts, and at the corners, in semi-circular swirls.

On those occasions in her life when she tried to pray, begging for an experience, Meg Hogben would fail, but return to the attempt with clenched teeth. Now she did so want to think of her dead aunt with love, and the image blurred repeatedly. She was superficial, that was it. Yet, each time she failed, the landscape leaped lovingly. They were driving under the telephone wires. She could have translated any message into the language of peace. The wind burning, whenever it did not cut cold, left the stable things alone: the wooden houses stuck beside the road, the trunks of willows standing round the brown saucer of a dam. Her too candid, grey eyes seemed to have deepened, as though to accommodate all she still had to see, feel.

It was lovely curled on the back seat, even with Mum and Dad in front.

'I haven't forgotten, Margret,' Mum called over her shoulder.

Fortunately Dadda wasn't interested enough to inquire.

'Did Daise owe anything on the home?' Mrs Hogben asked. 'She was never at all practical.'

Councillor Hogben cleared his throat.

'Give us time to find out,' he said.

Mrs Hogben respected her husband for the things which she, secretly, did not understand: Time the mysterious, for instance, Business, and worst of all, the Valuer General.

'I wonder Jack Cunningham,' she said, 'took up with Daise. He was a fine man. Though Daise had a way with her.'

They were driving. They were driving.

When Mrs Hogben remembered the little ring in plaited gold.

'Do you think those undertakers are honest?'

'Honest?' her husband repeated.

A dubious word.

'Yes,' she said. 'That ring that Daise.'

You couldn't very well accuse. When she had plucked up the courage she would go down to the closed house. The thought of it made her chest tighten. She would go inside, and feel her way into the back corners of drawers, where perhaps a twist of tissue-paper. But the closed houses of the dead frightened Mrs Hogben, she had to admit. The stuffiness, the light strained through brown holland. It was as if you were stealing, though you weren't.

And then those Whalleys creeping up.

They were driving and driving, the ute and the sedan almost rubbing on each other.

'No one who hasn't had a migraine,' cried Mrs Hogben, averting her face, 'can guess what it feels like.'

Her husband had heard that before.

'It's a wonder it don't leave you,' he said. 'They say it does when you've passed a certain age.'

Though they weren't passing the Whalleys he would make every effort to throw the situation off. Wal Whalley leaning forward, though not so far you couldn't see the hair bursting out of the front of his shirt. His wife thumping his shoulder. They were singing one of their own versions. Her gums all watery.

So they drove and drove.

'I could sick up, Leslie,' Mrs Hogben gulped, and fished for her lesser handkerchief.

The Whalley twins were laughing through their taffy forelocks.

At the back of the ute that sulky Lum turned towards the opposite direction. Meg Hogben was looking her farthest off. Any sign of acknowledgement had been so faint the wind had immediately blown it off their faces. As Meg and Lummy sat, they held their sharp, but comforting knees. They sank their chins as low as they would go. They lowered their eyes, as if they had seen enough for the present, and wished to cherish what they knew.

The warm core of certainty settled stiller as driving faster the wind payed out the telephone wires the fences the flattened heads of grey grass always raising themselves again again again

Clay

When he was about five years old some kids asked Clay why his mother had called him that. And he did not know. But began to wonder. He did, in fact, wonder a great deal, particularly while picking the bark off trees, or stripping a flower down to its core of mystery. He too, would ask questions, but more often than not failed to receive the answer because his mother could not bring herself to leave her own train of thought.

Mrs Skerritt said: 'If only your father hadn't died he'd still be putting out the garbage the bin is too much for me the stooping not to mention the weight in anyone short of breath but you Clay I know will be good to your mum and help when you are older stronger only that is still a long way off.'

So that it was Clay's turn not to answer. What could you say, anyway?

Mrs Skerritt said: 'I wouldn't ask anything of anyone but there are certain things of course I wouldn't expect a gentleman to stand up for me in the tram while I have my own two legs only it's the sort of thing a gentleman ought to do and ladies take Mrs Pearl for instance what she expects of her husband and him with the sugar diabetes too.'

Clay mooned about the house listening to his mother's voice boring additional holes in the fretwork, for fretwork had been Dadda's hobby: there was fretwork just about everywhere, brackets and things, even a lace of fretwork hanging from table-top and doorway. Stiff. Sometimes while his mother's voice bored and sawed further Clay would break off pieces of the brown fretwork and hide it away under the house. Under the house was full of fretwork finally.

Or he would moon about the terraces of garden, amongst the collapsing lattices, flower-pot shards crackling underfoot, legs slapped by the straps of dark, leathery plants, lungs

118

filled with suffocating bursts of asparagus fern. He would dawdle down to the harbour, with its green smell of sea-lettuce, and the stone wall, scribbled with the white drop-pings of gulls. The house itself leaned rather far towards the harbour, but had not fallen, because some men had come and shored it up. There it hung, however.

So Clay mooned. And would return often to the photo-graph. It was as though his childhood were riveted to the wedding group. There was his father, those thick thighs, rather tight about the serge crutch (unlike the Dadda he remembered lying Incurable in bed), and the influential Mr Stutchbury, and Auntie Ada, and Nellie Watson (who died), and someone else who was killed in action. But it was to his mum that Clay was drawn, before and after all, into the torrential satin of the lap, by the face which had just begun to move out of its fixture of fretted lace. And the shoe. He was fascinated by the white shoe. Sometimes its great boat would float out from the shore of frozen time, into the waters of his imagination, rocking his cargo of almost transparent thoughts.

Once Mrs Skerritt came into the room and caught him at it, though she did not exactly see Clay for looking at herself.

'Ah dear,' she said, 'in the end things is sad.'

She would often half cry, and at such moments her hair would look more than ever like so many lengths of grey string, or on windy days, a tizz of frayed dish-cloth.

On this particular day when she caught Clay looking at the photograph, his throat swelled, and he dared to ask:

'Why is my name Clay, Mum?'

Because by that time he was seven, and the kids were asking worse than ever, and bashing him up (they were afraid that he was different).

'Why,' she said, 'let me think your father wanted Percival that is after Mr Stutchbury but I could not bring myself I said there are so many things you don't do but want take a name a name is yours take pottery I said I've half a mind to try my hand if I can find some feller or lady you never know I may be artistic but didn't because well there isn't the time always so much to do the people who have to be told and who have to be told and then Dadda's incurable illness so I did not do that only thought and thought about it and that I believe is why you was called Clay.'

Then she went out the back to empty the tea-pot on a bed of maidenhair which tingled perpetually with moisture.

So the kids continued to bash Clay up, and ask him why he was called that, and he couldn't tell them, because how could you even when you knew.

There were times when it got extra bad, and once they chased him with a woman's old cast-off shoe. He ran like a green streak, but not fast enough in the end – they caught him at the corner of Plant Street, where he had been born and always lived, and the heel of their old shoe bored for ever in his mind.

Later, when he had let himself in, into the garden of the leaning house, lost amongst collapsing lattices and the yellow fuzz of asparagus fern, he cried a bit for the difference to which he had been born. But smeared his eyes dry at last, and his nose. The light was rising from the bay in all green peacefulness, as if the world of pointed objects did not exist alongside that of the dreamy bridal shoe.

But he did not embark. Not then. His ribs had not subsided yet.

Once Clay dreamed a dream, and came down into the kitchen. He had meant to keep the dream to himself. Then it was too late, he heard, he was telling it to his mum. Even though his mouth was frozen stiff he had to keep on, to tell.

'In this dream,' he said, 'the steps led on down.'

His mum was pushing the rashers around, which went on buckling up in the pan.

'Under the sea,' said Clay. 'It was beautiful.'

He was sorry, but he could not help it.

'Everything drawn out. Hair and things. And weeds. The knotted ones. And the lettucy kind. Some of the fish had beards, Mum, and barked, well, like dogs.'

His mum had put the fried bread on a plate to one side, where the little squares were already stiffening.

'And shells, Mum,' he said, 'all bubbles and echoes as I went on down. It felt good. It felt soft. I didn't have to try. But just floated. Down.'

He could see his mother's behind, how it had begun to

quiver, and he dreaded what might happen when he told. There was no avoiding it, though, and his mum went on prodding the bacon in the pan.

'When I got to the bottom,' he said, 'and the steps ended, you should have seen how the sea stretched, over the sand and broken bottles. Everything sort of silvery. I don't remember much else. Except that I found, Mum,' he said.

'What?' she asked.

He dreaded it.

'A cloud, Mum,' he said, 'and it was dead.'

Then Mrs Skerritt turned round, it was dreadful, how she looked. She opened her mouth, but nothing came out at first, only Clay saw the little thing at the back. Raised. When suddenly it began to act like a clapper. She began to cry, she began to create.

'Whatever are you gunna do to me?' she cried, as she pummelled and kneaded the moist grey dough of her cheeks.

'On top of everything else I never ever thought I'd have a freak!'

But Clay could only stand, and receive the blows her voice dealt. It was as though someone had taken a stick and drawn a circle round him. Him at the centre. There was no furniture any more.

The bacon was burning in the pan.

When Mrs Skerritt had thought it over, and used a little eau-de-Cologne, she took him up to McGillivray's. It was late by then, on a Saturday morning too. All the way Clay listened to her breathing and sometimes the sound of her corset. McGillivray was already closing, but agreed to do Mrs Skerritt's lad. McGillivray was kind.

'We want it short short Mr McGillivray please,' Mrs Skerritt said.

As the barber snipped Clay could hear his mum breathing, from where she sat, behind his back, under the coloured picture of the King.

Mr McGillivray did his usual nice job, and was preparing to design the little quiff when Mrs Skerritt choked.

'That is not short Mr McGillivray not what I mean oh no oh dear but it is difficult to explain there is too much involved and I left school when I turned fourteen.'

PATRICK WHITE

McGillivray laughed and said: 'Short is not shorn!'

'I don't care,' she said.

Clay could only look at the glass, and suck his cheeks in.

'Short is what I said and mean,' Mrs Skerritt confirmed. 'I was never one for not coming to the point.'

McGillivray was a gentle man, but he too began to breathe, he took the clippers, and shore a path through his subject's hair. He shore, and shore. Till there Clay was. Exposed.

'That suit?' McGillivray asked.

'Thank you,' she said.

So meek.

Then they went home. They crunched over the asphalt. They were that heavy, both of them.

As they went down the hill towards the turn where the milko's cart had plunged over, Mrs Skerritt said:

'There Clay a person is sometimes driven to things in defence of what we know and love I would not of done this otherwise if not to protect you from yourself because love you will suffer in life if you start talking queer remember it doesn't pay to be different and no one is different without they have something wrong with them.'

Clay touched his prickly hair.

'Let me remind you,' she said, 'that your mum loves you that is why.'

But Clay could no longer believe in love, and the kids bashed him up worse than ever, because his no-hair made him a sort of different different.

'Wot was you in for?' the kids asked, and did windmills on his stubble. 'Old Broad Arrer!' they shouted, and punched.

Actually Clay grew up narrow. He was all knuckle, all wrist. He had those drawn-out arms. He had a greenish skin from living under too many plants. He was long. And his eyes overflowed at dusk, merged with the street lights, and the oil patches on lapping water.

'Are you lonely, Clay?' Mrs Skerritt asked.

'No,' he said. 'Why?'

'I thought perhaps you was lonely you should get out and meet other young people of your own age you should get to know nice girls otherwise it is not normal.'

Then she drew in her chin, and waited.

122

But Clay stroked his prickly hair. For he went to McGillivray's every so often since it was ordained. When his voice broke the others no longer bashed him up, having problems of their own. The blackheads came, the pimples and moustaches.

Sometimes Mrs Skerritt would cry, sitting on the rotten veranda overlooking the little bay in which cats so often drowned.

'Oh dear Clay,' she cried, 'I am your mother and have a responsibility a double one since Dadda went I will ask Mr Stutchbury but cannot rely totally do you know what you want to do?'

Clay said: 'No.'

'Oh dear,' she moaned worse than ever, 'how did I deserve a silent boy who loves what I would like to know himself perhaps himself.'

In fact Clay did not know what he loved. He would have liked to think it was his mother, though it could have been Dadda. So he would try to remember, but it was only cold yellow skin, and the smell of sick sheets. When he had been forced to approach his father, lying Incurable in the bed, his heart could have tumbled down out of the belfry of his body.

Once his mother, it was evening, clutched his head against her apron, so that she must have pricked her hands.

'You are not my son,' she clanged, 'otherwise you would act different.'

But he could not, did not want to. Sometimes, anyway, at that age, he felt too dizzy from growing.

'How?' his voice asked, or croaked.

But she did not explain. She flung his long body away.

'It's not a matter,' she said, 'that anybody can discuss I will ask Mr Stutchbury to see what we must do and how.'

Mr Stutchbury was so influential, as well as having been a mate of Herb Skerritt's all his life. Mr Stutchbury was something, Mrs Skerritt believed, in the Department of Education, but if she did not clear the matter up, it was because she considered there was not all that necessity.

She bought a T-bone steak, and asked him round.

'What,' she asked, 'should we do with Clay I am a widow as you know and you was his father's friend.'

Mr Stutchbury drew in his moustache.

'We will see,' he said, 'when the time comes.'

Then he folded his moist lips over a piece of yellow fat from the not so tender T-bone steak.

When it was time, Mr Stutchbury thought up a letter to some fellow at the Customs and Excise.

> Dear Archie (he composed)
>   This is to recommend the son of an old friend. Herb Skerritt, for many years in the Tramways, died in tragic circumstances – of cancer to be precise . . .

(Clay, who of course opened the letter to see, got quite a shock from a word his mother never on any account allowed to be used in the home.)

> . . . it is my duty and wish to further the interests of the above-mentioned boy. In brief, I would esteem it a favour if you could see your way to taking him 'under your wing'. I do not predict wonders of young Skerritt, but am of the opinion, rather, that he is a decent, average lad. In any event, wonders are not all that desirable, not in the Service anyway. It is the steady hand which pushes the pen a lifetime.
>   I will not expatiate further, but send you my
>
> > > > Salaams!

The young lady whom Mr Stutchbury had persuaded to type the letter had barely left the room, when his superior called, with the result that he forgot to add as he intended: 'Kindest regards to Mrs Archbold.' Even persons of influence have to consider the ground they tread on.

But Clay Skerritt started at the Customs, because Mr Archbold was not the sort to refuse Mr Stutchbury the favour he asked. So Clay took the ferry, mornings, in the stiff dark suit his mother had chosen. His long thin fingers learned to deal in forms. He carried the papers from tray to tray. In time he grew used to triplicate, and moistened the indelible before writing in his long thin hand the details, and the details.

Clay Skerritt did not complain, and if he was ignored he had known worse. For he was most certainly ignored, by the gentlemen who sat amongst the trays of papers, by the young ladies of the Customs and Excise, who kept their nails so beautifully, who took their personal towels to the toilet, and giggled over private matters and cups of milky tea. If they ever laughed at the junior in particular, at his tricky frame, his pimples, and his stubble of hair, Clay Skerritt was not conscious of it. Why should he be? He was born with inward-looking eyes.

That all was not quite in order, though, he began to gather from his mother.

'When I am gone Clay,' she said – it was the evening the sink got blocked up, 'you will remember how your mother was a messer but found she only scraped the dishes into the sink because her mind was otherwise engaged with you Clay your interests always some practical young lady will rectify anything your mother ever did by good intention I would not force you but only advise time is not to be ignored.'

But on days when the wind blew black across the grey water Mrs Skerritt might remark, peering out from the arbours of asparagus fern:

'Some young woman clever with her needle lighter-handed at the pastry board will make you forget your poor mum well it is the way.'

Her son was bound to ignore what he could not be expected to believe. He would take a look at the wedding group. All so solidly alive, the figures appeared to announce a truth of which he alone could be the arbiter, just as the great white shoe would still put out, into the distance, for destinations of his choice.

His mother, however, continued in her mistaken attempts to celebrate the passing of reality. There was the day she called, her voice intruding amongst the objects which surrounded him:

'Take my grey costume dear up to the dry cleaner at the Junction tomato sauce is fatal when a person is on the stoutish side.'

Clay acted as he had been told. Or the streets were acting round him, and the trams. It was a bright day. Metal sang. The brick homes were no longer surreptitious, but opened up to disclose lives. In one window a woman was looking into her armpit. It made Clay laugh.

At the cleaner's a lady finished a yarn with the young girl. The lady said from alongside her cigarette:

'I'll leave you to it, Marj. I'm gunna make tracks for home and whip me shoes off. My feet are hurting like hell.'

Then the bell.

Clay was still laughing.

The young girl was looking down at the sheets of fresh brown paper, through the smell of cleaning. She herself had a cleaned, pallid skin, with pores.

'What's up?' she asked, as the client continued laughing.

She spoke so very flat and polite.

'Nothing,' he said, but added: 'I think perhaps you are like my mother.'

Which was untrue, in a sense, because the girl was flat, still, and colourless, whereas his mother was rotund, voluble, and at least several tones of grey. But Clay had been compelled to say it.

The girl did not reply. She looked down at first, as though he had overstepped the mark. Then she took the costume, and examined the spots of tomato sauce.

'Ready tomorrow,' she said.

'Go on!'

'Why not?' the girl replied. 'We are a One-day.'

But flat and absent she sounded.

Then Clay did not know why, but asked: 'You've got something on your mind.'

She said: 'It's only that the sink got blocked yesterday evening.'

It sounded so terribly grey, and she looking out with that expression of permanence. Then at once he knew he had been right, and that the girl at the dry cleaner's had something of his mother: it was the core of permanence. Then Clay grew excited. For he did not believe in impermanence, not even when his mother attempted to persuade, not even when he watched the clods of earth tumble down on the coffin lid. Not while he was he.

So he said: 'Tomorrow.'

It sounded so firm, it was almost today.

Clay got used to Marj just as he had got used to his mum, only differently. They swung hands together, walking over the dead grass of several parks, or staring at animals in cages. They were already living together, that is, their silences intermingled. Each had a somewhat clammy palm. And if Marj spoke there was no necessity to answer, it was so flat, her remarks had the colour of masonite.

Marj said: 'When I have a home of my own, I will turn out the lounge Fridays. I mean, there is a time and place for everything. There are the bedrooms too.'

She said: 'I do like things to be nice.'

And: 'Marriage should be serious.'

How serious, Clay began to see, who had not told his mum.

When at last he did she was drying the apostle spoons, one of which she dropped, and he let her pick it up, on seeing that it was necessary for her to perform some therapeutic act.

'I am so glad, Clay,' she said, rather purple, after a pause, 'I cannot wait to see this nice girl we must arrange some we must come to an agree there is no reason why a young couple should not hit it off with the mother-in-law if the home is large it is not so much temperament as the size of the home that causes friction.'

Mrs Skerritt had always known herself to be reasonable.

'And Marj is so like you, Mum.'

'Eh?' Mrs Skerritt said.

He could not explain that what was necessary for him, for what he had to do, was a continuum. He could not have explained what he had to do, because he did not know, as yet.

All Mrs Skerritt could say was: 'The sooner we see the better we shall know.'

So Clay brought Marj. Their hands were clammier that day. The plants were huge, casting a fuscous tinge on the shored-up house.

Mrs Skerritt looked out of the door.

'Is this,' she said, 'I am not yet not yet ready to see.'

Clay told Marj she must go away, for that day at least, he would send for her, then he took his mother inside.

Mrs Skerritt did not meet Marj again, except in the mirror, in which she saw with something of a shock there is no such thing as permanence.

Shortly after she died of something. They said it was her ticker.

And Clay brought Marj to live in the house in which he had been born and lived. They did not go on a honeymoon, because, as Marj said, marriage should be serious. Clay hoped he would know what to do as they lay in the bed Mum and Dadda had used. Lost in that strange and lumpy acre Clay and Marj listened to each other.

But it was good. He continued going to the Customs. Once or twice he pinched the lobe of Marj's ear.

'What's got into you?' she asked.

He continued going to the Customs. He bought her a Java sparrow in a cage. It was a kind of love poem.

To which Marj replied: 'I wonder if it's gunna scatter its seed on the wall-to-wall. We can always spread a newspaper, though.'

And did.

Clay went to the Customs. He sat at his own desk. He used his elbows more than before, because his importance had increased.

'Take this letter away, Miss Venables,' he said. 'There are only two copies. When I expected five. Take it away,' he said.

Miss Venables pouted, but took it away. She, like everybody, saw that something had begun to happen. They would watch Mr Skerritt, and wait for it.

But Marj, she was less expectant. She accepted the houseful of fretwork, the things the mother-in-law had put away – sets of string-coloured doilies for instance, once she came across a stuffed canary in a cardboard box. She did not remark, but accepted. Only once she failed to accept. Until Clay asked:

'What has become of the photo?'

'It is in that cupboard,' she said.

He went and fetched out the wedding group, and stuck it where it had been, on a fretwork table. At least he did not ask why she had put the photo away, and she was glad, because she would not have known what to answer. The bits of your husband you would never know were bad enough, but not to understand yourself was worse.

So Marj stuck to the carpet sweeper, she was glad of the fluff under the bed, she was glad of the pattern on the lino, the cartons of crispies that she bought – so square. Even light is solid when the paths lead inward. So she listened to the carpet-sweeper.

All this time, she realized, something had been happening to Clay. For one thing his hair had begun to grow. Its long wisps curled like feather behind his ears. He himself, she saw, was not yet used to the silky daring of hair, which formerly had pricked to order.

'Level with the lobes of the ears, Mr McGillivray, please,' Clay would now explain.

McGillivray, who was old by this, and infallibly kind, always refrained from commenting.

So did the gentlemen at the Customs – it was far too strange. Even the young ladies, who had been prepared to giggle at first, got the shivers for something they did not understand.

Only when the hair had reached as far as Mr Skerritt's shoulders did Mr Archbold send for Clay.

'Is it necessary, Mr Skerritt?' his superior asked, who had the additional protection of a private office.

Clay replied: 'Yes.'

He stood looking.

He was allowed to go away.

His wife Marj decided there is nothing to be surprised at. It is the only solution. Even if the fretwork crackled, she would not hear. Even if the hanging basket sprouted hair instead of fern, she would not see. There were the chops she put in front of her husband always so nicely curled on the plate. Weren't there the two sides of life?

One evening Clay came up out of the terraced garden, where the snails wound, and the sea smells. He stood for some considerable time in front of his parents' wedding group. The great shoe, or boat, or bridge, had never appeared so structural. Looking back he seemed to remember that this was the occasion of his beginning the poem, or novel, or regurgitation, which occupied him for the rest of his life.

Marj was certain that that was the evening he closed the door.

She would lie and call: 'Aren't you gunna come to bed, Clay?'

Or she would stir at the hour when the sheets are greyest, when the air trembles at the withheld threat of aluminium, Marj would ungum her mouth to remark: 'But Clay, the alarm hasn't gone off yet!'

From now on it seemed as though his body never stayed there long enough to warm the impression it left on the bed. She could hardly complain, though. He made love to her twice a year, at Christmas, and at Easter, though sometimes at Easter they might decide against – there was the Royal Agricultural Show, which is so exhausting.

All this is beside the point. It was the sheets of paper which counted, on which Clay wrote, behind the door, of that little room, which his wife failed to remember, it was soon so long since she had been inside. One of the many things Marj Skerritt learned to respect was another person's privacy.

So Clay wrote. At first he occupied himself with objects, the mysterious life which inanimacy contains. For several years in the beginning he was occupied with this.

'. . . the table standing continues standing its legs so permanent of course you can take an axe and swing it cut into the flesh as Poles do every once in a while then the shriek murder murder but mostly nothing disturbs the maps the childhood journeys on the frozen wave of wooden water no boat whether wood or iron when you come to think satin either ever sails from A to B except in the mind of the passenger so the table standing standing under an electric bulb responds unlikely unless to determination or desperation of a Polish kind . . .'

One night Clay wrote:

'I have never observed a flower pot intimately until now its hole is fascinating the little down of green moss it is of greater significance than what is within though you can fill it if you decide to if you concentrate long enough. . . .'

Up till now he had not turned his attention to human beings, though he had been surrounded by them all his life. In actual fact he did not turn his attention to them now, he was intruded on. And Lova was not all that human, or not at first, a presence rather, or sensation of possession.

That night Clay got the hiccups, he was so excited, or nervous. The reverberations were so metallic he failed to hear his wife Marj, her grey voice: 'Aren't you gunna come to bed, Clay?'

Lova was, by comparison, a greenish-yellow, of certain fruits, and plant-flesh.

'*Lova Lova Lova*,' he wrote at first, to try it out.

He liked it so much it surprised him it had not come to him before. He could have sat simply writing the name, but Lova grew more palpable.

'*. . . her little conical breasts at times ripening into porepores detachable by sleight of hand or windy days yet so elusive fruit and shoes distributed amongst the grass . . .*'

In the beginning Lova would approach from behind glass, her skin had that faint hot-house moisture which tingles on the down of ferns, her eyes a ferny brown that complemented his own if he had known. But he knew no more than gestures at first, the floating entanglement of hair in mutual agreement, the slight shiver of skin passing over skin. She would ascend and descend the flights of stone steps, inhabiting for a moment the angles of landings of old moss-upholstered stone. The leaves of the *monstera deliciosa* sieved her at times into a dispersed light. Which he alone knew how to reassemble. On rare occasions their mouths would almost meet, at the bottom of the garden, where the smell of rotting was, and the liquid manure used to stand, which had long since dried up. She was not yet real, and might never be. No. He would make her. But there were the deterrents. The physical discords.

Marj said: 'My hands are that chapped I must ask Mr Todd's advice. You can enjoy a chat with a chemist, doctors are most of them too busy pushing you out.'

And Lova got the herpes. Clay could not look at her at first. As she sat at her own little table, taking the fifteen varieties of pills, forcing them into her pig's snout, Lova would smile still, but it was sad. And soon the sore had become a scab. He could not bring himself to approach. And breath, besides.

For nights and nights Clay could not write a word. Or to be precise, he wrote over several nights:

'*. . . a drying and a dying . . .*'

If he listened, all he could hear was the rustle of Lova's assorted pills, the ruffling of a single sterile date-palm, the sound of Marj turning in the bed.

Then it occurred to his panic the shored-up house might break open. It was so rotten, so dry. He could not get too quickly round the table, scattering the brittle sheets of paper. Motion detached itself from his feet in the shape of abrupt, leather slippers. Skittering to reach the door.

Clay did not, in fact, because Lova he now saw locking locking locked it, popping the key afterwards down between.

Lova laughed. And Clay stood. The little ripples rose up in her throat, perhaps it was the cold key, and spilled over, out of her mouth, her wet mouth. He knew that the private parts of babies tasted as tender as Lova's mouth.

He had never tried. But suspected he must.

She came to him.

'Bum to you!' Lova said.

She sat in his lap then, and with his free hand he wrote, the first of many white nights:

'At last my ryvita has turned to velveeta life is no longer a toast rack.'

'Golly,' said Lova, 'what it is to be an educated feller! Honest, Clay, it must be a great satisfaction to write, if only to keep one of your hands occupied.'

She laughed again. When he had his doubts. Does every face wear the same expression unless it is your own? He would have liked to look at the wedding group, to verify, but there were all those stairs between, and darkness. All he could hear was the sound of Marj breaking wind. Marj certainly had said at breakfast: 'It is the same. Whatever the manufacturers tell you, that is only to sell the product.'

But Lova said: 'It is different, Clay, as different as kumquats from pommygranates. You are the differentest of all perhaps. I could lap up the cream of your genius.'

She did, in fact, look at moments like a cat crouched in his lap, but would close at once and open, like a knife.

'I would eat you,' she repeated, baring her pointed teeth, when he had thought them broad and spaced, as in Mum or Marj.

Although he was afraid, he wrote with his free right hand:

'I would not trust a razor-blade to any but my own . . .'

When Lova looked it over.

Shoot!' she said. 'That is what I am!'

He forgot about her for a little, for writing down what he had to write.

' . . . Lova sat in my lap smelling of crushed carrot tops she has taken the frizz out of her hair but cannot make it smell less green I would not trust her further than without meaning to cast aspersions you can't trust even your own thoughts past midnight . . .'

'Chip Chip Chip chipped off his finger,' Lova said. 'Anyway it begins with C.'

'Oh dear,' C began to cry. 'Oh dear dear dear oh Lova!'

'When does D come in?' she asked.

'D isn't born,' he said, 'and pretty sure won't be. As for A, A is in bed. No,' he corrected 'A am not.'

Suddenly he wished he was.

He realized he was eye to eye with Lova their lashes grappling together in gummy agreement but melancholy to overflowing. They were poured into each other.

After that, Clay finished, for the night at least, and experienced the great trauma of his little empty room, for Lova had vanished, and there were only the inkstains on his fingers to show that she had ever been there.

There was nothing for it now but to join Marj in the parental bed, where he wondered whether he could ever be able to rise again. He was cold, cold.

Actually Marj turned over and said: 'Clay, I had an argument with Mr Tesoriero over the turnips. I told him you couldn't expect the public to buy them flabby.'

But Clay slept, and in fact he did not rise, not that morning, the first in many years, when the alarm clock scattered its aluminium trays all over the house.

Clay Skerritt continued going to the Customs. They had got used to him by then, even to his hair, the streaks in it.

He realized it was time he went to McGillivray's again, but some young dago came out, and said:

'Nho! Nho! McGillivray gone. Dead. How many years? Five? Six?'

So Clay Skerritt went away.

It was natural enough that it should have happened to McGillivray. Less natural were the substances. The pretending houses. The asphalt which had lifted up.

Then he saw the pointed heel, caught in the crack, wrenching at it. He saw the figure. He saw. He saw.

When she turned round, she said:

'Yes. It's all very well. For you. With square heels. Bum bums.'

Wrenching at her heel all the while.

'But Lova,' he said, putting out his hands.

She was wearing a big-celled honeycomb sweater.

'Oh, yes!' she said.

And laughed.

'If that's how you feel,' he answered.

'If that's how I *feel*!'

His hands were shaking, and might have caught in the oatmeal wool.

'I'm not gunna stand around exchanging words with any long-haired nong in the middle of Military Road. Not on yours!'

'Be reasonable,' he begged.

'What is reasonable?' she asked.

He could not tell. Nor if she had asked: what is love?

'Aren't you going to know me then?' he said.

'I know you,' she said, sort of flat – two boards could not have come together with greater exactitude.

'And it is time,' she said, 'to go.'

Jerking at her stuck heel.

'I've come here for something,' he remembered. 'Was it bird seed?'

'Was it my Aunt Fanny!'

Then she got her heel free and all the asphalt was crackling up falling around them in scraps of torn black tinkly paper.

If he could only have explained that love cannot be explained.

All the while ladies were going in and out, strings eating into their fingers together with their rings. One lady had an alsatian, a basket suspended from its teeth, it did not even scent the trouble.

It was Saturday morning. Clay went home.

That evening, after they had finished their spaghetti on

toast, because they were still paying off the Tecnico, Marj said:

'Clay, I had a dream.'

'No!' he shouted.

Where could he go? There was nowhere now.

Except on the Monday there was the Customs and Excise. He could not get there quick enough. To sharpen his pencils. To move the paper-clips the other side of the ink eraser.

When what he was afraid might happen, happened.

Lova had followed him to the Customs.

The others had not spotted it yet, for it could have been any lady passing the day at the Customs in pursuit of her unlawful goods. Only no lady would have made so straight for Mr Skerritt's desk, nor would she have been growing from her big-celled oatmeal sweater quite so direct as Lova was.

She had those little, pointed, laughing teeth.

'Well,' she opened, 'you didn't reckon on this.'

She was so certain of herself by now, he was afraid she might jump out of her jumper.

He sat looking down, at the letter from Dooley and Mann, Import Agents, re the Bechstein that got lost.

'Listen, Lova,' he advised. 'Not in here. It won't help find the piano.'

'Pianner? A fat lot of pianner! You can't play that one on me.'

'You may be right,' he answered.

'Right!' she said. 'Even if I wasn't. Even if I was flippin' wrong!'

She put her hand-bag on the desk.

'If anyone's gunna play, I'm the one,' she said.

Sure enough the old black upright slid around the corner from behind Archbold's glassed-in office, followed by the little leather-upholstered stool, from which the hair was bursting out. Lova seemed satisfied. She laughed, and when she had sat down, began to dish out the gay sad jazz. Playing and playing. Her little hands were jumping and frolicking on their own. The music playing out of every worm hole in the old, sea-changed piano.

Clay looked up, to see Archbold looking down. Miss Titmuss had taken her personal towel, and was having trouble with her heels as she made her way towards the toilet.

When Lova got up. She was finished. Or not quite. She began to drum with her bum on the greasy, buckled-up rashers of keys of the salt-cured old piano.

'There!' she shouted.

She came and sat on the corner of his desk. She had never been so elastic. It was her rage of breathing. He was unable to avoid the pulse of her suspender, winking at him from her thigh.

One or two other of the Customs officials had begun to notice, he observed, desperately through the side-curtains of his hair.

So he said: 'Look here, Lova, a scene at this stage will make it well nigh impossible for me to remain in the Service. And what will we do without the pension? Marj must be taken into account. I mean to say, it is the prestige as much as the money. Otherwise, we have learnt to do on tea and bread.'

Lova laughed then.

'Ha! *Ha!* HA!'

There is no way of writing it but how it was written on the wall. For it was. It got itself printed up on the wall which ran at right angles to Archbold's office.

Clay sat straight, straight. His adam's apple might not endure it much longer.

'Scenes are so destructive,' he said, or begged.

So his mum had told him.

'If that is what you want,' said Lova, 'you know I was never one for holding up procedure for the sake of filling in a form.'

And she ripped it off the pad from under his nose. Her hands were so naked, and could get a whole lot nakeder. He was afraid he might be answerable.

'I would never suggest,' she shouted, 'that the pisspot was standing right end up when it wasn't.'

But he had to resist, not so much for personal reasons as for the sake of public decorum, for the honour of the Department. He had to protect the paper-clips.

Because their hands were wrestling, troubling the desk. Him and Lova. At any moment the carton might burst open.

At any. It happened quite quickly, breathily, ending in the sigh of scatteration.

'I will leave you for now,' she said, getting off the corner of the desk, and pulling down her sweater, which had rucked up.

Almost every one of his colleagues had noticed by this, but all had the decency to avoid passing audible judgment on such a very private situation.

When it was over a little while, Miss Titmuss got down and gathered up the paper-clips, because she was sorry for Mr Skerritt.

He did not wait to thank or explain, but took his hat, treading carefully to by-pass the eyes, and caught the ferry to the other side.

Marj said: 'Aren't you early, Clay? Sit on the veranda a while. I'll bring you a cuppa, and a slice of that pound cake, it's still eatable I think.'

So he sat on the veranda, where his mother used to sit and complain, and felt the southerly get inside his neckband, and heard the date-palm starting up. Sparrows gathered cautiously.

Marj said: 'Clay, if you don't eat up, it'll be tea.'

You can always disregard, though, and he went inside the room, which he did not even dread. There she was, sitting in the other chair, in the oatmeal sweater. Her back turned. Naturally.

'Lova,' he began.

Then she came towards him, and he saw that she herself might sink in the waters of time she spread before him cunningly the nets of water smelling of nutmeg over junket the steamy mornings and the rather shivery afternoons.

If he did not resist.

She was just about as resistant as water not the tidal kind but a glad upward plume of water rising and falling back as he put his hands gently lapping lapping. She was so gentle.

Marj began to knock on the door.

'Tea's getting cold, Clay,' she announced.

It was, too. That is the way of things.

'I made you a nice devilled toast.'

She went away, but returned, and held her ear to the dry rot.

'Clay?' she asked. 'Don't you mind?'

Marj did not like to listen at doors because of her regard for privacy.

'Well,' she said, 'I never knew you to act like this.'

It could have been the first time in her life that Marj had opened a door.

Then she began to scream. She began to create. It was unlike her.

She could not see his face because of all that hair. The hair and the boards between them were keeping it a secret.

'This is something I never bargained for,' she cried.

For the blood had spurted out of the leg of the table. Just a little.

And that old shoe. He lay holding a white shoe.

'I never ever saw a shoe!' she moaned. 'Of all the junk she put away, just about every bit of her, and canaries and things, never a shoe!'

As Clay lay.

With that stiff shoe.

'I don't believe it!' Marj cried.

Because everyone knows that what isn't isn't, even when it is.

PETER COWAN

The Voice

The staff-room was warm. He closed the door on the wind that seemed concentrated along the corridor as if it had blown nowhere else. He crossed to the fire in the glass fronted fireplace, one pane of glass missing so that beyond the small cube the flames held a sudden reality, before he saw that she was sitting in the easy chair by the long window.

He had thought he might have, briefly, the room to himself, like some respite from the endless impact of personalities, from the words that must be found, the demand of faces.

He said, 'Cold enough. Still.'

'Yes. This room is warm, though.'

He looked up quickly from the fire. He saw her every day, without particular note. Quite a time ago she had deepened her hair in colour to black. Before that he seemed to remember indeterminate shades, neutral, in keeping with her rather broad, quiet face, that her glasses with their emphasized rims seemed to guard. It was a face that revealed little, he thought, except a rather determined pleasantness, and he was aware suddenly how slight had been his curiosity or his interest. And nothing that he saw as he looked at her now would have changed his feeling. But her voice was so altered that for a moment it seemed grotesque, as if some joke had been played on him.

She smiled faintly, as if she read his thought.

'Laryngitis. Isn't it stupid? I'm helpless in class.'

'Yes,' he said. Her voice had ordinarily been different, a little high-pitched, with something of a childish quality. Now it seemed to hold authority, and something that eluded him. He could have laughed at a certain wariness in himself, afraid still this might be some trick.

'I'm going home last period. I've no class then.'

141

'It's the only thing to do,' he said. 'I remember a head-master once, more noted for his voice than any minor qualities such as intelligence, saying to me when I'd had the flu, "You're pretty helpless without a voice." It was the nearest I ever saw him come to self-revelation. And to smiling.'

He realized as he spoke that his joke was not communicable and he was irritated with himself for having placed the pointless words between them. But she smiled and said, 'That wouldn't have been Pete?'

'Yes. Did you know him?'

'He terrified me. When I was just out of training college. I can still hear his voice booming down corridors.'

'Always.' He laughed. 'It's a few years since I knew him. He retired quite a while back.'

She nodded. He thought probably she did not want to talk, but he would have liked to hear her voice. The change intrigued him, its tone somehow provocative, what one might have called, he thought suddenly, suggestive. He almost smiled. It was exaggerated, a bit stagy, as if she were acting in some not very competent theatrical. He looked at her quiet, rather serious face that he had always felt to be too plainly reserved, prim, and he thought how incongruous the voice was. But her eyes met his and she might somehow have shared his amusement, so that he was suddenly uncertain.

'I've nothing to read,' she said. 'You haven't a good thriller, something light?'

'I don't know – I don't think so. Not here. What would you like?'

'As long as it's not serious I don't care. I've finished all the exam marking and I just want to relax. And with this throat on top of it all I'm a bit fed up.'

'As are we all,' he said. 'I'll see what I can find in the library.'

'I've looked.'

'Oh. Nothing?'

'Not that I haven't read. It doesn't matter. It was only for tonight.'

She stretched herself, her arms lifting, and then let her

hands fall suddenly, her fingers spread, her palms upturned towards him. He looked down at the fire.

'I'm getting lazy here.'

'Why not?' he said.

'In this hive? It must be the fire.'

'I could get you a couple of books,' he said. 'I think I've some would do.'

'It doesn't matter.'

'It's no trouble. I could run them round to you.'

Once or twice, after late staff meetings, he had taken her home, with two other teachers who lived in the direction of his own suburb.

'Do you think you could?'

'Yes. I've a games practice after school, I may be a bit late –'

'After tea,' she said. 'There's no hurry. It's good of you –'

The bell broke the classrooms to sound and deliberate disorder. He looked up towards the window and the rain was moving greyly across the buildings and the black quadrangle.

The flat was on the ground floor of a small block of four. As the door opened and she stood beneath the light of the small entrance hall he felt a surprise that he realized she perhaps perceived. He had expected some evidence of the invalid. Heavy clothes. A thick sweater, perhaps. Even a scarf about her throat. Now that he thought of it, a bandage would have been possible. It would not have been out of keeping with the practicality he had always associated with her nature. Just as in winter she wore a shapeless grey raincoat like a man's. And heavy flat shoes.

'Come in,' she said. Her voice was deep, faintly strained. He had wanted to hear it again. But as he followed her into the room he had not been prepared for the white blouse, short sleeved, the thin brown skirt that suggested so plainly her hips and thighs. He could no longer remember the anonymity of the clothes she wore to the school. She looked quickly at him, perhaps aware of his comparison.

'My voice is strained,' she said. 'It's not the flu or anything like that. I'm not really an invalid.' She smiled. 'It was good of you to bother with these.'

He handed her the books.

'You said something light –'

'Thank you. These look just what I wanted. Sit down, Max.'

There was a heater near the fireplace. She went across to the corner of the room and turned on the television. He looked at the meaningless images that steadied to a pattern he did not bother to encompass.

'Mother is out,' she said. 'She plays bridge on Tuesdays.'

He looked about the room that seemed crowded with small pieces of furniture that achieved no particular balance, and he wondered if the personalities of herself and her mother had somehow reached a stalemate in the furnishings of this main room of the flat. It might have been that the furnishings of two different periods found an uneasy common ground, the old, ornately carved china cabinet and the clear, rather sharp lines of the low coffee table, the wide, high-backed settee and the chrome television chairs, contrasts so obvious as to seem deliberate. He had never met her mother.

She asked him about one of the books he had brought, and they discussed the writer, neither of them, he realized, interested, the words giving them excuse. About her wrist she wore two thin silver bracelets that slipped along her arm, they drew his gaze, for he could not remember her affecting any such adornment at the school.

He said suddenly, 'We've both been round at the school quite a time.'

She laughed, seeming not to find his remark unexpected.

'I suppose so. I was going to get a transfer about a year ago, but nothing came of it.'

'I'm used to the place,' he said. 'Probably I'll stay until I'm moved perforce.'

'That doesn't sound very cheerful.'

'Well – you know yourself, there are enough times it seems an insane asylum, and the warders the least sane.'

'Oh yes.'

He shrugged. 'Somehow one stays.'

'Perhaps we're afraid to go outside,' she said.

He looked at her quickly, but she was watching the television. Her fingers moved the thin bracelets back along her arm. For a time they allowed the shadows that moved in the diminutive world to hold them. Once or twice he noticed her lift her hand to her throat, and he wondered if her voice was painful to use, despite her denial. But it seemed to him that the evening had somehow broken, deriding them, as if it had offered some promise now withdrawn. Or perhaps, he thought, promise that had existed only in his own mind, unformed and now unlikely to find form. There was the beginning of uneasiness between them. He could find no words that might confirm their own reality, that after all this time they should be here, in the room of her flat, and she met his few obvious commonplaces too quickly. As the inanity of advertising filled the small screen before them, she stood up, smoothing briefly her thin skirt.

'I'll make some coffee. I won't be a moment.'

While she was out of the room he went across to the bookshelf and looked at the neat, even lines of the books. There was one strong section of travel, perhaps her mother's, he thought, but the rest held a queer neutrality almost like some disguise of a personality, the books perhaps expected of a teacher, of one who had been educated. As she came in he turned away.

She said, 'Nothing very much there.'

He stood close to her, taking the cup from the small tray. Her features were attractive, he thought in faint surprise, no longer marked with the air of rather conscientious worry she had always seemed to affect, and which he had found irritating. She smiled at him suddenly, and he had again the sense that his feeling must have been obvious, but the restraint between them seemed to have passed, and they talked without awkwardness, content to allow pauses to lengthen between them while they looked idly at the film, which reflected some of the tinsel of another age.

When again advertising without subtlety broke upon the screen as if to cancel all that had existed before it, he said,

'I must go. I've kept you late, and with your throat like that – you must be tired –'

'Oh no.' She rose with him. 'Those old films are curious – to think we felt like that – accepted all that as valid –'

He laughed. 'And the same will happen to today's.'

'Yes.'

He said, 'Your voice – I'd like you to go on talking –'

'My voice –' She laughed.

He was standing close to her, and seemingly without volition he reached towards her, touching her arms, and she
looked up at him. He thought she seemed without coquetry
or evasion as she was without the forced jollity, the careful
good fellowship he had associated with her.

'It's not yours, really, I suppose.'

'Isn't it? How do you know?'

The television screen was suddenly blank, and she smiled,
moving to turn it off.

He said, 'I didn't know it was as late as that.'

'It's not really.'

He said, 'If someone – suddenly isn't that person –'

She began to laugh and he said, 'It's very confusing.'

'It must be. How could it happen, Max?'

'I'm not sure.'

They heard the front door of the flat open, and he thought
that for a moment she looked startled, and her mother came
quietly into the room.

'Hullo,' she said. She looked at them as they stood near the
television set. 'I wondered how you were. We finished early,
so I came straight home to make sure you were all right. And
meet Mr Webster. Evelyn said you would lend her some
books. It was good of you.'

As they spoke, and he made his excuses for leaving, he
looked at the small woman, whose quiet manner held something of authority. There was a certain fussiness about her, as
though she did not like things disturbed, or to be
unexpected, a suggestion of the fixity of routine that was
perhaps also in the younger woman who came to the door
with him, thanking him again for the books.

She did not come to school the next day. He had thought of
ringing to ask how she was, but in the haste of activity that
seemed so often meaningless he did not get to the phone.
The following day, just before morning break, he came into
the staff room and she was standing by the window, talking
to the history teacher. He went towards them and she looked
up. As soon as she spoke he knew that the kind of strain, the

depth, the faint suggestiveness her voice had seemed to hold was gone.

He said, 'You're better.'

Her smile had a briskness. 'Oh yes. A day home worked wonders.'

'Something we could all do with more often.' The history teacher laughed at his own commonplace.

As he looked at them she seemed so much as he had always known her that he thought perhaps his feeling had been imagination, that he had somehow, on the verge of making a humiliating revelation, been reprieved. Or, as he listened to her laugh which echoed only an impersonal gesture, he thought it might have been that a mask had been replaced, the revelation not his alone, and he would suddenly have spoken to her. But she was offering some triteness to match that of the history teacher, the mask would perhaps not slip again. He turned away as the bell rang for the morning break.

OLGA MASTERS

A Rat in the Building

Maud was just ready when Vera came.

She (Maud) had just blown dust out of the teacups and set them back on their saucers when Vera's tap was heard on the door.

'I'm just ready!' Maud cried letting her in. 'Just ready this very minute!'

She smiled a broad false-toothed smile on Vera who slid in and sat where she usually did close to the door. Maud fussed with the cushion behind her.

Dear me, she's depressed again, thought Maud feeling her own spirits rise.

She took her pleased face to the window and told herself she was allowing Vera a little time to recover.

There is something I'll point out to her, Maud thought with self congratulations on her generous nature.

'Look at the pretty flowers out in Mrs Morris's window box! They must have just come out. Violets they look like.'

'I saw them this morning,' Vera said, her broad flat face the colour of an old brown blanket with two raisins for eyes. She stood then sat again, a gesture of protest. 'They're not violets. She poked some plastic flowers in among that green stuff. I wish you could've seen the violets I grew Maud.'

Maud stood still her hands folded at her waist.

'There was this big rock at the back of the house,' Vera said in a near trembling voice. 'I grew the violets under it.

'It was cool and damp and I used to go at dusk every day and stand and smell.'

Vera drew air into her nostrils and Maud did too.

'I'll get you a drink! I didn't offer you a drink when you came,' Maud said when they had both exhaled.

She went briskly though an opening leading to a kitchen and returned with Vera's drink.

'And I didn't kiss you!' Maud said and kissed Vera over the glass of ginger beer causing the contents to wobble and almost spill on Vera's dress, a navy blue crepe patterned in brown, fraying around the buttonholes.

Vera took a sip of her drink and Maud watched her face for a change. There was none.

'I lost the house, you know Maud. It was in his name.'

Maud knew. She gave her sitting room a brief but loving glance.

'I'll get myself a little drink too,' she said and rose and did so.

They sipped alternately until Maud felt it was time to say something more.

'Irene should be in presently,' she said.

'She still got her rat?' Vera said a thin stream of envy running into her mournful voice.

They both glanced at the floor and Maud who was quite proud of her slim feet in their medium heel beige shoes lifted them and folded one behind the other resting only one toe on the floor.

Vera lifted her feet too. She wore large boat-shaped shoes, some of the creases breaking into cracks and bulbous where her corns had taken over their shaping. She too placed one upon the other ready at a given moment to climb the chair leg.

Maud smiled a very tolerant smile.

'I saw her on the stairs yesterday and she said she couldn't sleep the night before and when she put the light on there it was sitting up looking at her.

'It made no attempt to go back into the hole, she said.'

Maud and Vera looked stealthily around the visible areas of Maud's skirting board.

'We mustn't tell Mabel,' said Maud.

She put a thumb under her chin pushing it upwards looking wisely on Vera.

'Mabel talks to Henderson.'

'Runs after Henderson!' corrected Vera. There was the bark of a fox in her voice. Indeed she looked a lot like a large navy blue fox with age squashing its features and straggling its coat.

She tossed her head and opened her mouth as if she was ready to snap her jaws on Henderson, caretaker of the flats where they lived.

Her eyes strayed to the floor and so did Maud's and stayed there until there was a tap on the door.

Both jumped and swept their legs upwards.

'Oh dear,' said Maud recovering first and standing up she smoothed down her dress and her hair even sweeping both hands down her cheeks.

She opened the door to Irene.

Irene sidled in.

She was unmarried while Vera was divorced Mabel widowed and Maud married to Bert not yet retired who worked as a storeman in a firm in the city.

Irene was long like a pencil with a small round head at one end and surprisingly big feet at the other. She had been tall and hard and skinny in her youth while other girls were rosy, warm and fleshy. The result was that Irene bent herself sideways in an attempt to shorten herself on one side at least. She remained bent in her old age and looked like a dandelion weathered by rain and wind with its head gone colourless and tufty. Irene had taken lately to hiding her colourless and tufty hair under an ancient dusty straw hat with a mauve flower made of some faded flimsy material sitting above her forehead.

Irene's face beamed under the flower with a sort of shy and ugly radiance.

'You look so happy dear!' Maud cried watching her while she seated herself sideways on a settee.

'Doesn't she look happy Vera?' said Maud.

'She's got her rat!' said Vera with a short sharp bark.

'Oh Maud,' Irene said, 'I left the light on last night and out he came – here I am saying "he".'

'We always say "he",' Vera said. 'God knows why but we always say "he"!'

'I shouldn't be saying "he" Maud,' said Irene, 'Because it raised itself up Maud –'

Irene raised her two hands like the front paws of a rat and Maud and Vera looked around their feet and lifted them clear of the floor.

'And I saw these little pink titties! Little pink titties peeping out of the white fur!' said Irene. 'Maud it was trying to tell me something.'

'Well, it better not tell Henderson!' said Vera.

'We're keeping it from Mabel,' said Maud running her eyes over the floor before fixing them on the bobbing flower on Irene's hat. 'In case she lets something drop.'

'Before the rat does!' cried Vera looking for the first time almost pleased.

'I'll get Irene a drink,' said Maud getting up and bringing it from the kitchen.

'And I didn't kiss her!' she said wisely crushing a cheek against the flower before putting the glass into Irene's agitated hands.

Irene held her drink on her lap with a fixed expression ahead of her and the hint of a smile causing Maud and Vera to nervously follow her gaze.

Maud cleared her throat.

'We're not saying anything to Mabel dear,' she said speaking louder than necessary. 'Because she talks to Henderson and might say something.'

'You can't bring anything into this place!' said Vera.

'I didn't bring it here,' said Irene. 'It might have been here first!'

'The notice says no pets of any kind,' said Maud.

'No dogs!' said Vera.

'No cats!' said Maud.

'No caged birds!' said Vera.

'No pot plants on concrete surfaces!' said Maud.

'No climbing plants in window boxes!' said Vera. 'No rats! Certainly no rats!' There was something close to relish in her voice.

Irene whose eyeballs swam in some colourless liquid like pale brown glue gripped her drink harder and was gripping it when Mabel knocked on the door.

'Mabel, oh Mabel!' cried Maud in greeting as Mabel came in large and showily dressed in tan coloured jersey splashed all over with huge flowers pale pink in colour and sprouting centres that ran into the hemline and the edge of her sleeves finishing at the elbows. She had a large head with frizzy gingerish hair making it appear larger and her shoes were freshly caked with white cleaner.

Vera who hadn't cleaned her shoes backed them under her chair.

'She's got her hibiscus dress on!' cried Maud. 'We all love Mabel's hibiscus dress!'

'And she's brought the deaths! Oh thank you dear!'

Maud kissed Mabel remembering this time to do it at once something which caused Vera's raisin eyes to flash into hard little currants.

Mabel had a folded paper under an arm which she went to put on a little table near Vera then decided not to.

It was the section of a daily newspaper that contained the columns of death notices.

Mabel confiscated this when a tenant on her floor separated it from the news section and dumped the unwanted pages into a receptacle left for waste paper.

None of them bought a daily paper although Maud's Bert read one for free at his works.

Maud took the paper from Mabel and Mabel took the chair that appeared to be waiting for her and laid her large flowery arms along the chair arms.

Maud without her glasses held the paper at arms' length squinting and grimacing as if this would help her eyesight, then tucked it under her arm.

'I'll see them later! I'll get Mabel her drink!'

Vera put up a hand.

'I'll have a look!'

She raised the paper which she read easily without glasses and Mabel looked hard at the back of it.

'Put it where Maud can find it easy!' said Mabel loudly as if the paper was a wall she had to shout through.

Maud bringing Mabel a drink gave her a soothing smile which Vera saw while folding the paper.

'Anyone there we know dear?' said Maud with a little soothing smile to Vera which Mabel also saw.

'No one there I'd like to be there if you know what I mean!' said Vera.

Maud arranged her features sympathetically.

'Would they come to the funeral if I died before them?'

Vera said. 'Would he come by himself? Would she come? I wonder!'

'They mightn't know,' said Mabel.

'Of course they'd know!' said Vera the bark back in her voice. 'Everyone's death goes in the death columns, doesn't it Maud?'

'I would think so dear,' said Maud taking biscuits from a barrel and arranging them in a pattern on a plate. 'What about the door? Shall we open it a little for Mabel to hear her phone if it rings?'

'Mabel's phone never rang once since we've been coming to Maud's on a Thursday!' barked Vera. 'We could be blown to the GPO but the door has to be left open for Mabel's phone!'

Maud with some hesitancy opened the door a couple of inches. 'There! That shouldn't worry anyone!'

Irene's eyes full of watery dreams fixed themselves on the opening at floor level.

Maud looked down at her feet and moved them and Vera lifted hers.

Mabel looked down at her caked footwear and smoothed a hibiscus on her thigh.

'There has to be someone to put your death notice in the paper. It doesn't get there by itself does it Maud?' Mabel said. (Mabel had a married daughter living in the country.)

'He would put it in! I know he would!' said Vera.

'How would he know you died?' said Mabel. 'He'd have to find out first.' Her eyes were gingerish like her hair and they flashed from Vera to Maud.

'They're pretty busy with their little place. I doubt they'd even have time to read your name in the deaths let alone put it there. What do you say Maud?'

Maud was moving four cups and saucers on the cloth worked by herself for her glory box when she first met Bert.

She paused and like Irene assumed a dreamy air. Bert was several years younger so it was likely she would die first. She pictured his droopy face above some papers he was shuffling looking for her full name.

'Maud Florence!' she said suddenly into the silence and Vera jumped and looked at her feet.

'Oh dear,' Maud said going red.

'How would you know they're busy, Mabel?' said Vera as if gnawing a bone she was reluctant to put down. 'You don't have to pass there to go to Dr Powers! You go the back way by Railway Street. It's shorter!'

'I can go to Dr Powers whatever way I like, Vera,' said Mabel. 'Anyway I made a special trip to have a look at the little place.'

Vera for the moment could not raise a bark.

'They were busy too,' said Mabel.

'When?' said Vera.

'Friday if you must know.'

'You can't take any notice of Friday trade. All pubs are busy on a Friday! On other days there wouldn't be a soul there,' said Vera.

'Well there was plenty of souls there when I looked in,' said Mabel. 'It was early in the day too. I saw her. She was flat out behind the bar. She had her hair all done up. Bouffant I think they call it. It looked real nice.'

Maud stood.

'I'll put the jug on shall I?' she said.

Mabel mesmerized Maud to stillness with her eyes.

'They were busy when you and Bert were there, weren't they Maud?' Mabel said.

'You've never been there, Maud!' cried Vera.

'Oh yes she has,' said Mabel. 'Maud had a little stickybeak just like I did. Bert too!'

'Talk about rats!' cried Vera.

Irene grasped her bony knees in agitation and Maud sat suddenly lifting her feet from the floor. Vera looked wildly around the skirting board before finding Maud's face.

'Bert and I just took a little walk and when we were passing there Bert felt thirsty,' Maud said her corseted body upright.

'Ryan's is across the road and Tattersall's next door! Why didn't you go there?'

'Bert wasn't thirsty then,' said Maud.

'He got his thirst up in a hell of a hurry!' cried Mabel.

Maud reached out a hand and laid it on the ginger beer bottle.

'Have another little drink, Vera.'

'No thank you Maud! You bought that drink from them! Did you?'

'Of course I don't buy drink anywhere but the supermarket!' said Maud.

'You left them a tip, I suppose! To pay for her bouffant hairdo!'

'Of course not, Vera! Bert never tips!'

After a moment Maud looked Irene's way and gave her a small anxious smile. 'You all right there, dear?' she said.

'She's all right' cried Vera and lifted her feet so that they looked like a pair of boats about to start in a race against each other.

Maud raised hers too leaving the tips of her toes barely touching the floor.

Mabel glanced from one pair of feet to the other and looked around her own two great white blobs on Maud's carpet.

Irene's feet remained glued to the floor and her eyes on the thin opening at the doorway.

Maud followed her gaze and half rose.

'Perhaps we could close the door while we have our tea?'

'Close it if you want to! Don't worry about me!' cried Mabel.

'I do worry about you Mabel,' Maud said. 'I worry about all of you.'

'You worry about me all right!' said Vera.

'I worry about you most of all, Vera!' Maud said.

'Well thanks very much but don't worry about me!' said Vera.

'We're all like sisters. I say that all the time,' said Maud.

Mabel lifted her arms from the chair arms and dropped them over the side where they hung like two huge floral bats.

'You said it last Wednesday in the queue for the matinée,' Mabel said. 'You said "you and I are like sisters, Mabel. We're even closer than sisters!" '

'Youse went to the pictures!' cried Vera darting her eyes from one to the other and seeing Maud lower her eyes and Mabel wave her sleeves.

'We were all in here last Thursday and youse had been to the pictures the day before and not a word was said! Did Irene go?'

Irene did not shake her head. She didn't need to. Her beatific gaze was fixed on the pencil of light through the doorway. Maud and Vera looked too and lifted their feet.

Angrily Vera clamped hers down and Maud jumped.

'Dear me,' she said looking around the floor.

'Dear me all right!' cried Vera. 'Do you know what I did on Wednesday afternoon?' She plunged inside the neck of the navy blue crepe for a handkerchief and blew her nose. 'I sat by the window and watched the bloody traffic go by! That's what I did!'

'It wasn't that much of a programme, was it Mabel?' Maud said.

Mabel swung her bat-like arms up and down and arranged a small smile on her face.

'We thought of asking you to come along,' said Maud. 'Didn't we Mabel?'

'I don't remember if we did,' said Mabel opening and shutting her little ginger eyes.

'Irene's not getting upset about it,' said Maud with a soothing little smile taking in both Irene and Vera. 'Are you dear?'

'She wouldn't be upset!' said Vera. 'She'd be busy rat sitting!'

'What rat sitting?' cried Mabel lifting her feet so suddenly and violently some of the white flaked off her shoes and scattered on the floor.

'Irene's got a rat!' said Vera. 'Hasn't she, Maud?'

Maud wet her lips and looked towards the kitchen where the electric jug should be plugged in, avoiding Mabel's snapping accusing eyes.

'Maud knows about Irene's rat,' said Vera with great calm and only a cursory look around the skirting board and her feet just clear of the floor.

Mabel raised her feet and wound them around the legs of her chair. The white cleaner streaked the brown polished wood.

'Oh, Mabel my best chair!' cried Maud. 'I'll have to get that off before Bert gets home!' She moved forward as if to go at once for a cleaning cloth but sat back and lifted her feet an inch or two from the floor.

Mabel leaned back and rolled her ginger head on the chair back.

'Oh dear that sounds so funny!' she said stretching both legs out with her feet well above the floor.

Maud's eyes clung to Mabel's closed eyes.

Then she opened them and leaned forward.

'Tell Bert I marked the chair, Maud! He won't mind!'

'You don't know my Bert, Mabel!' Maud cried.

'Don't say "my Bert" Maud! It might become a habit. And habits are hard to break!' Mabel with her large arms loose over the chair arms rolled her head from side to side, her eyes closed again.

Maud had gone white.

Vera saw and put her head back too and laughed raising her feet with abandon and clapping her boat shoes together.

'There's more than one rat scuttling about the building!'

'My little rat doesn't scuttle anywhere! He just comes to me!' Irene cried.

'It's a "she" don't forget!' said Vera.

Irene intending to lean forward towards Mabel jerked sideways until she hung over the edge of the settee. She addressed the corner of the room past Mabel's chair.

'Don't tell Henderson! Don't tell Henderson!'

Mabel's hibiscus sleeve fell back to her elbow when she lifted an arm and looked with meditation on a raised hand quite well shaped with nails painted Maud noticed with a wildly beating heart.

'Come to think of it Bert doesn't scuttle about the building either,' Mabel said. 'He just comes to me!'

'Oh Mabel, he doesn't!' Maud cried out. 'How can you be sure, Mabel?'

Maud looked wildly around her. 'Bert goes to work and comes home!'

'So you say Maud,' said Mabel placidly looking at her hand again.

'Oh Mabel, stop joking!' Maud went to stand then sat and looked around her feet as if in search of something but she had forgotten what.

'It's no joke,' said Mabel. 'You can't watch Bert every minute of the day Maud.' She paused blinked her eyes rapidly. 'Or night.'

'Bert sleeps in his bed all night!'

'All night?'

'He gets up with his bladder! I hear him!'

'You hear him get up *or* go back to bed Maud. Not both.'

'Mabel, stop it!' Maud cried getting up and briefly glancing at her ankles before returning her wide and blazing eyes to Mabel.

'Bert wouldn't hurt anyone! I know he wouldn't!'

'He certainly doesn't hurt me, Maud,' said Mabel. 'Quite the opposite.'

'Oh my God!' shrieked Vera rocking herself with delight. 'This is better than the pictures! I didn't miss anything after all!'

'She's joking. She's never met Bert!' said Maud.

'You hustle us out of here every Thursday before Bert gets home,' Mabel said. 'You don't want us to meet him, do you Maud?'

Maud took a pace or two towards Mabel but stopped before she could stand over her. She did not look at her feet.

'Get out of my house!'

Mabel stood both hands brushing down in a flowing movement her hibiscus dress.

'That's right! Say "my house", Mabel! It's a good start!'

'Get out!' cried Maud.

'I'm going,' said Mabel.

'Surely not before you've made a date for the pictures!' cried Vera, but she too was on her feet and just behind Maud when she flung the door open.

They went into the hall with Irene behind when Henderson came towards them on one of his routine inspections of the building.

Maud as if in a race against Mabel cried out: 'There's a rat in the building, Mr Henderson!'

No one spoke although Irene was about to. Her gnarled purple hand crushed to her mouth caused nothing to emerge but a thin squeak.

They all leapt and looked at their feet. Henderson had trouble with his legs and they creaked and wavered while his trousers always worn too long seemed in danger of tangling him up.

'It's in Miss Crump's flat, Mr Henderson!' Maud cried. 'It's upsetting us all, isn't it Mabel? But Mr Henderson will get rid of it, won't you Mr Henderson?'

But Mabel's head was up and her back towards them sailing away like a floral boat in the direction of her door.

ELIZABETH JOLLEY

Five Acre Virgin

'There's a five acre virgin for sale.' Mother scooped up her avocado pear and drank her cocoa quickly. She pushed the country towns and properties into her shopping bag. 'We'll have a look later,' she said. 'Might be just right for Mr Hodgetts.' She looked at the clock. 'We'll have to hurry if we're going to get all the rooms done today.' Some days I helped Mother like today when I had a half day from the toy shop where she had got me this little job to keep me occupied, as she said, during the long summer holidays. I was screaming mad in that shop, it was so quiet in there. Like yesterday I only had two people in all day, just two little boys who looked at everything, opened all the boxes and took things off the shelves, spilled all the marbles and kept asking me, 'What's this?' and 'How much is this?' And then in the end they just bought themselves a plastic dagger each. I preferred to go with Mother on her cleaning jobs. She had all these luxury apartments in South Heights to do. We got a taste of the pleasures of the rich there and it had the advantage that Mother could let people from down our street in at times to enjoy some of the things which rich people take for granted like rubbish chutes and so much hot water that you could have showers and do all your washing and wash your hair every day if you wanted to. Old Mrs Myer was always first in to Baldpate's penthouse to soak her poor painful feet.

Just now Mother was terribly concerned over Mr Hodgetts our lodger. He was a surgeon in the City and District Hospital; he worked such long and odd hours Mother felt sure a piece of land was what he needed to relax him.

'He don't get no pleasure poor man,' Mother said. 'There's nothing like having a piece of land to conquer,' she said. 'It makes a man feel better to clear the scrub and have a good burning off.' All doctors had yachts or horses or farms and it would be quite fitting for Mr Hodgetts to have some acres of his own.

Mr Hodgetts never stopped working. He used to come home clomping his boots across the verandah. Mother said his firm heavy step was Authority walking. She said it was the measured tread of a clever man pondering over an appendix.

His room opened off the end of the verandah so we had to pass it going in and out of our own place. He needed privacy, Mother said, and she put a lace curtain over the glass part of the door and she got my brother to fix up a little plate with his name on. The plate had to be right at the bottom of the door as this was the only part they could make holes in for the screws.

'Who ever heard of a surgeon being a lodger,' my brother said.

'Well anyone might be a lodger temporarily,' Mother said. 'If the Queen came she'd have to stay somewhere till the council got a palace built for her.'

'Not in a crappy place like this.' My brother shoved at the window to open it and the whole thing fell into the yard.

'Well, Mr Hodgetts hasn't said he's the Queen, has he?' Mother had to go out to get something for tea then. Thinking what to get Mr Hodgetts and my brother for their tea was a real worry.

'What about lamb's fry and bacon?' I said, but Mother said she thought she had better prepare something elegant like sardines. She was always on about the elegance of sardines and brown bread and butter.

'You'll be giving us celery and yoghurt next!' my brother looked disgusted. 'You know I can't stand fish,' he said, 'and tell your surgeon he can take off his cycle clips in the house.' With that he slammed off out. Sometimes he was in a terrible mood, Mother said it was because he couldn't tolerate the false values of society and didn't know how to say so.

'I'll have to hurry,' Mother said. 'It's Mr Hodgetts' ear nose and throat clinic tonight.'

Mother always assisted Mr Hodgetts. He just presumed she would wash and iron his white coat and every night he stood with his arms out waiting for her to help him into it.

The first time I saw them dressed in white with bits of cloth tied over their faces I nearly died laughing. I had to lean against the door post it was killing me laughing so much. Mother gave me such a kind look.

'Just you sit down on that chair,' she said to me, 'and you can be first in, Mr Hodgetts will see you first.'

'But I don't want to see Dr Hodgetts, there's nothing wrong with me.'

'It's *Mr* Hodgetts,' Mother said ever so gently. 'Surgeons is always Mr not Dr.'

That shut me up I can tell you. So every Friday I had my throat examined and Mr Hodgetts sat there with a little mirror fixed to a band round his head. He peered into my ears too and made notes on a card. Mother fixed up his medical book between the cruet and the tomato sauce on the sideboard. The whole thing was covered with a cloth. Every day we had to bake cloths in the stove to make them sterile for Mr Hodgetts. And Mother made and changed appointments for the people down our street in the back of my old home science note-book.

When Mr Hodgetts went on the night shift Mother took the opportunity to suggest we go to have a look at the five acres.

'We can go on the eight o'clock bus,' she said to him, 'and come back on the one o'clock and you can have time for your sleep after that. We could have a nice outing and take Mrs Myer, it's been a while since she was taken anywhere.'

Mr Hodgetts pondered and then said, 'That's right. The lists don't start till eight p.m.'

'The list,' Mother explained to us, was the operations.

'Who ever heard of operations being done all night,' my brother was scornful. 'And they don't wear boiler suits in the operating theatre and who ever heard of a surgeon having his own vacuum polisher and taking it on the bus.'

'Well, he can't take it on his bike, can he,' Mother said.

It was true the wash line was heavy with grey boiler suits; every day Mother had this big wash, white coat and all.

'Just you hush!' Mother said as I was about to ask her something. 'And you mind what you're saying!' she said to my brother. Mr Hodgetts was clomping through the verandah.

'Oh!' I said very loud. 'I could have sworn I saw a cat

hunched on the window.' Of course there was no cat there, I said it so Mr Hodgetts wouldn't think we were discussing him.

'Oh, that's nothing,' Mother said, 'your Aunty Shovell once saw a black umbrella walk right round the room of itself.'

Just then there was a knock on the kitchen door and who should come in but our Aunty Shovell.

'Oh!' Mother had to sit down. 'Talk of angels!' she said white as a sheet. 'We just this minute said your name and you walk in through that door!'

'Nothing I wouldn't say about myself, I hope.' Aunty Shovell dropped her parcels, lemons rolled from her full shopping bag and she sank, out of breath, on to the kitchen chair. 'Got a kiss for me, then?' My brother obediently gave her a little kiss and Aunty Shovell smiled at him lovingly. She had a special place in her heart for my brother, she always said. She even carried a photo of him as a little boy in her handbag. Mother would never look at it. She said there was too much shy hope and tenderness and expectation in his face.

'Who's our gentleman?' Aunty Shovell indicated the verandah with a toss of her head. The firm footstep was on its way back from the wash-house.

'Anyways,' she said before Mother could explain, 'a man who walks like that could never be a thief.' She settled herself comfortably and didn't make any attempt to leave till she got Mother to ask her to tea the next day.

In the morning we nearly missed our bus, as my brother wouldn't get out of bed and Mr Hodgetts took so long writing up his kidneys and then old Mrs Myer was late too.

Mother was half under the bus.

'I think there's a big nail drove right into your tyre,' she called up to the impatient driver. 'You better come down and have a look.' Mrs Myer was waddling up the street as fast as she could. Everyone just made it into the front seats of the bus by the time the driver had climbed down and been under to check the tyre which seemed to be all right after all.

We found the piece of land but Mr Hodgetts did not seem very impressed.

'Look here's a few fencing posts, probably thrown in with the price,' Mother pointed out the advantages. 'And over there there's a little flat part where you could put your shed and I'm sure these rocks could be useful for something.' Her face was all flushed from the fresh air and her nose had gone red the way it does if she's excited about things.

'There's no money in wool,' Mr Hodgetts said slowly.

Mother agreed. 'Too right! There's nothing in wool these days and, in any case, if you put sheep here they'd break their necks in no time,' she said. 'And there's nothing for them to eat.'

It was a terrible piece of land, even if it was virgin. There was no shade and it was so steep we had to leave Mrs Myer at the bottom.

'Oh, it's so fragrant!' Mother said. 'You know, land isn't just for sheep. It's for people to enjoy themselves.' She waved her arms. 'I'm sure there are masses of flowers here in the spring, you must agree it's a wonderful spot!'

Mr Hodgetts stroked his chin thoughtfully.

'I feel this land is very strong,' Mother urged, 'and what's more it's only two hundred dollars deposit.'

'Why pay two hundred dollars to kill yourself,' my brother said, 'when you could do it for nothing,' and he pretended to slip and fall down the steep rock.

'Halp! I'm falling!' he called and his thin white fingers clutched at the fragments of scrub. 'Halp!' His long thin body struggled on the rock face as he went on falling. He put on his idiot's face with his eyes turned up so only the whites showed. 'Haaalp!'

'Oh Donald, be careful!' Mother called. As he fell and rolled we had to see the funny side and we both roared our heads off while Mr Hodgetts stood there in his good clothes and boots.

Suddenly we saw smoke curling up from below.

'Quick!' Mother cried. 'There's a fire down there, Mrs Myer will get burned to death!' She began to scramble down. 'Fire always goes up hill,' she said. 'Hurry! Hurry! We must stop it! Don't be afraid, there's my good girl!' she said to me and we got down that hill much faster than we got up it.

'I am josst boilink my kettle,' Mrs Myer explained from the

middle of her fire. 'I sought ve vould all hev tea. I bring everyding in my begs,' she said. 'My leetle cookink is surprise for you!' I don't think I have ever seen Mrs Myer look so happy. My brother was already stamping out the little runs of flame and the rest of us quickly did the same while Mrs Myer busied herself with her teapot.

Mother had a lot on her mind on the way home. It was clear Mr Hodgetts had no feeling for the land.

'And another thing,' she said to me in a low voice. 'There isn't a soul for his outpatients clinic tonight. The street's all been. Wherever am I going to find someone else to come.' She seemed so tired and disappointed. And of course she would have extra to do at South Heights to make up for not being there today.

'What about Aunt Shovell?' I said. 'She's never been examined.' Mother shook her head.

'Shovell's never believed in doctors,' she said. And another burden settled on her. 'Whatever shall I get for *her* tea tonight?'

All through the meal Mr Hodgetts never took his eyes off Aunt Shovell. Mother had asked him into the kitchen as it seemed a shame for him to eat off his tray all alone.

'Mr Hodgetts, this is my sister Miss Shovell Hurst, Shovell, this is Mr Hodgetts who lodges with us.'

'Pleased to meet you Cheryl.' Mr Hodgetts leaned over the table and shook hands and after that it was all Cheryl. He kept getting up to pass her the plate of brown bread and butter. He kept telling her things too, starting every remark with, 'Cheryl, I must tell you,' and 'Cheryl, have you heard this . . .?' And then he asked her a riddle. 'Cheryl, what lies at the bottom of the ocean and shivers?'

'Oh,' she said, 'now let me see, what lies at the bottom of the ocean and shivers? I give up!'

'A nervous wreck.' Mr Hodgetts laughed his head off nearly, so did Aunt Shovell. And then she said, 'Pass your cup, I'll read your tea leaves and tell your fortune,' so we all listened while Aunt Shovell predicted a long life of prosperity and happiness for Mr Hodgetts.

'Romance is to be yours,' she said leaning right across the

table. 'Miss Right is nearer to you than you think!' Mr Hodgetts sat there amazed.

'Is that so, Cheryl,' he said. 'Well, I never,' and after tea he asked her if he could take her home before going to his own job.

'We never had the clinic,' I said to Mother when Mr Hodgetts had left for the hospital, walking Aunty Shovell to her bus on the way to his. 'Mr Hodgetts forgot about his clinic.'

'Never mind!' Mother said.

'I never knew Aunty Shovell's name was Cheryl.'

'Yes, Shovell, like I said, Shovell,' Mother said.

'Is Aunty Shovell a virgin then?' I asked.

'Nice girls don't ask things like that,' Mother said.

'There's pretty near five acres of her, whatever she is,' my brother said.

I thought Mother would go for him for saying that but she only asked him, 'Is my nose red?' as if he cared.

'Just a bit,' he said.

'I expect it's the fresh air,' Mother said and she began to sing,

How do you feel when you marry your ideal . . .

'. . . it's a popular song from my youth,' she explained.

How do you feel when you marry your ideal,
ever so goosey goosey goosey goosey,

and she laughed so much we thought she must be really round the bend this time.

Frederick the Great
Returns to Fairfields

'Why can't the father, the father of your – what I mean is, why can't he do something.'

'I've told you, he's dead.'

'How can you say that, he was on the phone last night. I could tell by your voice that's who it was.'

'He's dead. I've told you.'

At last the day has come when I must leave for Fairfields. It is all arranged. I have been there once already and know it to be a place of grated raw vegetables and children with restless eyes. It is also a place of poetry and music and of people with interesting lives and ideas.

'I simply can't understand you. How could you with your education and your background breed like a rabbit –'

'You're always saying that, for years you've said it. I've told you rabbits have six, I only one.'

'How can you speak to me, your mother, like that.'

'Oh shut up and remember this. I'm never coming back. Never!'

'And another thing, Helena looks like a miner's child dressed up for an outing!' My mother does not like the white frock and the white socks and the white hair ribbons. I tie Helena's hair in two bunches with enormous bows and do not remind my mother that she bought the white frock, and the white socks and the white ribbons.

'She'll get a headache, her hair pulled tight like that. And why white for a train journey, two train journeys. Oh Vera!' My mother, I can see, has tears in her eyes, 'Leave Helena here with me, your father and I would like to have her here with us, please! Besides, she is happy with us.'

But I will not be parted from my child. I throw a milk bottle across the kitchen, it shatters on the tiles and I am pleased because my mother is frightened. 'What's wrong with miners and their children and their outings,' I shout at her.

Perhaps Helena would be happier with her grandmother. I do not want to think this and it is painful to be told.

My father comes with us to the station.

'That's a nice coat,' he says carrying it for me. It is my school winter coat, dark green and thick. It would not fit into my case so I have to carry it or wear it.

'It's a new coat, is it?' he says feeling the cloth with his hands. I don't reply because I have been wearing the coat for so many years.

We are too early for the train. The platform is deserted.

'It looks like a loden,' he is still talking about the coat. 'Like the Austrian loden cloth.' He is restless, my father, very white faced and he holds Helena's hand and walks up and down the platform, up and down. The coat on his other arm.

Always when my father sees off a train he is at the station too soon. And then, when the train is about to leave, when the whistle is being blown and the doors slam shut, one after the other down the whole length of the train, he rushes away and comes back with newspapers and magazines and pushes them through the window as he runs beside the now moving train. As the engine gets up steam and the carriages clank alongside the platform my father increases his speed keeping up a smiling face outside the window.

His bent figure, his waving arms and his white face have always been the last things I have seen when leaving. I know too from being with him, seeing other people off, that he stands at the end of the platform, still waving, long after the whole train has disappeared.

Walking up and down we do not speak to each other. The smell of the station and the sound of an engine at the other platform remind me of Ramsden and of the night several years earlier when I met her train. Ramsden, Staff Nurse Ramsden, arriving at midnight. There was a thick fog and her train was delayed.

'I've invited Ramsden to come and stay for a few days,' I said to my mother then, assuming a nonchalance, a carelessness of speech to hide Ramsden's age and seniority.

'Why, of course Vera, a nursing friend is always welcome . . .' There had been a natural progression from school friend to nursing friend. My father never learned to follow, to keep up with this progression.

'And is Miss Ramsden a good girl?' would be his greeting, a continuation of, 'And is Jeanie a good girl?' He would say it to Ramsden without seeing the maturity and the elegance and without any understanding of the superior quality of her underclothes.

'My parents are looking forward to meeting you,' I invited Ramsden knowing already these other things.

Ramsden, with two tickets to Beethoven, in our Town Hall, prepared herself to make the long journey.

Putting off the visit, in my mind, from one day to the next, reluctantly, at last I was in the Ladies Only waiting room, crouched over a dying fire, thin-lipped and hostile with the bitter night. My school coat heavy but not warm enough and my shoes soaked.

Ramsden, who had once, unasked, played the piano for my tears, arrived at last. I could see she was cold. She was pale and there were dark circles of fatigue round her eyes. She came towards me distinguished in her well-cut tailored jacket and skirt. Her clothing and manner set her apart immediately from the other disembarking passengers.

'Miss Ramsden will have to share the room,' my mother said before I left for the station, 'your sister's come home again.' Shrugging and blinking I went on reading without replying. Reading, getting ready slowly, turning the page of my book, keeping one finger in the page while I dressed to go and meet the train.

Ramsden came towards me with both hands reaching out in leather gloves. At once she was telling me about the Beethoven, the Choral Symphony, and how she had been able to get tickets. There was Bach too, Cantata Eighteen. Remember? she said. *For as the rain cometh down and the snow from heaven* she, beating time with one hand, sang, *so shall my word be that goeth forth out of my mouth*. . . In the poor light of the single mean lamp her eyes were pools of pleasure and tenderness. She did not mind the blackout she said when I apologised for the dreariness of the station. 'Ramsden,' I said, 'I'm most awfully sorry but there's been something of a tragedy at home. I couldn't let you know . . . I'm so most awfully sorry . . .'

'Not –?' concern added more lines to Ramsden's tired face. I nodded turning away from the smell of travelling which hung about the woollen cloth of her suit.

'Oh Wright! I am so sorry. Veronica.' It was the first time she had spoken my first name, well almost the first time. I glanced at her luggage which stood by itself on the fast emptying platform. The case seemed to hold in its shape and leather the four long hours of travelling, the long tedious journey made twice as long by the fog.

There would be a stopping train to London coming through late, expected at three in the morning the porter said as Ramsden retrieved her case from its desolation.

A glance into the waiting room showed that the remnant of the fire was now a little heap of cold ash. Perhaps, she suggested, even though there was no fire it would be warmer to sit in there.

'I'm so sorry,' I said, 'I shall not be able to wait for your train.' So sorry I told her, I must get back, simply must get back.

'Is it –?' more concern caused Ramsden to raise her dark eyebrows. The question unfinished, I drew my arm away from her hand's touch. I thought of the needlework and embroidery book I had chosen from her room, too nervous with my act, then, to read the titles when, to please me, she said to choose a book to have to keep, as a present, from her shelf. The badly chosen book I thought, at the time, made me feel sick. I began that day, almost straight away, to feel sick.

We walked along the fog-filled platform. 'I've come to you all the way from London,' Ramsden drawing me to her began in her low voice. 'I'd hoped . . .' I turned away from the clumsy embrace and her breathed-out whispered words, knowing her breath to be the breath of hunger.

'I'm sorry,' I said again stiffening away from her, 'but I'll have to go.'

'To them,' she said, 'yes of course, you must,' she nodded her understanding and her resignation.

'I am sorry I can't wait till your train comes. I can't wait with you. I'm most awfully sorry!' trying to change, to lift my accent to match hers.

She nodded again. I knew from before, though I couldn't see them, what her eyes would be like.

I had to walk the three miles home as there were no buses at that time of night. The fog swirled cold in my face. The way was familiar but other things were not. My own body, for one thing, for I was trying, every day, to conceal my morning sickness.

I turn away trying to avoid the place on the platform where Ramsden tried to draw me towards an intensity of feeling I could not be a part of that night.

'She wasn't on the train,' I told my mother the next morning standing on purpose behind her flowered overall and keeping to the back of her head which was still encased in metal rollers. She was hurrying to get to the Red Cross depot. Her war effort.

'It was a dreadful night for travelling,' my mother said, not turning from the sink, 'perhaps your Miss Ramsden will send a letter. You can invite her again, perhaps in the spring, we'll have more space then, perhaps by then your sister will be better.'

My father, running now beside the moving train, pushes a magazine and a comic through the window. I, because I feel I must, lean out and see him waving at the end of the platform. Helena, clinging to my skirt, cries for her Grandpa.

Unable to stop thinking of Ramsden I wonder why do I think of her today after all this time of forgetting her. I never write to her. I never did write even when she wrote to me saying that she was still nursing and that she lived out, that she had a little flat which had escaped the bombs and if I liked to stay she would love to have me stay as long as I liked, 'as long as you feel like it'. I never answered. Never told her I had a child. Never let her into my poverty and never let her into my loneliness.

London is full of people who seem to know where they are and to have some purpose in this knowing. I drag my case and the coat and Helena and change stations and at last we are travelling through the fields and summer meadows of

Hertfordshire. The train, this time, is dirty and has no corridor and immediately Helena wants the lavatory. I hate the scenery.

At last we are climbing the steep field path from the bus stop to the school. Fairfields, I have been there once already and know the way. The path is a mud path after it leaves the dry narrow track through the tall corn which is turning, waving and rippling, from green to gold, spotted scarlet with poppies and visited by humming hot weather insects. I have seen before that the mud is caused by water seeping from two enormous manholes in the trees at the top of the hill. Drains, the drains of Fairfields School.

'Who is that?' Helena stops whimpering. And I see a man standing quite still, half hidden by trees. He does not seem to be watching, rather it is as if he is trying to be unseen as we climb higher. He does not move except to try and merge into a tree trunk. With the case I push Helena on up the steepest part of the path and I do not look back into the woods.

In the courtyard no one is about except for a little boy standing in the porch. He tells me his Granny will be coming to this door, that he is waiting to be fetched by her. 'My Granny's got a gas stove,' he tells me. I think suddenly of my mother's kitchen and wish that I could wait now at this door for her to come and fetch me and Helena. Straight away I want to go back.

Miss Palmer, the Principal, the one they call Patch – I know this too from my earlier visit – carrying a hod of coke, comes round from an outhouse.

'Ah!' she says. 'I see you mean to stay!' she indicates my winter coat, 'so this is Helena!' she glances at my child. 'She's buttoned-up, I daresay.' I know this to mean something not quite explained but I nod and smile. Patch tells me that no one is coming to fetch Martin. 'He's new, he hasn't', she says, 'adjusted yet.'

She shows me my room which I am to share with Helena. It is bare except for a cupboard and two small beds. It is bright yellow with strong smelling distemper. There is a window, high up, strangled with creeper.

'Feel free to wander,' Patch says, 'tea in the study at four. Children's tea in the playroom at five and then the bathings.

Paint the walls if you feel creative.' She has a fleshy face and short, stiff hair, grey like some sort of metal. I do not dislike her.

'Thank you,' I say narrowing my eyes at the walls as if planning an exotic mural.

Helena, pulling everything from the unlocked case, intones a monologue over her rediscovered few toys. I stare into the foliage and the thick mass of summer green leaf immediately outside the window.

Later the Swiss girl, Josepha, who has the room opposite mine, takes me round the upstairs rooms which are strewn with sleeping children. We pull some of them out of bed and sit them on little chipped enamel pots. There is the hot smell of sleeping children and their pots.

Josepha tells me the top bathroom is mine and she gives me a bath list. The face flannels and towels hang on hooks round the room.

Josepha comes late to breakfast and takes most of the bread and the milk and the butter up to her room where her sweetheart, Rudi, sleeps. I heard their endless talk up and down in another language, the rise and fall of an incomprehensible muttering all night long, or so it seemed in my own sleeplessness.

The staff sit at breakfast in a well-bred studied shabbiness huddled round a tall copper coffee pot and some blue bowls of milk. Children are not allowed and it seems that I hear Helena crying and crying locked in our room upstairs. Patch does not come to breakfast but Myles, who is Deputy Principal, fetches prunes and ryvita for her. She is dark-eyed and expensively dressed like Ramsden but she has nothing of Ramsden's music and tenderness. She is aloof and flanked by two enormous dogs. She is something more than Deputy Principal. Josepha explains.

'Do not go in,' Josepha points at Patch's door, 'if both together are in there.'

When I dress Helena I take great trouble over her hair ribbons and let her, with many changes of mind, choose her dress because I am sorry for leaving her alone, locked in to cry in a strange place. I have come to Fairfields to work, with the idea that it will give Helena school and companionship and already I have tried to persuade her, to beg her, and finally rushed away from her frightened crying because staff off-spring (Myles' words) are not allowed at staff meals. I take a long time dressing Helena and find that Josepha has dressed all the children from my list as well as her own. I begin to collect up the little pots.

'No! Leave!' Josepha shouts, and tying the last child into a pinafore, she herds them downstairs. Moving swiftly Josepha can make me, with Helena clinging to my dress, seem useless.

Josepha does the dining room and I am to do, with Olive Morris, the playroom where the smaller children have their meals. Mrs Morris has a little boy called Frank but Helena will not sit by him. She follows me with a piece of bread and treacle and I have to spend so much time cleaning her that Olive Morris does the whole breakfast and wipes the tables and the floor. She does not say anything, only gets on with ladling cod liver oil, which is free, into the children as they leave the little tables.

I discover that Olive Morris has three children in the school and that Josepha feels it is morally right that Olive should work more than anyone else because of this. Josepha is always dragging children off to have their hair washed. She has enormous washing days and is often scrubbing something violently at ten o'clock at night. The smell of scorching accompanies the fierceness of her ironing.

'Do not go in there,' she points to the first floor bathroom, 'when Patch and Tanya in there,' she says, 'and do not tell Myles!'

Tanya teaches art. She looks poor but Josepha says she is filthy rich and wears rags on purpose.

Tanya, on my first day, was painting headless clowns on the dining room walls. She stepped back squinting at her work. 'They are going to play ball with the heads,' she explained bending down over her paint pots as if she had been talking to me for years.

'What a good idea,' I said, ashamed of my accent and trying to sound as if I knew all about painting.

That day she asked me what time it was, saying that she must hurry and get her wrists slashed before Frederick comes back from his holiday.

Later, in the pantry, she is there with both arms bandaged. 'Frederick the Great,' she says, 'he'll be back. Disinfectant, fly spray, cockroach powder and mouse traps. He will,' she says, 'ask you to examine his tonsils.'

Olive Morris looks ill. Sometimes when I sit in my room at night with an old cardigan round the light to keep it off Helena's bed I think of Olive and begin to understand what real poverty is; her dreadful little bowls of never-clean washing, the rags which she is forever mending and her pale crumpled face from which her worried eyes look out hopelessly.

I have plenty of pretty clothes for Helena. And then it suddenly comes to me that this is the only difference. My prospects are the same as Olive's. I have as little hope for the future as she has. It just happens that at present, because of gifts from my mother, Helena, for the first years of her life, has been properly fed and is well dressed.

One hot afternoon I sit with the children in the sandpit hoping that they will play. There are only two little spades and the children quarrel and fight and bite each other. It is hard to understand why the children can't enjoy the spacious lawns and the places where they can run and shout and hide among the rose bushes. Beyond the lawns is deep uncut grass bright with buttercups and china blue harebells. I am tired, tired in a way which makes me want to lie down in the long grass and close my eyes. Helena, crying, will not let me rest. The children are unhappy. I think it is because they do not have enough food. They are hungry all the time.

I do lie down and I look up at the sky. Once I looked at the sky, not with Ramsden but after we had been talking together. I would like to hear Ramsden's voice now. It is strange to wish this after so long. Perhaps it is because everyone here seems to have someone. Relationships, as they are called here, are acceptable. And I, having no one, wishing for someone, vividly recall Ramsden. She said, that time in the morning before I went for my day off to sleep among the spindles of rosemary at the end of my mother's garden, that love was infinite. That it was possible, if a person loved, to believe in the spiritual understanding of truths which were not fully understood intellectually. She said that the person you loved was not an end in itself, was not something you came to the end of, but was the beginning of discoveries which could be made because of loving someone.

Lying in the grass, pushing Helena away, I think about this and wonder how I can bring it into the conversation at the four o'clock staff tea and impress Patch and Myles. I practise some words and an accent of better quality.

Because of being away from meadow flowers for so long I pick some and some of the delicate grasses adding their glowing tips to the bunch, wondering with bitter uneasiness, how I can get them unseen to my room. I can see Patch and Myles at the large window of Patch's room. Instead of impressing them I shall simply seem vulgar, acquisitive and stupid, clutching a handful of weeds, ineffectually shep-herding the little children towards their meagre plates of lettuce leaves and Patch-rationed bread.

In the evening there is a thunderstorm with heavy rain. I am caught in the rain on the way back from the little shop where I have tried to buy some fruit. The woman there asks me if I am from the school and if I am, she says, she is unable to give me credit. In the shop there is the warm sweet smell of newspapers, firelighters and cheap sweets, aniseed, a smell of ordinary life which is missing in the life of the school. Shocked I tell her I can pay and I buy some poor quality carrots, as the apples, beneath their rosy skins, might be rotten. I will wash the carrots and give them to Helena when I have to leave her alone in our room in the mornings.

The storm is directly overhead, the thunder so loud I am afraid Helena will wake and be frightened so I do not shelter in the shop but hurry back along the main road, through the corn and up the steep path. I am wet through and the mud path is a stream. The trees sway and groan. I slip and catch hold of the undergrowth to stop myself from falling. When I look up I see that there is someone standing, half hidden, quite near, in the same place where a man was standing on that first afternoon. This man, I think it is the same man, is standing quite still letting the rain wash over him as it pours through the leaves and branches. His hair is plastered wet-sleeked on his round head and water runs in rivulets down his dark suit. He, like me, has no coat. He does not move and he does not speak. He seems to be looking at me as I try to climb the steep path as quickly as I can. I feel afraid. I have never felt or experienced fear like this before. Real terror, because of his stillness, makes my legs weak. I hurry splashing across the courtyard and make my way, trembling, round to the kitchen door. Wet and shivering I meet Olive Morris in the passage outside my room. She is carrying a basin of washing. Rags trail over her shoulder and her worn-out blouse, as usual, has come out of her skirt.

I tell her about the man in the woods. 'Ought I to tell Patch?' I try to breathe calmly. 'It's getting dark out there. He's soaked to the skin. I ought to tell Patch.'

Olive Morris's shapeless soft face is paler than ever and her lips twitch. She looks behind her nervously.

'No,' she says in a low voice. 'No, never tell anyone here anything. Never!' She hurries off along to the other stairs which lead directly up to her room in the top gable of the house.

While I am drying my hair Olive Morris, in a torn rain coat, comes to my door.

'I'm going down to post a letter,' she says putting a scarf over her head. 'So if I see your stranger in the trees I'll send him on his way – there's no need at all to have Myles go out with the dogs. No need at all.'

My surprise at the suggestion that Myles and the dogs might hunt the intruder is less than the feeling of relief that I need not go to Patch's room where Myles, renowned for her sensitive nudes, will be sketching Patch in charcoal and reading poetry aloud. They would smile at each other, exchanging intimate glances while only half-listening to what I had to say. Earlier, while Patch pretended to search her handbag for a ten-shilling note as part of the payment owing to me, Myles had looked up, gazing as if thoughtfully at me for a few minutes and then had resumed her reading of the leather-bound poems.

Josepha is on bedroom duty and the whole school is quiet. Grateful that Helena has not been disturbed by the storm, I lie down in my narrow bed.

Instead of falling asleep I think of the school and how it is not at all as I thought it would be. Helena stands alone all day peering through the partly closed doors watching the dancing classes. She looks on at the painting and at the clay modelling and is only on the edge of the music.

There must be people who feel and think as I do but they are not here as I thought they would be. I want to lean out of a window in a city full of such people and call to some passer-by. I am by my own mistakes buried in this green-leafed corruption and I am alone.

My day off, which Josepha did not tell me about till all the children were washed and dressed, was a mixture of relief and sadness. A bus ride to town. Sitting with Helena in a small café eating doughnuts. Choosing a sun hat for Helena. Buying some little wooden spades and some coloured chalks. Trying to eat a picnic lunch of fruit and biscuits on a road mender's heap of gravel chips. I can hardly bear to think about it. As I handed Helena her share and saw her crouched on the stones with her small hands trying to hold her food without a plate, I knew how wrong it was that she was like this with no place to go home to.

I think now over and over again that it is my fault that we are alone, more so than ever, at the side of the main road with cars and lorries streaming in both directions.

There is a sudden sound, a sound of shooting. Gun shots. I go into the dark passage. From Josepha's room comes the usual running up and down of their voices, first hers and then his. I am afraid to disturb them. A door further down clicks open and I see, with relief, it is Tanya.

'Oh, it's you, Tanya! Did you hear anything just now?'

'Lord no. I never hear a thing m'dear and I never ask questions either so if you've been letting anyone in or out I just wouldn't know darling.'

I tell her about the shot.

'Lord!' Tanya says, 'that's Frederick. Back from his leave. Frederick the Great, literature and drama. Room's over the stables. Never unpacks. Got a Mother. North London. Cap gun. Shoots off gun for sex. The only trouble is darling,' Tanya drawls, 'the orgasm isn't shared.' She disappears into the bathroom saying that she's taken an overdose and so must have her bath quickly.

I go on up the next lot of stairs to Olive's room. I have never been there. I must talk to someone. Softly I knock on the door. At once Olive opens it as if she is waiting on the other side of it.

'Oh, it's you!' her frightened face peers at me.

'Can I come in?' I step past her hesitation into her room. It is not my intention to be rude, I tell her, it is my loneliness. Olive catches me by the arm. Her eyes implore. I am suddenly ashamed for, sitting up in bed wearing a crumpled shirt and a tie, is a man. The man I had seen standing with sinister patience in the rain.

'Oh, Olive, I am so sorry. I do beg –'

'This is Mr Morris, my husband. This is Vera Wright, dear,' Olive whispers a plain introduction.

'Pleased to meet you I'm sure,' Mr Morris says. I continue to mumble words of apology and try to move backwards to the door.

The three Morris children are all in a heap, asleep in a second sagging double bed up against the gable window. Washing is hanging on little lines across the crowded room and Mr Morris's suit is spread over the bed ends to dry.

'Mr Morris is on his way to a business conference,' Olive begins to explain. I squeeze her arm. 'I'll see you tomorrow,' I say. We are wordless at the top of the steep stairs. She is tucking her blouse into her too loose skirt. It seems that she will go on performing this little action for ever. Repeating it for ever even when she has no clothes on.

'No one at all knows that Mr Morris is here,' she says in a breaking whisper.

At breakfast I wish I had someone to whom I could carry, with devotion, bread and butter and coffee. I could not envy Myles because of Patch or Josepha because of Rudi. Tanya must be feeling as I feel, for she prepares a little tray for Frederick and is back almost at once with a swollen bruised bleeding nose and quite quickly develops two black eyes which, it is clear, will take days to fade.

It would be nice for Olive to sail into breakfast and remove a quantity of food bearing it away with dignity to the room in the top gable.

'I suppose you know,' I say to Patch when we meet by chance in the hall, 'that Olive Morris's husband arrived unexpectedly last night and will be with us for a few days.'

Patch says, 'Is he dear?' that is all.

Mr Morris, who is a big man, wears his good suit every day, thus setting himself somewhat apart from the rest of us. He comes to supper and tells us stories about dog racing. His dogs win. He tells us about boxing and wrestling. He has knocked out all the champs. He knows all their names and the dates of the matches. He knows confidence men who treble their millions in five minutes. His brothers and sisters teach in all the best universities and his dear old mother is the favourite Lady-in-Waiting at Buckingham Palace. Snooker is his forté, a sign, he tells us, of a misspent youth. He sighs.

Patch comes to supper every night. Josepha stops shouting at Olive, Mr Morris calls Olive 'Lovey' and reminds her, for us all to hear, of extravagant incidents in their lives. He boasts about his older children, regaling us with their exam results and sporting successes. Olive withers. She is smaller and paler and trembles visibly when Patch, in a genial mood, with mockery and amusement in her voice, leads Mr Morris into greater heights of story-telling. While he talks his eyes slide sideways as he tries to observe us all and see the effects of his fast moving mouth.

Mr Morris, we have to see, is the perfect husband and father. During the day he encourages his children and the other children to climb all over him. He organizes games and races, promising prizes.

He gives all sorts of presents, the table in the kitchen is heaped with chickens and ducks, ready for the oven, jars of honey and expensive jams and baskets of apples and fresh vegetables. Patch prepares the meals herself. Our vegetarian diet was only because the local butchers, unpaid, no longer supply the school.

Frederick, refusing to come to meals, refusing to leave the loft, has a bucket on a string into which Josepha, he will not take from anyone else, puts chicken breasts and bread and butter and a white jug of milk. Tanya says if there is any wormy fruit or fly-blown meat Frederick the Great will get it.

He, she explains, because of always searching for them, attracts the disasters in food.

'Where is Mr Philbrick?' Patch asks, correcting quickly what she calls a fox's paw, a slip of the tongue. 'Mr Morris? Why isn't he here?' She is carving, with skill, the golden chickens and Myles is serving the beans and baby carrots which shine in butter. Olive can hardly swallow a mouthful.

'What's keeping Mr Morris?' I ask her loud enough for Patch's ears. 'Anything wrong?' devouring my plateful, 'is someone ill?'

'No. No – it's nothing at all,' she whispers.

Towards the end of the meal Mr Morris comes in quietly and sits down next to the shrinking Olive. Patch, with grease on her large chin, hands a plate of chicken to him. Thickset, stockily at the head of the table, she sings contralto as if guarding a secret with undisturbed complacency.

There is a commotion in the hall and the sound of boots approaching.

'It's the Politz!' Josepha, on bedroom duty, calls from the stairs. Mr Morris leaps up.

'Leave this to me, dear Lady,' he says to Patch. And, with a snake-like movement, he is on his way to the door.

We follow just in time to see Mr Morris suddenly small and white-faced being led in handcuffs to the front door and out to a car which, with the engine running, is waiting.

I want to say something to Olive to comfort her.

'It's better this way,' she says, 'better for him this way, better than them getting him with dogs. And the children,' she says, 'they didn't see anything.' I don't ask her what Mr Morris has done. She does not tell me anything except that Mr Morris finds prison life unbearable and that he has a long stretch of it ahead.

Patch walks about the school singing and eating the ends off a crusty loaf. When the bills come addressed to her for all the presents from Mr Morris she laughs and tosses them into the kitchen fire.

One of the little boys rushing through the hall stops to glance at Tanya's latest painting.

'How often do you have sexual intercourse?' he pauses long enough in his flight to ask.

'Three times a week,' Tanya steps back to squint at her work, 'never more, never less,' she says.

Tanya says that Frederick the Great is coming down from the loft and will be at supper. I wash my hair and put on my good dress and go down to the meal early, rejoicing that it is Olive's night to settle the children. I am looking forward to meeting Frederick. Perhaps, at last, there will be someone for me. Olive scuttles by with her tray which she must eat upstairs. I hear the uproar from the bedrooms and smile to myself.

Frederick is bent in a strange contortion over the sink in the pantry. He is trying to see into his throat with a torch and a small piece of broken mirror stuck into the loose window frame. I am glad to be able to meet him without Josepha and Tanya.

'Would you mind looking at my throat,' he says straightening up. He is very tall and his eyes enclosed in gold-rimmed spectacles do not look at me. 'I've been trying a new gargle.' He hands me the torch and I peer into his throat.

'Is it painful?' I feel I should ask him.

'Not at all,' he says taking back the torch.

In the dining room Frederick has a little table to himself in the corner. He eats alone quickly and leaves at once. I sit in my usual place. One of the children is practising on the pantry piano. I listen to the conscientious stumblings. Ramsden played Bach seriously, repeating and repeating until she was satisfied and then moving on to the next phrases.

In my head I compose a letter to Ramsden . . . *this neck of the woods*, this is not my way but it persists, *this neck of the woods is not far from London. Any chance of your coming down one afternoon? Staff tea is at four. I'd love to see you and show you round . . .*

There is so much I would tell Ramsden.

For as the rain cometh down, and the snow from heaven, and returneth not thither, but watereth the earth, and make it bring forth and bud, that it may give seed to the sower, and bread to the eater: so shall my word be that goeth forth out of my mouth:

I want to write to Ramsden. After that night and after almost five years how do I address her. Dear Ramsden? Dear Staff Nurse Ramsden. She might be Sister Ramsden. She might not be nursing now, though she did go on after the end of the war. She might be married though I think that is unlikely, perhaps she is on concert platforms . . .

Dear Ramsden I have no way at all of getting away from this place. Please Ramsden can you come? Please?

Patch and Myles come in to supper. Ignoring me they devotedly help each other to mountains of grated raw carrots and cabbage.

ELIZABETH HARROWER

The Cost of Things

Dan Freeman shut the white-painted garage doors and went across the paved courtyard to the house which was painted a glossy white, too. *A lovely home.* Visitors always used these words to describe it and Dan always looked intent and curious when they did, as if he suspected them of irony. But the house did impress him for all that he wasn't fond of it.

When the Freemans bought the place they said apologetically to their friends that they couldn't afford it *but* . . . People just looked unfriendly and didn't smile back. Then came the grind, the worry, fear, boredom, paring down, the sacrifices large and small of material and, it really did seem, spiritual comforts, the eternal use of the negative, habitual meanness, harassment. And it wasn't paid for yet, not *yet*. They had been careful, he and Mary, though, to see that the children hadn't – to use Mary's phrase – gone without.

Lately Dan had begun to think it mightn't have done any harm if Bill and Laura *had* been a bit deprived. They might now be applying themselves to their books occasionally, and thinking about scholarships. But, oh no! They had no doubt their requirements would all be supplied just for the wanting. Marvellous! The amount of work they did, it would be a miracle if either of them matriculated.

'Hullo. You're late. Dinner's ready,' Mary called as the back door closed.

Leaning round into the kitchen, he looked at her seriously and sniffed the air. 'What is it?'

'Iced soup. Your special steak. Salad with –'

He rolled his eyes. 'There's the paper. Five minutes to get cleaned up and I'm with you.'

Mary was an excellent cook. The Freemans had always eaten well, but since Dan had come home from his six months' interstate transfer, she had outdone herself. 'I experimented while you were away,' she explained, producing dinners nightly that would have earned their house several stars in the *Guide Michelin* had it ever been examined in this light.

'Experimented!' Dan laughed in an unreal, very nearly guilty way the first time she said this, because he was listening to another voice in his head reply smartly, 'So did I! So did I!'

Feeling the way he felt or, rather, remembering the name Clea, he was shocked at the gleeful fellow in him who could treat that name simply as something secret from Mary. And he thought *I am ashamed* although he did not *feel* ashamed to find himself taking pride in the sombre and splendid addition to his past that the name represented. Clea, he thought, as if it were some expensive collectors' item he had picked up, not without personal risk, for which it was not unnatural to accept credit. At the sound of that guilty laugh or the puffing of vanity, Dan mentally groaned and muttered, 'I'm sorry. I'm sorry.'

For the first weeks after his return to Melbourne, he had blocked all memories of those Sydney months since he could not guarantee the behaviour of his mind, and if to remember in such ways was to dishonour, he had emerged out of a state of careful non-consideration with the impression that to remember truly might not be wise. But lately, lately . . . He realized that lately when he was alone he sat for hours visualizing his own hand reaching to grasp hers. And each time he produced this scene its significance had to be considered afresh, without words, through timeless periods of silence. Or he pictured her walking away from him as he had once seen her do. An occasion of no significance at all. She had merely been a few steps in front of him. And he pictured her arms rising. For hours, weeks, he had watched her walk away. Then for nights, days and weeks he had looked at the movement of her arms.

He could not see her face.

Wrenching his mind back with all his energy and concentration, he set about tracking down her face, methodically collecting her features and firmly assembling them. The results were static portraits of no one in particular, faded and distant as cathedral paintings of angels and martyrs. These faces were curiously, painfully undisturbing, as meaningless as the dots on a radar screen to an untrained observer.

In their elaborate dining-room, he and Mary sat at the long table dipping spoons into chilled soup.

'Where are the kids?'

'Bill's playing squash with Philip, and Laura's over at Rachel's. They're all going on to a birthday party together.'

'At this time of night?'

'They have to go through some records.'

'What about their work? I thought they agreed to put in three hours a night till the end of term?'

'You can't keep them home from a party, Dan. All the others are going.'

'All the others don't want to be physicists! Or they've got wealthy fathers and don't have to win scholarships. These two'll end up in a factory if they're not careful.'

Mary looked at him. 'You *are* in a bad mood. Did something go wrong at the office?'

'They're irresponsible. If they knew what a depression was like, or a war –'

'Now don't spoil your dinner. How do you like the soup? At the last minute I discovered I didn't have any parsley and I had to use mint. What do you think? Is it awful?'

She hadn't altered her hair-style since they were married. She still chose dresses that would have suited her when she was twenty and wore size ten. Her face was bare of make-up except for a rim of lipstick round the edge of her mouth. And there was something in the total of all this indifference that amounted to a crime.

How easily she had divested herself of the girl with the interests and pleasant ways. And what contempt she had felt for him and shown him, for having been so easily deceived, when she was sure of her home, her children. She had transformed herself before his eyes, laughing.

Anyway, he gave in when she wanted this house, which was pretentious and impossible for them, really. But he even thought he might find it a sort of hobby, a bulwark, himself. You have to have something.

'What are you looking at? Dan? Is it the mint? Is it awful?'

She was really anxious. He lifted another spoonful from his plate and tasted it. Mary waited. He felt he ought to say something. 'Mary . . .' What had they been discussing? 'It's – extra good,' he said very suddenly.

'*Extra* good.' She gave a little scoffing laugh. 'You sound like Bill.'

Not raising his eyes, he asked, 'What sort of a day have you had?' and Mary began to tell him while the creamy soup slid weirdly down his throat, seeming to freeze him to the marrow. He shivered. It was a warm summer night. Crickets were creaking in the garden outside.

'– and Bill wants to start golf soon. He asked me to sound you out about a set of clubs. And while I'm at it, Laura's hinting she'd like that French course on records. She says it'd be a help with the accent.'

'*Mary*,' he protested bitterly and paused, forgetting. 'For God's sake!' he added on the strength of his remembered feeling, gaining time. Then again, as before, the weight descended – the facts he knew, the emotions. 'What are you trying to do? You encourage them to want – impossible things. Why? To turn me into a villain when I refuse? You know how we stand. Your attitude baffles me.' Mary's expression was rather blank but also rather triumphant. He went on, and stammered slightly, 'I want them to have – everything. I grudge them nothing. But these grown-up toys – it can't be done. If Laura would stay home and work at her French – and Bill already has so many strings to his bow he can't hold a sensible conversation about anything. They'll end up bus conductors if they're not careful.'

Mary looked at him sharply. 'Have you been drinking, Dan?'

'Two beers.'

'I thought so! . . . Really, if I have to hear you complain about the cost of their education for the next six years, I don't think it would be worth it. Not to them either, I'm sure.'

He said nothing.

'*We* aren't going without anything. We've got the house and car. And the garden at week-ends. It isn't as if we were young.' Mary waved an arm. 'But if you feel like this, ask them to re-pay you when they've qualified. They won't want to be indebted to you.'

He stared at her heavily, lifted his formal-looking squarish face with its blue eyes and stared at her, saying nothing. Mary breathed through her nose at him, then collected his plate and hers and went away to the kitchen.

'Clea . . .' It was a groan. Tears came to his eyes. It was the night he had thought to go away with her. They could *not* be parted. How could he explain? It was against nature, could not *be*. He would sell everything and leave all but a small essential amount with Mary and the children. Then he and Clea would go – far away. And great liners trailing music and streamers sailed from Sydney daily for all the world's ports. Now that he'd found Clea, he would find the circumstances he had always expected, with their tests that would ask more of him than perseverance, resignation. They would live – somewhere, and be – very happy.

Commonsense had cabled him at this point: this would all be quite charming except for one minor problem that springs to mind.

What would they live on? A glorified clerk, his sole value as a worker lay in his memory of a thousand details relating to television films bought by the corporation. Away from the department he had no special knowledge, no money-raising skills. Could he begin to acquire a profession at forty-five? Living on what, in the meantime?

'There. At least there's nothing wrong with the steak.' Mary looked at him expectantly, and he looked at the platter of food for some seconds. 'It's – done to a turn.'

'*Over*done?'

'No.' He thought of saying to her pleased face, 'I thought of deserting you, Mary.' And he had, oh, he had. 'What? . . . Yes, everything's fine.' The only trouble was that unfortunately, unfortunately, he was beginning to feel sick.

'Dan, I forgot to mention this since you got back. You're never here with all this extra work –'

'Yes?' Here it came: the proof that he had been right to return, that he and Mary *did* have a life in common. How often had he pleaded with Clea in those last days, 'You can't walk out on twenty years of memories.' (Not that she had ever asked or expected him to.)

'It's the roof. The tiles. There was a landslide into the

azaleas while you were away. I thought you'd notice the broken bushes.'

'Oh.'

'So do you think I should get someone to look over the whole roof?'

'Yes, I suppose so.'

'Well, it's important to get it fixed before we start springing leaks.'

'Yes. All right. Ring Harvey. Get him to give us an estimate.'

'Dan? Where are you going? You haven't touched your dinner!'

'I'm sorry. I've got to get some air. No, stay here. Eat your dinner.'

'Aren't you well?' She half-rose from her chair, but he warded her off and compelled her to sink back to the table with a large forbidding movement of his arm. Mary shrugged, gave a tiny snort of boredom and disdain, and resumed eating.

Sydney . . . At the end of a week he had begun to look forward to getting back to Mary's cooking. The department wasn't lavish with away-from-home expenses for officers on his grade, and he had the usual accounts flying in from Melbourne by every post, in addition to an exorbitant hotel bill for the very ordinary room he occupied near the office. The hotel served a 'continental' breakfast and no other meals. At lunchtime he and Alan Parker leapt out for beer and a sandwich which cost next to nothing, then by six o'clock he was famished. Somehow surreptitiously, he started to treat himself to substantial and well-cooked dinners in restaurants all over the city. In Melbourne he only patronized places like these once a year for a birthday or anniversary. He felt rather ill-at-ease eating, so to speak, Mary's new dress or the children's holidays, and he was putting on flesh. But – everything was hopeless. You had to have something. But money harassed him. He felt a kind of anguished dullness at the thought of it. It made him dwell on the place where it was cheaper and less worrying to be: home.

As the representative of his department, he was invited one Friday evening to an official cocktail party. A woman entered the building as he did, and together they ran for the row of automatic lifts, entered one, were shot up to some height between the fourth and fifth floors and imprisoned there for over half an hour. Clea.

Dan's first thought was that she looked a bit flashy. Everything about her looked a fraction more colourful than was quite seemly: the peacock-blue dress, and blonde hair – not natural, the make-up and, in another sense, the drawling low-pitched voice. (This would certainly have been Mary's view.)

Then while the alarm bell rang and caretakers and electricians shouted instructions at one another, they stood exchanging words and Dan looked into her eyes with the usual polite, rather stuffy, slightly patronizing expression.

He was surprised. Under gold-painted lids, her blue eyes glanced up and actually saw him, with a look that twenty years, fifteen years, ago he had met daily in his mirror. It was as familiar as that. She wasn't *young*. It wasn't a young look. It was alarmingly straight. It was the look by which he had once identified his friends.

At the party when they were finally released, however, Clea treated him with wonderful reserve, recognizing nothing about him. She remained steadfastly with the group least likely to succeed in charming the person Dan imagined her to be, smiling a lazy gallant smile, bestowing gestures and phrases on their sturdy senses. Showing pretty teeth, laughing huskily, she stood near them and *was*. When Dan approached, though, that all appeared to have been illusory. She was merely quiet, watchful, sceptical, an onlooker.

Ah, well! He put her from him. He expected nothing. It had been a momentary interest, and this wasn't the first time, after all, that circumstances had separated him from someone whom he would in some way always know.

But he met her one day in the street accidently. (Though Sydney is two million strong, people who live there can never lose touch, eager though they might be to do so.) He remembered they said something about the party, and something else about the lift, and then they said goodbye and parted. It wasn't till he had gone some eight or nine steps that Dan realized he had walked backwards away from her.

The following Saturday night they met at another inter-departmental party and after that there were no backward steps till this inevitable, irrevocable return to hearth and home.

Clea had a flat – kitchen, bathroom, bed-sitting room – in a converted habourside mansion, and a minor executive job with a film unit that paid rent and food and clothing bills. Once she had been an art student but at the end of four years she stopped attending classes and took a job.

'You were too critical of yourself,' Dan said. 'Your standards were too high.'

She smiled.

In her spare time she had continued to paint, she told Dan, and he had an impression of fierceness and energy and he felt he knew how she must have looked. So she had painted. And it was why she was sane. And why people who knew nothing whatever about her liked to be near her. But ages ago, and permanently, she had laid it aside. That is, laid aside the doing, but not the looking, not the thinking, not finally herself.

Dan insisted on being shown the few pieces of work that she hadn't destroyed, and he examined them solemnly, and felt this discarded talent of Clea's was a thing to respect. In addition (and less respectably, he knew) he saw it as a decoration to her personality not unflattering to himself. From talk of art, which he invariably started, he would find he had led the way back to that perennially sustaining subject – their first meeting.

'At the party that night, why were you so – cold?'

'For good reasons. Which you know. How many times do you think I can survive this sort of thing?'

They were in Clea's room on an old blue sofa by the fire. Dan turned his head away, saying nothing. She said. 'It's no fun. You get tired. Like a bird on the wing, and no land. It's – no fun. You feel trapped and hunted at the same time. And the weather seems menacing. (No, I don't mean now. But there have been times.) And in the long run, it's so much less effort to stay where your belongings are ... Wives shouldn't worry too much. And even other women shouldn't. By the time they find themselves listening to remorseful remembrances of things past they're too – killed to care. And they find they can prompt their loved one with considerable detachment when he reels off the well-known items – old clothes and family illnesses, holidays and food and friends . . . Make me stop talking.'

It mattered very little to them where they went, but they walked a lot and saw a few plays. They went to some art galleries. And once they had a picnic.

'It's winter, but the sun never goes in,' he said.

'Except now and then at night. Sydney's like that.'

In the evenings Clea sometimes read aloud to Dan at his suggestion. And he would think: *The fire is burning. I am watching her face and listening to her voice.* And he felt he knew something eternal that he had always wanted to know. One night Clea read the passage in which Yury Zhivago, receiving a letter from his wife after their long and tragic separation, falls unconscious.

Because Clea existed and he was in her presence, Dan felt himself resurrected and so, though what she read was beautiful and he thought so, he laughed with a kind of senseless joy as at something irrelevant when she stopped.

'All right, darling, I suppose it is wonderful. That Russian intensity. If *I* could ever totter to a sofa and collapse with sheer strength of feeling, I'd think: "Congratulations, Freeman! You're really living." '

Clea laughed, too, but said, 'Ah, don't laugh. Because if you can laugh, you make it impossible . . .'

One thing Clea could not do was cook. It took Dan some weeks to accept this, because she wasn't indifferent to food. If they ate in a restaurant, she enjoyed a well-chosen meal as much as he did. But when he discovered that she could tackle any sort of diet with much the same enthusiasm, he was depressed.

'What do you live on when I'm not around?' he demanded, a little disgruntled.

She thought. 'Coffee.'

He was proud of her. He even liked her a lot. But he couldn't help saying, 'I get hungry.'

She looked abstracted. 'Dan, I – You're *hungry*. Oh . . . We had steak?'

'Yes, but no – no *trimmings*,' he tried to joke. 'No art.'

'Dan –'

'I take it back about no art.'

'I'll – tomorrow –'

'I take it back about no art.'

'I will do better.' And after this she tried to cook what she thought were complicated meals for him, and he didn't discourage her.

It was the night they came back from their picnic in the mountains that he had the brilliant idea of asking her why she had never married.

She laughed.

'You wouldn't have had any trouble,' he insisted, trying to see her face.

Still smiling, she said, 'The candidates came at the wrong time or they were too young for me when I was young.' She looked at him, raising her brows. 'How old were you? When you married.'

'Twenty-one.'

'I wouldn't have liked you then.'

'You'd have been right. But *you* – tell me.'

She moved restlessly on the sofa, and spread her arms along the back. He felt it was cruel to question her, but knew he would never stop. She said, 'Oh . . . I met someone, and bang went five years. Then some time rolled by while I picked myself up. Then I met – someone else who was married. Names don't matter.'

He looked at her.

'All right, they do. But not now . . . So, by the time you look round after that, you're well into your thirties. And a few of the boys have turned into men, but they're married to girls who preferred them – quite young.'

'Are you saying this to blame me? You are, aren't you?' He heard the rhetorical note in his voice. He knew he had asked her.

Clea seemed to examine the stitches of the black hand-knitted sweater he was wearing. She jumped up quickly and out in the kitchen poured whisky into two glasses, carrying one back to him.

'I can only say, Clea – if things were different – things

would be different . . . All right, it sounds lame. But I *mean* it. What do you *want* me to do?'

'And what would you *like* me to say? You'll go back to Mary. Do you want me to plead with you?'

He could see that it was neither reasonable nor honourable in him to want that, but in her it would have been more *natural*, he felt. He said so.

Clea was biting the fingernails of her left hand, cagily. He saw again that it was cruel to talk to her like this, but he knew he would never stop.

She glanced at him over her hand. 'You're beginning to think about your old clothes and family holidays just as I said. And why shouldn't you? These intimate little things are what count in the end, aren't they?'

And she disposed of her hand, wrapping it round her glass as she lifted it from the floor to drink. She rolled a sardonic blue eye at Dan and he gave the impression of having blushed without a change in colour, and frowned and drank, too. Because of course his mind *had* turned lately in that direction. He *had* begun to remember the existence of all that infinitely boring, engulfing domesticity, and his vital but unimportant part in it. It was all *there*, and his. What could he do about it?

Clea knew too much, drank too much, was nervy, pushed herself to excess, bit her fingernails. She was the least conditioned human being he had ever encountered. She was like a mirror held up to his soul. She was intelligent, feeling and witty. He loved her.

'Many thanks.' But she wouldn't meet his eyes.

'Marriage,' he said, harking back suddenly. 'When I think of it! And you're so independent. What could it give you? Really? No, don't smile.'

Still, she did smile faintly, saying nothing, then said irritatingly, 'Someone to – set mouse traps and dispose of the bodies.'

He brushed this away. 'You hate the office. Why?'

'Dan.' She was patient.

'Why do you hate the office?' He did feel vaguely that he was torturing her. 'Why?'

'I don't see the sun. I lose the daylight hours. The routine's exacting, but the work doesn't matter. It takes all my time from me and I see nothing beautiful.'

'And just what would you do with this time?' he asked, somehow scientifically. He would prove to her how much better off . . .

With her left hand, distracted, she seemed to consider the length and texture of the hair that fell over her ear. 'Oh. Look about. Exist.'

Dan thought of Mary. 'Some wives are busy all day long.' He was positive that Mary would be in no way flattered if it were ever suggested that *she* had had time to practise as a student of life. 'In fact,' he went on, 'though cultivation is supposed to be the prerogative of the leisured classes, I think women in your position form a sort of non-wealthy aristocracy all to themselves.'

'Do you?' Clea shifted the dinner plate from her lap and went over to the deal table where she had a lot of para-phernalia brought home from the office spread out. At random she picked up a pencil and tested its point against the cushion of her forefinger saying, 'That's an observation!'

'No, don't be angry.' He turned eagerly to explain to her over the back of the sofa. 'What I mean is that however busy you are from nine till five, you have all the remaining hours of the day and night to concentrate on yourself – your care, cultivation, understanding, amusement . . .'

She smiled at him. 'Don't eat that if you can't bear it. I'll make something else.'

He said, 'Forgive me.'

They quarrelled once, one Thursday evening when he passed on Alan and Joyce Parker's invitation to drive out into the country the following Sunday.

Alan Parker was a tall mild man of fifty, who clerked with dedication among the television films of the library. His wife, whom both Clea and Dan had met at official parties, was friendly and chatty. The Parkers knew Dan was married, and they knew that (as they put it) Dan and Clea had a thing about each other. But they liked Dan because he wasn't disagreeably ambitious though he was younger than and senior to Alan, and they implied a fondness for Clea. Dan guessed that they would be the subject of Joyce's conversation for a week after the trip, but he couldn't find it in his heart to dislike anyone to whom he could mention Clea's name.

But she said swiftly, 'Oh no, I couldn't go with them.'

He paused, amazed, in the act of kicking a piece of wood back into the fire. 'What do you mean? Why not?'

'No, I just couldn't go,' she said definitely, beginning to look for her place in the book she was holding.

'But *why*?' Dan fixed the fire, buffed some ash from his hands and turned to sit beside her on the sofa. He took the book from her, thrust it behind his back, and forced her to lift her head.

Her look daunted him. He said in parenthesis, 'I'm addicted to that eye-shadow.' He said reasonably, 'Only last week you talked about getting out of town.'

'I'd be bored, Dan.'

'Bored? I'd be there!' he rallied her, smiling in a teasing way. 'And Joyce's going to produce a real French picnic lunch.'

There was a smile in her that he sensed and resented.

She said, 'I'm sorry.'

'And *I'm* sorry if the fact that I like to eat one meal a day is offensive to you.'

'Darling. Please go, if you'd like to. No recriminations. Truly.'

Mondays to Fridays he didn't see her all day. He couldn't have borne to lose hours of her company. Six months, he'd had, just days ago. Now there were ten weeks.

He said unpleasantly, 'You do set yourself up with your nerves and your fine sensibility, Clea. When you begin to feel that a day in the company of nice easy-going people like the Parkers would be unbearably boring, *I* begin to feel you're carrying affectation too far. If you pander to yourself much more you'll find you're unfit to live in the world at all!'

She didn't answer that, or appear to react. Instead she caught his wrist in her right hand and smoothed her thumb against the suede of his watchstrap. 'In their car, Dan, I'd feel imprisoned. I have to be able to get away. I'd be bored, Dan.' She said, 'I don't love them.'

He stared, jerked his arm away, gave a short incredulous laugh and stood up. 'Don't *love* them!'

She added, 'As things are.'

Throwing on his coat he went to the door still uttering sarcastic laughs. 'Don't *love* them! Well – *good – night – Clea!*'

In ten minutes he returned. And the ten weeks passed.

'Dan? How are you now?' Mary peered down at him, then glanced abruptly right and left, bringing her chin parallel with each of her shoulders in turn. It was dark on the balcony. 'Do you still want your dinner? It'll be ruined, but it's there if you want it . . . Dan!' She leant over him.

'What?'

'Well, for heaven's sake, you can still answer when I speak to you! I thought you'd had a stroke or something, sitting there like an image.' She bridled with relief and exasperation.

'No.'

In a brisk admonitory voice she said, 'Well, I think you'd better get yourself along to Dr Barnes in the morning. It's all this extra work. And you're not eating. Sometimes I think you don't even know you're home again.'

He said something she couldn't catch.

'What? Where's *what*? . . . Your dinner's in the oven.' Mary waited for him to speak again. 'Smell the garden, Dan . . . We'd better get ready, then. Jack and Freda'll be over soon.'

'What?' He stirred cautiously in the padded bamboo chair. He felt like someone who has had the top of his head blown off, but is still, astonishingly, alive, and must learn to cope with the light, the light, and all it illuminated.

'I told you this morning,' Mary accused him. 'You hadn't forgotten?'

Carefully he hauled himself up by the balcony railing. 'I'll be bored,' he said.

In the soft black night, Mary went to stand in front of him, tilting her face to look at him. 'Bored, Dan?' She sounded nervous. 'You know Jack and Freda,' she appealed to him, touching his shirt sleeve.

'I don't care for them,' he complained gently, not to her. And added, 'As things are.'

'Oh, Dan!' Mary swallowed. Tears sprang to her eyes. She

caught his arm and walked him through the front door, and down the carpeted hall to their bedroom. 'Lie down, Dan. Just lie there.'

He heard her going to the telephone. She rang the doctor. Then she rang Freda and Jack to apologize and ask them not to come. He heard her crying a little with fright as she repeated his uncanny remark in explanation.

And Dan took a deep breath, and looked at the ceiling, and smiled.

The Meeting

Just before the meeting, which was fixed for three thirty, Flinders took a walk in the Organization's rose garden. This garden was set in a protected angle of the buildings and looked towards the river. Seagulls – for the river was in reality part of an estuary – swooped over Flinders' head as he crunched up and down the pebbled paths between beds of wintry spikes tagged 'Queen Frederika' or 'Perfect Peace' or 'British Grenadier'. About him, plane trees scored the sky and frozen lawns rolled down to the cold river. With the exception of two uniformed guards and a statue ferociously engaged in beating swords into ploughshares, Flinders was the only human figure in sight. The grounds were closed to the public at this season, and the staff were sealed in their narrow cells, intent on the Organization's business.

Enclosed on three sides by the congested streets of a great city, the Organization was nevertheless well laid out in the ample grounds of its foundation-granted land, and stood along the banks of the river with something of the authority that characterizes Wren's buildings on the Thames at Greenwich. Here as at Greenwich the river's edge was faced with a high embankment and bordered, where the lawn ended, by a narrow walk. From this walk one looked across the river to the low-lying labyrinth of docks and factories, surmounted by an immense Frosti-Cola sign. Behind the Organization's back, the skyscrapers of the city rose as abruptly as the Alps, an ascending graph of successful commerce. The setting impressed all newcomers, and still had an effect on even those members of the staff who had been with the Organization since the signing of its Founding Constitution. Flinders, who had spent the past two years in a North African town, was all but overwhelmed by it.

A forester and agricultural conservationist, Flinders had

been recruited by the Organization two years before to serve as an expert in its Project for the Reforestation of the Temperate Zone. With a single stop here at Headquarters for briefing, he had flown from his home town in Oregon to a still smaller town some hundred miles to the south of the Mediterranean. Now, on his way home with his mission at an end, he was at Headquarters once more in order to report on his work and to be – although the word was yet unknown to him – debriefed.

He had no idea of what he should say at the meeting. He had never attended meetings at all until he got involved with the Organization. His profession had kept him out of offices. His two years in North Africa could not be contained within reportable dimensions in his mind. Throughout his assignment he had, as instructed, sent in quarterly technical reports to his opposite number at Headquarters, a certain Mr Addison. These Reports on Performance in the Field (an expression which allowed Flinders to fancy himself capering in a meadow) had given a faithful account of his initial surveys, the extent and causes of erosion in the area, the sampling of soils, availability of water, and ultimately the selection and procurement of young trees and the process of their planting.

In addition, he had reported in person, as he was required to do every few weeks, to the Organization's regional office at Tangier. Apart from these trips to the coast, he had lived a solitary life. At El Attara, where the Organization had provided him with a comfortable house, he dealt with the local farmers and landowners, who were cheerful and polite, and with the local officials – who, though less cheerful, treated him well. He kept two servants and a gardener for the overgrown terraces that surrounded his little house. In the evenings he strolled in the medina and drank mint tea in the café, or he stayed at home studying Arabic by an oil lamp. He wore the djellaba – in summer a white one, in winter one of rough brown wool. He learned to walk as the Arabs do, with a long stride designed to cover many miles, and to ride sideways on a donkey when necessary. He drove his jeep to his work in the hills, and sometimes camped at the planting sites for days at a time. At the beginning he was appallingly lonely, and for the first two months crossed off the single days on a Pan American calendar he had tacked up on his bedroom wall. But he was accustomed to an independent, outdoor existence and gradually became absorbed in his work and in the simple life of the town. The silence in the hills, the peace and variety of the countryside pleased him immensely. During his obligatory trips to Tangier, he swam in the ocean, ate French food, bought books and toothpaste, and took out an enigmatic girl named Ivy Vance who worked at the Australian Consulate. When Ivy Vance's tour of duty presently came to an end and she was posted to Manila, Flinders began to postpone even these short trips away from his work.

By the time his mission was over, he had completed not only his own assignment but also that of two other experts, once promised him as assistants, who had never materialized. No mention of this appeared in the communications he received from Mr Addison; nor did Flinders expect or wish for any. Flinders had no complaint. His salary cheques, having been afflicted by some early confusion, were arriving regularly by the second year of his stay: there was nothing to spend money on at El Attara and he saved a useful sum. Also towards the end of his mission he received full instructions for his return journey, and a large envelope containing a Briefing Kit that outlined the work for which he had been engaged and that had been omitted at the outset. Otherwise, all had gone smoothly. Mr Addison had replied to his letters with reasonable punctuality – five weeks having been the maximum delay – and had run up a creditable score of answers to questions asked. Flinders had no complaint.

Flinders had no complaint. This fact alone, had it been known, would have made him an object of curiosity in the Organization.

Two days before, on his return to Headquarters, he had met Mr Addison – a singularly small person to have been selected as opposite number to a man as tall as Flinders. Mr Addison greeted him pleasantly and introduced him to his secretary, to whom Flinders gave, for typing, a sheaf of handwritten pages containing his suggestions for conserving and extending the plantations at El Attara. The tentative enquiries he made of Mr Addison mostly seemed to fall within the competence of some other authority. Mr Addison had replied anxiously, 'Mr Rodriguez-O'Hearn will tell you about that,' or 'That belongs in the province of Mr Fong,' or 'You'd better ask Miss Singh in Official Records.' And, 'Sorry your final cheque isn't ready. Our accountant is on leave without pay.' Otherwise, all had gone smoothly.

Mr Addison explained to Flinders that he was himself under great pressure of work, at the same time producing a ticket for a guided tour of the building. The secretary to whom Flinders had handed his manuscript then showed him where to take the Down elevator and gave him a yellow slip on which was written the time and place of this afternoon's meeting.

Flinders looked at his watch, and turned back towards the main building. The gravel paths were narrow and at each of his impractical long strides his coat was clawed by Gay Flirtation or Pale Memory. His Rush Temporary Pass had not yet been issued and he was obliged to explain his business to the guard at the door, and once again at the cloakroom where he collected his brief-case and papers. It was exactly three-thirty when he took the elevator to the meeting.

Patricio Rodriguez-O'Hearn, short, bald, blue-eyed and in his fifties, came from Chile. His reserve was unusual in a man of Latin and Irish blood, but would not otherwise have been noticeable. He was calm and courteous and, since he made a policy of being accessible to his staff, often looked exhausted in the afternoons. Within DALTO – the Department of Aid to the Less Technically Oriented – he was responsible for the overseas assignments of experts. It was to Mr Rodriguez that Mr Addison and his colleagues in the Opposite Numbers Unit reported, and Mr Rodriguez reported in his turn to the Chief Coordinator of DALTO. Rodriguez had been married twice, had a number of young children, and was known to play the piano rather well. When he sat at his desk or, as at this moment, at the head of a conference table, he would occasionally follow imaginary notes with his fingers while waiting for discussion to begin.

Mr Addison was quite far from Rodriguez, having been placed midway down the table. A large lady sat on Flinders' right, and Addison had naturally been seated opposite. There were some fifteen other members of the meeting, and Flinders found that he was not the only expert reporting that afternoon. On his left, a shock-headed young man named Edrich, back from a three-year assignment as a Civic Coordination expert in the Eastern Mediterranean, was leafing confidently through an envelope of documents. Senior members of DALTO were taking their seats, and there were, in addition, representatives from political departments of the Organization – a thin gentleman with a tremor from the Section on Forceful Implementation of Peace Treaties, and a young woman in a sari from Peaceful Uses of Atomic Weapons. A secretary was distributing pads of white paper and stunted yellow pencils. The room was low-ceilinged, without windows, and carpeted in yellowish-green. At one end of it stood a small movie-screen and at the other a projector. At Flinders' back, a bookcase contained a 1952 *Who's Who*, and a great number of Organization documents.

Flinders, having turned to look at the bookcase, soon turned back to the table. By assuming an alert expression he tried to include himself in various conversations taking place around him, but no one paid him any attention. A young man next to Addison said, 'These problems are substantive, of course, not operational,' and Addison replied, 'Obviously.' 'Essential elements,' declared a Japanese, and 'Local infrastructure,' responded a Yugoslav. The Forceful Implementation man looked very angry, and the girl from Peaceful Uses put her hand on his arm and murmured, 'Under great pressure.' Someone else said soothingly, 'We'll put a Rush on it.'

When all the places were taken, Rodriguez-O'Hearn coughed for silence, welcomed the two experts to Headquarters, and introduced them to the meeting. The large lady leant across Flinders to ask Edrich a question, but Edrich was nodding around the table and did not see her. Edrich, Flinders noted enviously, seemed to know everybody and had greeted several people by first name. Apart from Addison, who had gone into temporary eclipse behind the leaning lady, Flinders knew no one at all.

Mr Rodriguez-O'Hearn called on Edrich to describe his

work to the meeting; he then leant back in his chair and took off his glasses.

Edrich bent forward and put his glasses on. He placed on the table a list of points he had drawn up. 'I have,' he said, 'recently submitted, in six copies, my final report and this will shortly be available' – he turned up another paper – 'under the document symbol E dash DALTO 604' – he glanced again at the paper in his hand – 'slash two.' He therefore proposed, he said, to give only a brief summary of his work to the present meeting, and with this in mind had prepared a list of points on which emphasis might effectively be laid. (Flinders, looking over his shoulder, saw that there were fourteen of these, on which emphasis had already been effectively laid by underlinings.) Moreover, in accordance with instructions, Edrich had brought with him a short film showing various stages of his performance in the field.

Rodriguez-O'Hearn here suggested that the film be shown first, in order to give even greater reality to Edrich's list of points. A young man was sent for who, under Edrich's supervision, set up the reel in the projector. Rodriguez shifted his chair, and Flinders, who had his elbows on the table, was asked to move back so that the lady on his right might see the screen. Edrich borrowed a ruler from the outer office, the lights were put out, and the film was set, hissing and crackling, in motion.

Flinders was immediately struck by the similarity of the opening scene to the countryside he had just left. The eroded hills, though steeper, were garlanded with terraces of vines and fruit trees and glittered white in the meridional sunshine. The village, though even smaller than El Attar, was composed of the same whitewashed houses, the same worn steps and pitted doors. At the well, the women stood talking with their jars at their feet or their children in their arms, and outside the single tavern the old men played cards. The camera wavered over flat roofs and small peeling domes and squinted at stony hills. And upon the whole, as though marking a target, Edrich's ruler now described a great circle.

'This was the deplorable condition of the area when I arrived. Low level of overall production, cottage industries static for centuries, poor communications with neighbouring towns, no telegraph or telephone system, partial electrification, dissemination of information by shepherd's rumour, little or no interest in national or international events. In short, minimal adjustment to contemporary requirements, and incomplete utilization of resources.'

Screaming with laughter, a child raced into the camera's path in pursuit of a crowd of chickens.

'As you know,' Edrich continued, 'the object of the Civic Coordination Programme is to tap the dynamics of social change in terms of local aspirations for progress. These aspirations may be difficult to establish in a society where there has been no evolution of attitudes or change in value orientation for generations and where there are no new mechanisms for action within the community structure. In order to create a dynamic growth situation resulting in effective exploitation of community potential, aspirations must be identified in relation to felt needs. The individual thus feels himself able to function as a person, at the same time participating in implementation of community goals.'

'What are the group relationships?' The lady next to Flinders sat forward tensely for the reply.

'I'm glad you ask that, Miss Bass. Owing to traditional integration of the family as a unit, the individual seems reluctant to function in a group or sub-group situation. These social patterns may take some time to break down. And this is natural.'

'Yes. This is predictable.' Miss Bass relaxed in her chair.

'Immediately after my arrival, meetings were set up with local officials to alert them to Civic Coordination projects in the vicinity and to inform them of the terms of my assignment as agreed between their own government and the Organization.' Edrich returned to the film, where a herd of shaggy goats had appeared in the main street, followed by a donkey. 'A committee was appointed to evaluate needs and resources and to establish work priorities.' The scene changed to a row of sunburnt men in dungarees and open shirts. One was leaning self-consciously on a tall staff; another was waving at the camera. 'After a certain initial language confusion – owing to a particularly corrupt dialect spoken in this region – my project was accepted enthusiastically, although a slower timetable was eventually agreed upon.'

Here the film came to a splicing, and a series of horizontal black lines twitched frantically up the screen.

'I believe the pictures will speak for themselves from here on.'

There followed, when the film resumed, a succession of scenes involving prodigious bodily labour of all kinds. One by one the men and women of the town passed across the screen – carrying great baskets of earth, digging deep and narrow ditches, or with muscles braced and heads bowed, pushing against a boulder. Once Edrich himself was glimpsed sitting on a rock and mopping his brow. And once, to the horror of Flinders, a tree was chopped down. A bridge was built, across a stream whose course was subsequently diverted. A little blockhouse of raw brick was laboriously constructed among the whitewashed domes and in no time at all bore the legend 'Administration Building' in three languages. In the final episode, every able-bodied member of the community was shown on hands and knees, breaking stones for a road that would connect the area to the nearest industrial centre.

The film came to its end in a shower of black and white flecks, and the lights were turned on. Members of the meeting got up to stretch their legs and to question Edrich about his fourteen points. A concealed fan was switched on and vibrated with a slow hum. The technician was running the film back on to its spool. Watching him, Flinders regretted that the course of events could not be similarly rewound. What of the women at the well, he wondered? What of the laughing child that somewhere on the machine spun back to his former deplorable condition – and the flock of chickens now laying their eggs in electrified coops all through the night? What improvements were being inflicted on those static industries that had for centuries repeated themselves in the graceful jars about the well?

'Coordination,' the voices were insisting, and 'basic procedures'. Edrich was pulling out his chair and saying 'issue-oriented'. Flinders resisted claustrophobia: the room was like an upholstered bomb-shelter.

'You have your films with you, Mr Flinders?'

Rodriguez-O'Hearn was looking at him. Flinders brought up his brief-case from beside his chair and produced an envelope of coloured slides. 'Only a few stills, sir.'

The meeting was settling down again. He was being listened to. He knew that he cut a poor figure with his nine or ten slides, after Edrich's film. The Arabs had rather disliked being photographed, and in any case he had often forgotten to take a camera on field trips. He handed the envelope over to the technician with a sinking heart. 'They're not too clear,' he said.

Flinders had never made a speech before. He had been intimidated, too, by the eloquence of Edrich. His hands were shaking, and he placed them flat on the table before him. All the faces were turned, waiting for him to begin.

'In classical times,' he said, 'the lands bordering the Mediterranean were much more thickly vegetated. We know this, for example, from Euripides' description of the area around Thebes, or Homer's account . . .'

Here he paused to draw breath, and the Chief of Official Records asked if he had submitted his final report.

Mr Addison confirmed that a short account of Flinders' performance in the field was at that moment with his own typist.

'But your final report, Mr Flinders,' the Records Chief persisted with thinly veiled patience. 'Your evaluation of the success of your assignment, in six copies, your recommendations for future concrete measures.'

'Given the fluidity of the situation,' Edrich put in, with a sympathetic nod to Flinders.

Flinders said slowly that the success of a mission such as his must depend on the survival of trees which had only just been planted.

The Records Chief declared that such a condition could not be regarded as an obstacle to the submission of a final report.

'One must give them a chance,' Flinders said. 'The growth of a hybrid poplar or even a eucalyptus may be very little in the first season.'

'A long-term project, in other words,' said Edrich.

'In other words,' Flinders agreed.

Rodriguez-O'Hearn addressed him down the table. 'Why, Mr Flinders, have we been subjected to so much erosion since classical times?'

Flinders looked at him. 'In the main, sir, it is due to over-grazing.'

Edrich said, 'Correct.'

How does *he* know it's correct? Flinders wondered irritably. He went on to speak of the movement of soil at certain elevations and in certain winds, the presence of useful or destructive insects, the receptivity of the land – all the circumstances, in fact, which had led to the selection of the trees at El Attara. 'In conditions such as these,' he said, looking along the row of fatigued faces, 'the drought-resistant species has the only hope for survival.'

'And it is this type you are concerned with?' asked Rodriguez-O'Hearn.

Flinders nodded. 'Very often these don't give dramatic results. You see – some of the most valuable types in the world are unspectacular. But they hold their own by . . . per-severance.'

The slides had been set up, and the technician asked for permission to turn out the lights. Flinders got up and stood by the screen. In the dark he could not find Edrich's ruler, and at first, being a rather awkward man, he got in the way of the picture. The slides were in colour and, although Flinders had no skill whatever as a photographer, they did derive a certain clarity from the sharp air and splendid light of the countryside.

The first slide had been taken from a hilltop; it was a panorama of the area to the south of El Attara. The contours of this country were European rather than African, and Flinders had often found it possible there to imagine how France or Italy might have looked before spaciousness was diminished by overpopulation. The hills were sometimes covered by green grasses so short that after heavy rain the soil showed through in violet streaks. This picture, however, had been taken in summer, and the pebbled course of a dry stream wound through a valley of orange groves and cypress trees. The next pictures were of a depleted slope, furrowed by weather, on whose receding earth a number of sheep were pessimistically feeding.

Flinders said, 'This is the site we chose for the first plantation.'

The pictures that followed were so repetitious that he could not help wondering why he had taken them. The same hillside, and a large area nearby, were shown in various stages of preparation – but these preparations were so gradual and so little obvious to the layman that there seemed to have been no purpose in recording them.

'The work near El Attara,' Flinders said, 'serves as an experiment. The country has a conservation programme now, and the local authorities have their own plans for the future.'

Someone said uneasily, 'And this is good.'

Flinders said, 'Naturally.'

Edrich called out, 'Correct.'

Rodriguez-O'Hearn's voice enquired whether Flinders spoke Arabic.

'Not very well, sir, I'm afraid.' Flinders hesitated. 'I've been studying for three years. Semitic languages are difficult for Westerners.'

'You made yourself understood, however?'

Flinders smiled. 'As to that, sir,' he said, 'how does one know?'

The last slide came on to the screen. It was a shot taken by Flinders on the morning of the first planting. Half-way up a slope, a parked truck leant inwards on a narrow, unsurfaced road. The angle of the truck was made more precarious by the ditch into which it was partly sunk and the way in which the photograph had been taken. That the truck had just stopped was evident from the cloud of white dust still rising about its wheels. Nevertheless, the gate of the truck's open back was down, and two young men in djellabas had scrambled aboard. One was already handing down to a forest of up-stretched hands the first of the small trees with which the truck was loaded. The waiting peasants – the men in brown robes, the women mostly unveiled and wrapped in the bright colours of the country folk – reached up excitedly, but the youth on the truck held the plant with extreme care. Behind him in the truck, young trees were stacked up in even rows, their roots wrapped in burlap; on the hillside above the road, dozens of small craters had already been turned in the fresh earth.

Flinders had forgotten taking the picture, although now he remembered it with a pang of nostalgic pleasure – the brilliant January morning, the shouts of delight which greeted the arrival of the loaded truck, the many serious shakings of the hand, the good omens invoked, and the long day's work that followed. He recognized all the faces in the picture – most were from the vicinity of El Attara, and a few from villages close to the planting site. Everyone in the photograph seemed to be smiling, even two children who were rolling up stones for the wheels of the truck.

A voice in the dark said, '*They* look happy, at any rate.'

The technician said, 'I guess that's all.'

The lights went on, and the slide, remaining a moment longer on the screen, grew pale. Flat and dreamlike, the hillside stood at one end of the conference room, and the reaching figures threw up their arms on an empty wall.

With a click, the picture vanished. Addison lit a cigarette. The members of the meeting were looking at their watches and speaking of appointments, perhaps thinking of their afternoon tea. A girl with flat black hair had come in and was handing a message to Rodriguez-O'Hearn. The one or two questions asked of Flinders had, he felt, little to do with what he had said, and he thought this must be his fault. Addison made an appointment to lunch with him next day, and the girl from Peaceful Uses said shyly that she looked forward to discussing with him the effects of nuclear testing in the Sahara. In the meantime, Rodriguez-O'Hearn, whom Flinders had wanted to meet, had disappeared. A secretary came in to empty the ashtrays and align the empty chairs. It occurred to Flinders that another meeting was about to take place here: the very idea was exhausting.

He left the room and walked down a grey corridor. He wished he had gone to the trouble of taking a proper film, like Edrich, or had at least prepared the right kind of final report. At El Attara he had thought these things peripheral, but here they seemed to matter most of all. He should have been able to address the meeting in its own language – that language of ends and trends, of agenda and addenda, of concrete measures in fluid situations, which he had never set himself to master. At El Attara they had needed help and he had done what he could, but he found himself unable to speak with confidence about this work. He knew the problem of erosion to be immense; and the trees, being handed down that way, had looked so few and so small.

At the elevator he met Edrich. Edrich seemed older and shorter than he had in the conference room. Flinders would have told him what was in his heart, but he somehow felt that Edrich was not the right recipient for the information. They took the Down elevator together, and Edrich got off at the Clinic. Flinders continued to the main floor and, leaving the building by a side entrance, went out through the rose garden.

Rodriguez-O'Hearn put down the telephone. Hearing him ring off, his secretary brought him his afternoon coffee in a cardboard container.

'Thank you, Miss Shamsee.'

'Regular with sugar.' She pulled up a metal blind. In the early outside darkness, red and yellow lights were being turned on. The river icily reflected the crimson Frosti-Cola sign.

'Any other messages?'

She put a slip of paper in his calendar. 'Tomorrow afternoon, meeting at three-thirty. Two experts reporting: Suzuki in public accounting, and Raman, malaria control.'

'Better get up their files.'

'I've already sent for them.'

Rodriguez-O'Hearn drank his coffee, and made a space for the container among the papers on his blotter. He tipped back his chair. 'To think,' he said, 'Miss Shamsee, that when I was a young man I wanted to be the conductor of an orchestra.'

She took the empty container off the desk and dropped it in the waste-basket. 'That's what you are,' she said, 'in a manner of speaking.'

'No, no,' he said, but tipped his chair down again. 'Such mistakes we make,' he said.

When the girl went out he looked through his In-tray. He

then wrote a note asking Addison to bring Flinders to see him the following day, signed several recommendations for new experts, and began to read a report, making notes in the margin. When his secretary next came in, however, with an armful of files, she found him looking out of the window.

'Miss Shamsee,' he said gravely, 'I'm afraid we have suffered much erosion since classical times.'

She was used to him, and merely put the files in his In-tray. She saw, as she did so, that on the edge of his blotter he had drawn a small tree.

FAY ZWICKY

Hostages

I think I began to hate when I was twelve. Consciously, I mean. The war was then in its fourth year, there was no chocolate and my father was still away in Borneo. I barely knew him. Till then I had learnt to admire what my mother believed to be admirable. Striving to please with ascetic rigour, I practised scales and read Greek myths. Morality hinged on hours of piano practices achieved or neglected. I knew no evil. The uncommon neutrality of my existence as a musical child in wartime was secured in a world neither good nor malevolent. My place among men was given. Did I have feelings? I was not ready to admit them for there seemed to be rules governing their revelation which I either could not or would not grasp. Nameless, passionless, and without daring I repressed deepest candour. But *tout comprendre c'est tout pardonner*; what was once self-indulgence is now permissible revelation. Why, then, should shame crimp the edge of my reflection so many years after the event?

Sophie Lindauer-Grünberg, German refugee, piano teacher, used to visit our house once a week. Poor fat sentimental Sophie, grateful recipient of my mother's pity. I was to be her first Austalian pupil.

'But why me?'

'Because she needs help. She has nothing and you, thank God, have everything. She's been a very fine musician in her own country. You have to understand that this is someone who has lost everything. Yes, you can roll your eyes. *Everything*, I said. Something I hope, please God, that will never happen to you. So you'll be nice to her and pay attention to what she says. I've told Mr Grover he lives too far away for me to go on taking you to lessons twice a week.'

Suddenly dull and bumbling Mr Grover in his music room

smelling of tobacco and hair oil seemed like my last contact with the outside world. I was to be corralled into the tight, airless circle of maternal philanthropy.

The day of my first lesson a hot north wind was tearing at the huge gum in front of the house. Blinds and curtains were drawn against the promised heat. The house stood girded like an island under seige. My younger brother and sister had gone swimming. I watched them go, screwing up my eyes with the beginnings of a headache, envying their laughter and the way they tore sprigs off the lantana plants lining the driveway. I awaited my teacher, a recalcitrant hostage. The rooms were generous and high-ceilinged but I prowled about, tight-lipped, seeking yet more room. A deep nerve of anger throbbed in me and I prayed that she would not come. But she came. Slowly up the brick path in the heat. I watched her from the window, measuring her heavy step with my uneasy breath. Then my mother's voice greeting her in the hallway, high-pitched and over-articulated as if her listener were deaf, a standard affectation of hers with foreign visitors. 'Terrible day . . . trouble finding the house . . . Helen looking forward so much . . .' I ran to the bathroom and turned on the tap hard. I just let it run, catching sight of my face in the mirror above the basin.

Could I be called pretty? Brown hair hanging long on either side of high cheekbones, the hint of a powerful nose to come, a chin too long, cold grey eyes, wide mouth, fresh colour. No, not pretty. No heroine either. A wave of self-pity compensated me for what I saw and tears filled my eyes. Why me? Because she has to have pupils. Am I such a prize? No, but a Jew who has everything. 'Be thankful you were born in this wonderful country.' My mother's voice sounded loud in my ears. 'They're making them into lamp shades over there.' I had laughed, but shrank from the grotesque absurdity of the statement. Why the dramatics? All I remember is the enveloping anger directed at everything my life had been and was. I wanted to be left alone but didn't know how or where to begin. 'She has lost her whole family. Taken away and shot before her eyes . . .' So? Now she has me.

My mother and Miss Grünberg were talking about me as I stood in the doorway. My own hands were clammy as I moved forward to the outstretched, unfamiliar gesture. Hers were small, fat and very white, surprisingly small for such a tall, heavily built woman, like soft snuggling grubs. She herself looked like some swollen, pale grub smiling widely and kindly, a spinster of nearly sixty. Her little eyes gleamed through thick, round spectacles. On the skin beneath her eyes tiny bluish vessels spread their nets.

'So here is *unsere liebe Helene*!'

I raised my eyebrows insolently, as the girls did at school, after one of my ill-judged observations. It was essential to the code governing the treatment of victims. But this time I had the upper hand and didn't know how to handle my advantage. The cobbles of Cologne and Cracow rang hollow under my boots. The light from the pink shaded lamp fell on my new teacher. The wind blew in sharp gusts outside.

'Helen, this is Miss Grünberg.' My mother with a sharp look in my direction. 'I've been telling her about the work you've done so far with Mr Grover. Miss Grünberg would like you to have another book of studies.'

'Perhaps you will play *ein Stück* for me. Liszt perhaps?' She nodded ponderously at our Bechstein grand that suddenly took on the semblance of some monstrous piece of abstract statuary, out of all proportion to the scale of the room.

'Lord, no. I've never done him.' I fell into uncharacteristic breeziness. 'I'm not really in practice. Hardly anything going at the moment and I'm pretty stale on the stuff Grover had me on for the exams.' Deliberately fast, consciously idiomatic, enjoying, yes, *enjoying* the strain of comprehension on my victim's round, perpetually smiling face.

'You can *still* play those Debussy *Arabesques*,' said my mother, her neck flushed. 'I put the music on the piano,' and she gave me yet another warning look.

I opened the lid noisily and sat down with elaborate movements, shifting the metronome a few inches to the right, altering the position of the stand, bending to examine my feet fumbling between the pedals. The *Arabesques* moved perfunctorily. I kept my face impassive, looked rigidly ahead at the music which I didn't see. Even during the section I liked in the second piece, a part where normally I would lean back a little and smile. I had begun to learn how not to please. But the process of self-annihilation involved the destruction of others. *Tout pardonner* did I say?

Miss Grünberg arranged with my mother to return the following week at the same time.

'Why are you behaving like this?' asked my mother, red and angry with me after she had left in a taxi. The young blond driver had tapped his foot noisily on the brick path as Miss Grünberg profusely repeated her gratitude to my mother for the privilege of teaching her talented daughter. Moving rapidly away from them I conversed with him, broadening my vowels like sharks' teeth on the subject of the noon temperature. I was desperate that the coveted outside world and its tranquil normality should recognize that I was in no way linked with the heavy foreign accent involved in demonstrative leave-taking on our front lawn.

'Behaving like what?'

'You know what I mean. You behaved abominably to that poor woman.'

'I played for her, didn't I?' She came closer to me with a vengeful mouth.

'You could call it that. I don't know what's got into you lately. You used to be such a good child. Now you know the answers to everything. A walking miracle! What terrible things have we done, your father and I, that you should behave like a pig to a woman like that? We've given you everything. *Everything*! And because I'm good to an unfortunate refugee who needs help wherever she can find it, you have to behave like that! I'm sorry for you, *really* sorry for you!'

'Spare your sympathy for the poor reffoes!' The taxi driver's word burst savagely out of my mouth. She flew at me and slapped me across the face with her outstretched hand.

'One thing I do know,' she was trembling with rage, 'the one thing I'm sure of is that I've been too good to you. We've given you too much. You're spoilt rotten! And *one* day, my girl, one day you too may be old and unwanted and . . .'

'A lampshade perhaps? So what.' I shook with guilt and fear at the enormity of what I'd said, terrified of the holocaust I'd shaken loose and my mother's twisted mouth.

But the revolution didn't get under way, either that day or

that year. The heroine lacked (should one say it?) courage. Sealed trains are more comforting than the unknown wastes of the steppes. The following week Miss Grünberg toiled up our front path and I sat down to the new course of Moscheles studies and a movement of a Mozart concerto. *Her* music. Scored heavily in red pencil, the loved and hated language dotted with emotional exclamation marks. Her life's work put out for my ruthless inspection. She moved her chair closer to my stool to alter the position of my right hand. 'Finger *rund*, *Kleine*, always *rund*. Hold always the wrist supple, *liebe Helene*.' I shrank from the alien endearment and her sour breath but curved my fingers, tight and deliberate. Her smell hung over me, a static haze in the dry air. Musty, pungent and stale, the last faint reminder of an airless Munich apartment house. Her dress, of cheap silky fabric, rustled when she moved her heavy body. Breathing laboriously she tried to explain to me what I should do with the Mozart. She couldn't get used to the heat of the new country and was beginning to find walking difficult. But I didn't practise between her visits and gave only spasmodic attention to her gentle directions. I was shutting myself off from words and from music, beginning a long course in alienation. I seldom looked my mother in the eye in those days. I quarrelled bitterly with my sister, ignored my brother.

About six months after my lessons with Miss Grünberg started I was not much further advanced. I spent a lot of time reading in my room or just looking out of the window at the garden which was now bare. Squalls lashed the gum tree and drove the leaves from the weeping elm skittering across the grass. Miss Grünberg now had several pupils amongst the children of the Jewish community and even one or two gentiles from the neighbouring school. She lived in a very poorly furnished flat in a rundown outer suburb. She still travelled to her pupils' homes. Her breathing had become very short in the last few weeks. Inattentive and isolated as I was, I had noticed that she was even paler than usual.

My mother one day told me with some rancour how well the Lapin girl was doing with the piano. 'She never had your talent but what a worker! She's going to give a recital in the Assembly Hall next month.' I merely shrugged. The boots of the conqueror were no picnic. She was welcome to them. 'And while I'm about it, I've decided to tell Miss Grünberg not to come any more. I don't feel there's much point as you seem quite determined to do as little with music as possible. I've done all *I* can. At least she's on her feet now.' On her feet! Oh God! But I replied, 'That's all right with me', in as neutral a voice as I could summon.

But that night I ground my face into the covers of my bed, no longer a place of warmth and security but a burial trench. At the mercy of my dreams appeared Sophie Lindauer-Grünberg, pale as brick dust. Her face wasting, crumbling to ash, blasted by the force of my terrible youth. And, waking in fright, I mourned for the first time my innocent victim and our shared fate.

DAVID MALOUF

The Sun in Winter

It was dark in the church, even at noon. Diagonals of chill sunlight were stacked between the piers, sifting down luminous dust, and so thick with it that they seemed more substantial almost than stone. He had a sense of two churches, one raised vertically on gothic arches and a thousand years old, the other compounded of light and dust, at an angle to the first and newly created in the moment of his looking. At the end of the nave, set far back on a platform, like a miraculous vision that the arctic air had immediately snap-frozen, was a Virgin with a child at her knee. The Michelangelo. So this church he was in must be the Onze Vrouw.

'Excuse me.'

The voice came from a pew two rows away, behind him: a plain woman of maybe forty, with the stolid look and close-pored waxy skin of those wives of donors he had been looking at earlier in the side panels of local altars. She was buttoned to the neck in a square-shouldered raincoat and wore a scarf rather than a wimple, but behind her as she knelt might have been two or three miniatures of herself – infant daughters with their hands strictly clasped – and if he peeped under her shoes, he thought, there would be a monster of the deep, a sad-eyed amorphous creature with a hump to its back, gloomily committed to evil but sick with love for the world it glimpsed, all angels, beyond the hem of her skirt.

'You're not Flemish, are you?' she was saying, half in question (that was her politeness) and half as fact.

'No,' he admitted. 'Australian.'

They were whispering – this was after all a church – but her 'Ah, the *New* World' was no more than a breath. She made it sound so romantic, so much more of a venture than he had ever seen it, that he laughed outright, then checked himself;

but not before his laughter came back to him, oddly transformed, from the hollow vault. No Australian in those days thought of himself as coming under so grand a term. Things are different now.

'You see,' she told him in a delighted whisper, 'I guessed! I knew you were not Flemish – that, if you don't mind, is obvious – so I thought, I'll speak to him in English, or maybe on this occasion I'll try Esperanto. Do you by any chance know Esperanto?' He shook his head. 'Well, never mind,' she said, 'there's plenty of time.' She did not say for what. 'But you *are* Catholic.'

Wrong again. Well, not exactly, but his 'No' was emphatic, she was taken aback. She refrained from putting the further question and looked for a moment as if she did not know how to proceed. Then following the turn of his head she found the Madonna. 'Ah,' she said, 'you are interested in art. You have come for the Madonna.' Relieved at last to have comprehended him she regarded the figure with a proprietary air. Silently, and with a certain old world grandeur and largesse, she presented it to him.

He should, to be honest, have informed her then that he had been a Catholic once (he was just twenty) and still wasn't so far gone as to be lapsed – though too far to claim communion; and that for today he had rather exhausted his interest in art at the little hospital full of Memlings and over their splendid Van Eycks. Which left no reason for his being here but the crude one: his need to find sanctuary for a time from their killing cold.

Out there, blades of ice slicing in off the North Sea had found no obstacle, it seemed, in more than twenty miles of flat lands crawling with fog, till they found *him*, the one vertical (given a belltower or two) on the whole ring of the horizon. He had been, for long minutes out there, the assembly-point for forty-seven demons. His bones scraped like glaciers. Huge ice-plates ground in his skull. He had been afraid his eyeballs might freeze, contract, drop out and go rolling away over the ancient flags. It seemed foolish after all that to say simply, 'I was cold.'

'Well, in that case,' she told him, 'you must allow me to make an appointment. I am an official guide of this town. I am working all day in a government office, motor vehicle licences, but precisely at four we can meet and I will show you our dear sad Bruges – that is, of course, if you are agreeable. No, no – please – it is for my own pleasure, no fee is involved. Because I see that you are interested, I glimpsed it right off.' She turned up the collar of her coat and gave him an engaging smile. 'It is OK?' She produced the Americanism with a cluck of clear self-satisfaction, as proof that she was, though a guide of this old and impressively dead city, very much of his own century and not at all hoity-toity about the usages of the New World. It was a brief kick of the heels that promised fun as well as instruction in the splendours and miseries of the place.

'Well then,' she said when he made no protest, 'it is decided – till four. You will see that our Bruges is very beautiful, very *triste*, you understand French? *Bruges la Morte.* And German too maybe, a little? *Die tote Stadt.*' She pronounced this with a small shiver in her voice, a kind of silvery chill that made him think of the backs of mirrors. At the same time she gave him just the tips of her gloved fingers. 'So – I must be off now. We meet at four.'

Which is how, without especially wanting it, he came to know the whole history of the town. On a cold afternoon in the Fifties, with fog swirling thick white in the polled avenues and lying in ghostly drifts above the canals, and the red-brick façades of palaces, convents, museums laid bare under the claws of ivy, he tramped with his guide over little humpbacked bridges, across sodden lawns, to see a window the size of a hand-mirror with a bloody history, a group of torture instruments (themselves twisted now and flaking rust), the site, almost too ordinary, of a minor miracle, a courtyard where five old ladies were making lace with fingers as knobbled and misshapen as twigs, and the statue of a man in a frock coat who had given birth to the decimal system.

The woman's story he caught in the gaps between centuries and he got the two histories, her own and the city's, rather mixed, so that he could not recall later whether it was his lady or the daughter of a local duke who had suffered a fall in the woods, and her young man or some earlier one who had been shut up and tortured in one of the many towers. The building she pointed to as being the former Gestapo head-quarters looked much like all the rest, though it might of course have been a late imitation.

She made light of things, including her own life, which had not, he gathered, been happy; but she could be serious as well as ironic. To see what all this really was, she insisted – beyond the relics and the old-fashioned horrors and shows – you needed a passion for the everyday. That was how she put it. And for that, mere looking got you nowhere. 'All you see then,' she told him, 'is what catches the eye, the odd thing, the unusual. But to see what is common, that is the difficult thing, don't you think? For that we need imagi-nation, and there is never enough of it – never, never enough.'

She had spoken with feeling, and now that it was over, her own small show, there was an awkwardness. It had grown dark. The night, a block of solid ice with herrings in it, deep blue, was being cranked down over the plain; you could hear it creaking. He stamped a little, puffing clouds of white, and shyly, sheepishly grinned. 'Cold,' he sang, shuffling his feet, and when she laughed at the little dance he was doing he continued it, waving his arms about as well. Then they came, rather too quickly, to the end of his small show. She pulled at her gloves and stood waiting.

Something more was expected of him, he knew that. But what? Was he to name it? Should he perhaps, in spite of her earlier disclaimer, offer a tip? Was that it? Surely not. But money was just one of the things, here in Europe, that he hadn't got the hang of, the weight, the place, the meaning; one of the many – along with tones, looks, little movements of the hands and eyebrows, unspoken demands and the easy meeting of them – that more than galleries or torture cham-bers made up what he had come here to see, and to absorb too if he could manage it. He felt hopelessly young and raw. He ought to have known – he had known – from that invisible kick of the heels, that she had more to show him than this crumblingly haunted and picturesque corner of the past, where sadness, a mood of silvery reflection, had been turned into the high worship of death – a glory perhaps, but one that was too full of shadows to bear the sun. He felt suddenly a great wish for the sun in its full power as at home, and it burned up in him. He *was* the sun. It belonged to the world he had come from and to his youth.

The woman had taken his hand. 'My dear friend,' she was saying, with that soft tremor in her voice, '– I *can* call you that, can't I? I feel that we *are* friends. In such a short time we have grown close. I would like to show you one thing more – very beautiful but not of the past. Something personal.'

She led him along the edge of the canal and out into a street broader than the rest, its cobbles gleaming in the mist. Stone steps led up to classical porticoes, and in long, brightly-lit windows there were Christmas decorations, holly with red ribbons, and bells powdered with frost. They came to a halt in front of one of the largest and brightest of these displays, and he wondered why. Still at the antipodes, deep in his dream of sunlight and youth, he did not see at first that they had arrived.

'There,' the woman was saying. She put her nose to the glass and there was a ring of fog.

The window was full of funerary objects; ornamental wreaths in iridescent enamel, candles of all sizes like organ pipes in carved and coloured wax, angels large and small, some in glass, some in plaster, some in honey-coloured wood in which you saw all the decades of growth; one of them was playing a lute; others had viols, pan pipes, primitive side-drums; others again pointed a slender index finger as at a naughty child and were smiling in an ambiguous, un-otherworldly way. It was all so lively and colourful that he might have missed its meaning altogether without the coffin, which held a central place in the foregound and was tilted so that you saw the richness of the buttoned interior. Very comfortable it looked too – luxuriously inviting. Though the scene did not suggest repose. The heavy lid had been pushed strongly aside, as if what lay there just a moment ago had got up, shaken itself after long sleep, and gone striding off down the quay. The whole thing puzzled him. He wondered for a moment if she hadn't led him to the site of another and more recent miracle. But no.

'Such a coffin,' she was telling him softly, 'I have ordered for myself. – Oh, don't look surprised! – I am not planning to die so soon, not at all! I am paying it off. The same. Exactly.'

He swallowed, nodded, smiled, but was dismayed; he couldn't have been more so, or felt more exposed and naked, if she had climbed up into the window, among the plump and knowing angels, and got into the thing – lain right down on the buttoned blue satin, and with her skirt rucked up to show stockings rolled tight over snowy thighs, had crooked a finger and beckoned him with a leer to join her. He blushed for the grossness of the vision, which was all his own.

But his moment of incomprehension passed. His shock, he saw, was for an impropriety she took quite for granted and for an event that belonged, as she calmly surveyed it, to a world of exuberant and even vulgar life. The window was the brightest thing she had shown him, the brightest thing he had seen all day, the most lively, least doleful.

So he survived the experience. They both did. And he was glad to recall years after, that when she smiled and touched his hand in token of their secret sympathy, a kind of grace had come over him and he did not start as he might have done; he was relieved of awkwardness, and was moved, for all his raw youth, by an emotion he could not have named, not then – for her, but also for himself – and which he would catch up with only later, when sufficient time had passed to make them of an age.

As they already were for a second, before she let him go, and in a burst of whitened breath, said 'Now my dear, dear friend, I will exact my fee. You may buy me a cup of chocolate at one of our excellent cafés. OK?'

FRANK MOORHOUSE

From a Bush Log Book: Going into the Heartlands with the Wrong Person at Christmas

That Christmas he went into the Budawang Ranges with his decadent friend, Belle.

They had debauched in motel rooms and restaurants along the coast while he turned forty, bed sheets drenched with champagne and with all the smells and fluids that two bodies could be made offer up in such dark love-making as, in their curious way, he and Belle were drawn into. But the conversations in the restaurants had become unproductively sadistic as they exhausted amiable conversation.

He'd gone increasingly into interior conversation with himself about 'turning forty' because she was too young to have empathy with his turning forty. And he was trying to salve the loss of his young girlfriend who was overseas and 'in love'.

He also had some home-yearnings which came on at Christmas. His family was not in town for this Christmas, but anyhow his home-yearnings had been displaced over the years away from his family in the town to the bush about fifty kilometres away from, but behind, the coastal town where he had grown up – the Sassafras bush in the Budawang Ranges.

He'd put camping gear in the car when they'd left the city and they drove as deep into the bush as the road permitted and then left the car and backpacked their way.

As they walked deeper into the bush he kept glancing at Belle to see if she was being affected by the dull warm day and the bush. He knew the creeping hysteria and dread which the Australian bush could bring about.

She saw him looking back at her and said, 'I'm coping. Stop looking back at me all the time.'

They walked for an hour or so and came to what is called Mitchell Lookout.

'This is called Mitchell Lookout,' he said, 'but as you can see it is not a lookout in the Rotary sense.'

It was a shelf of rock with a limited view of the gorge.

'Lookouts are an eighteenth-century European act of nature worship which Rotary clubs have carried on. The growth is too thick – you can't see the river down there. You'll have to take my word for it.'

'I can see that the growth is too thick.'

'Laughably, the only thing you can see clearly from Mitchell Lookout is directly across the gorge – they could have another lookout which looked across at Mitchell Lookout.'

He saw her look across at the other side and back again. She made a small movement of her mouth to show that she didn't think it was particularly 'laughable'.

'I don't go into the bush for views,' he said.

'Tell me – what do you go into the bush for?'

'I go into the bush to be swallowed whole. I don't go into the bush to look at curious natural formations – I don't marvel at God's handiwork.

For reasons he could not explain and did not record in his log book, he decided to put the tent on the rock ledge overlooking the gorge.

'You'll find sleeping on the rock is OK,' he said, 'it is really much better than you imagine.'

'If you say so,' she said, dumping her backpack.

'I go into the bush for raw unanalysed sensory experience,' he said, 'I don't go in for naming things geologically or birds and so on.'

'You don't have to apologize for not knowing the names of the birds and the stones.'

He cut some bracken fern to lie on, more as a gesture towards the idea of what made for comfort.

'That'll do a fat amount of good,' Belle said.

'It's a gesture.'

He put up the tent, pinning each corner from inside with rocks and tying the guy ropes to rocks.

'I've even used rocks as pillows,' he said.

She sat, one leg crossed over the other, cleaning dirt from her painted fingernails with a nail file.

He instantly doubted whether she had ever used a rock for a pillow and whether sleeping on rock was in fact OK.

'There,' he said, 'the tent is up.'

She looked across at it, got up, went over and looked inside the tent but did not go in.

'How about a drink?' she said.

'Sure – it's the happy hour. Any hour can be a happy hour.' She laughed at this to herself.

He went about getting the drinks.

'I'll cook the Christmas dinner. That'll be my contribution,' she said.

'No,' he said, 'that's OK – I'm used to cooking on camp fires.'

'Look – you may be fourth-generation Australian but you're not the only one who can cook on a camp fire, for godsake.'

'All right, all right.'

As they had their bourbons he doubted whether she could cook on campfires. He thought about what they could salvage to eat.

'I came through the Australian experience too,' she said.

'Do you know what to do if you get lost in the bush?' he asked her.

'No, I didn't mean to invite a test, but you tell me, what do I do if I get lost in the bush?'

'You stay where you are, mix a dry Martini and within minutes someone will be there telling you that you're doing it wrong.'

'Ha ha. I wouldn't mind a Martini now this very minute.'

He had never seen her cook a meal. It was always restaurants and luxury hotels, that was their relationship.

'But it was my idea to come out here in the bush – let me cook it.'

'I'll cook it.'

'OK – if you feel happy about it.'

'I feel quite happy about it, Hemingway.'

She made a low, slow fire, just right, and rested the pannikins and camp cooking dishes on the coals. It wasn't quite the way he would have done it but he didn't say anything.

Wood coals look stable until things tilt and spill as the wood burns away.

She squatted there at the fire. She first put potatoes on the coals. She put on the rabbit pieces – which they had not themselves hunted, he hadn't brought the guns – after smearing them with mustard and muttered to herself *'lapin moutarde'*, laughing to herself. She wrapped the rabbit in tin foil and wormed them down into the coals with a flat stick. Then she crossed herself. She put the corn cobs on to boil, candied the carrots with sugar sachets from the motel, put on the beans. She then heated the lobster bisque, throwing in a dash of her bloody mary, again saying something to herself that he didn't catch.

Maybe a gypsy incantation.

She put the plum pudding on to be warmed and mixed a careful custard.

She squatted there at the smoking fire, stirring and moving the pots as needed, throwing on a piece of wood at the back at the right time for some quick heat, all with what he thought was primitive control. He swigged bourbon from a First World War officer's flask and passed it to her from time to time. He liked to think that the flask had belonged to one of his great-grandmother's lovers. She squatted there in silence, full of attention for what she was doing.

He swigged the bourbon and, from time to time, became a First World War officer. She had slipped into a posture which belonged to the primitive way of doing things – what? – a few thousand years ago when the race cooked on camp fires. Or more recently, back to Settlement.

He sat off on a rock and took some bearings using his Swiss compass and Department of Mapping 1:25 000 topographic maps, trying to identify some of the distant peaks.

'Shrouded God's Mountain,' he said.

'Good,' she said, not looking up.

He kept glancing at her, enjoying her postures.

He opened a bottle of 1968 Coonawarra Cabernet Shiraz.

'It's ready,' she said, muttering something.

She presented the meal with perfect timing, everything right, at the right time, no over-cooking, no cold food, no ash or grit in the food. She served it on the disposable plates they'd bought.

He complimented her.

'Don't sound so surprised,' she said.

They ate their Christmas dinner and drank the wine in the Guzzini goblets he'd bought for camping, and as they did, a white mist filled the gorge and stopped short of where they were so that they were atop of it, as if looking out the window of an aircraft above the clouds.

It came almost level with the slab where they were camped and were eating.

'Jesus, that's nice,' he said, staring down at the mist.

'I thought you didn't go in for God's handiwork.'

'Well, I don't go searching for it. When he does it before my very eyes, I can be appreciative.'

She looked down at the mist while chewing the meat off a rabbit bone, as if assessing the mist, aesthetically? theologically? She ate the meal with her fingers, with their painted nails.

'It's all right,' she said, emphatically.

It was warm and there were bush flies which worried her and she kept brushing them away with her hand, cursing at them.

'Piss off, you bastard,' she said.

'I've made peace with the flies,' he said. 'Sooner or later in the Australian bush you have to stop shooting the flies and let them be.'

'I'm not going to let them be,' she said, 'I'm going to give them a bad time.'

'Please yourself.'

'I will.'

'You did the meal perfectly.'

'Thank you – but you aren't the only person in Australia who can cook on a camp fire.' She then laughed, and said, 'Actually it was the first time I have cooked a meal on a camp fire.'

'It was perfect. You looked very primitive – you could have been out of the First Settlement.'

'I felt very primitive,' she said, 'if the truth be known.'

'I meant it in the best sense.'

'I assumed you did.'

They sat there with food-stained hands, smoky from the fire, food and wine on their breath. Belle exposed her legs to the misty sun.

She stared expressionlessly at him, her hand methodically waving away the flies, and she then began to remove her clothing. They had sex there on the rock slab surrounded by the mist. They played with the idea of her naked body on the rock slab, the bruising of it, the abrasion. He held her head by the hair and pinned her arms, allowing the flies to crawl over her face. She struggled but could not make enough movement to keep them off her face. She came and he came.

They drank and became drowsy watching, from a cool distance, the fire burning away.

During the night he got up because he liked to leave the tent in the dead of the night and prowl about naked. He said to himself that although he did not always feel easy in the bush, in fact, he sometimes felt discordant in it, he'd rather be out in it feeling discordant then not be there.

'What are you doing out there, for godsake?' Belle called from the tent.

'Having a piss.'

He crawled back into the tent.

'I thought for a moment you were communing,' she said.

'Just checking the boundaries.'

In the morning he said, 'Well, it wasn't unsleepable on the rock.'

'No, not unsleepable,' she said, and smiled, 'not unfuckable either.'

'The rock tells our body things our mind cannot comprehend.'

'Don't give me that bullshit.'

It was still misty and the air heavy with moisture but it was not cold.

Neither of them now wanted to stay longer in the bush although they'd talked initially of staying 'for a few days'.

He thought he might have stayed on if he'd been alone.

They struck camp.

'I liked having it off on the rock,' she said, 'I seem to be bruised.'

'But you were bruised enough?' he ritualistically asked, resolving that he would not make that joke again because of its tiredness, resisting what the tiredness meant about their relationship.

'Hah, hah.'

It was a grey sky. The dampness quietened everything down just a little more than usual and the dull sky dulled everything a little more, including their mood.

They hoisted on their backpacks and began walking.

'I know all about abjection and self-esteem but for a slut like me it's all a game now.'

He gestured to indicate that he wasn't making judgements about it.

'It's no longer the whole damned basis of my personality,' she said.

'You have to be a bit like that to go into the bush anyhow. It's very easy to make it self-punishing.'

'I was thinking that.'

They walked a few metres apart. They passed a stand of grey kangaroos some way off which speculatively watched them walk by. Belle and he indicated to each other by a glance that they'd seen the kangaroos.

'More of God's handiwork,' she called.

He realized as they walked out that he had a disquiet about being there with Belle. When he looked at the Christmas they'd just had together – on paper – it was untroubled, memorable, an enriched event – the mist in the gorge, the perfect camp-fire meal, the good wine. Belle naked on the rock, his standing on the ledge in the dead of night, the melancholy bush.

The disquiet came because Belle had been moved *out of place* in his life. The Budawang bush was the place of his childhood testing, his family's bush experience, touching base, touching primitive base. He had learned his masculinity here.

She did not belong in that album.

He looked back at her up the trail, plodding through the swampy part in her Keds dripping wet from the moisture of the bushes. He saw her again at the camp fire, primitively squatting. He felt a huge fondness for her.

They'd often said that they were not the sort of person either would really choose to spend Christmas or birthdays with, they were making do with each other.

By bringing Belle with him on his fortieth birthday and on Christmas he had left an ineradicable and inappropriate memory trace across the countryside.

But she was also somehow an embodiment of his great-grandmother, they'd divined that in Katoomba at his great-grandmother's grave. But this was not his great-grandmother's territory.

He was then struck by a splintering observation – the Budawangs and the Blue Mountains of Katoomba were part of the Great Dividing Range but in his head they were different mountains, different districts. His great-grandmother and Belle belonged at Katoomba, the decayed health resort and spa. It was there that his great-grandmother had used her charms and beauty to make her living, her fortune. The Budawangs were where he'd been the boy scout and the army officer.

The parts still didn't quite come together.

He caught up with Belle and touched her fondly.

'Sorry about the mud,' he said.

'I can cope. I can take it.'

This was where he'd learned as a boy how to 'take it'.

'I'll get you a new pair of Keds.'

'They come from the States.'

'I'll get a pair sent across.'

'You probably won't.'

In a motel on the coast they showered off the mud, dried off the dampness, turned up the air-conditioner to warm, and got slowly drunk, sprawled on the floor. Belle with a towel wrapped around her drying hair, in a silk kimono, was like a cat back in habitat.

He spread out the map of southern New South Wales.

This is my heartlands, he showed her, the English damp green tablelands of Bowral and Moss Vale, the old goldfields, the lakes of Jindabyne, the new snow resort, down to Bega where my father introduced me to the man who had a library of a thousand books of mystery and the supernatural, to Kiama where my girlfriend from school and I went for our miserable honeymoon after we married in the hometown Church of England.

And Milton, where I found ten years of *Champion* magazine in an old news agency.

He told her how he had been a rebellious but highly proficient scout, had played football up and down the coast, had been a soldier on manoeuvres there, had surfed the whole coast, camped out and hunted in all the bush.

'You're a very sentimental person,' she said, as she rubbed cream into a scratch on her leg.

'No, I don't think I am.'

'I think you are.'

'I think not.'

'A sentimental drunk, then.'

'There is another territory.'

He circled the Katoomba and Jenolan Caves district.

'My great-grandmother's territory.'

'We've done that.'

'And there is my grandfather's territory.' He circled the town. 'He committed suicide in the hotel there. But that was not his territory, maybe being what he was he had no territory.'

But neither were ever mentioned in this territory, he told her, pointing at the first circle.

Belle was leaning on his shoulder pretending an interest, for an instant she became someone else leaning on his shoulder looking at the map, a high-spirited late arrival at a dying party.

'Let's go,' he said, 'let's check out now and go back to the city. I think it's over.'

Two weeks later he went back to the Budawangs and camped again in the same place, alone. It was a trip to erase the mistake of having gone there with Belle.

He realized, as he sat there in the bush at Mitchell Lookout, that it was a misguided effort. Coming back to erase it had only more deeply inscribed it.

Now whenever he passed the place he would think of having gone there with the wrong person, of having taken his great-grandmother into the hard country where she didn't belong. He would laugh about Belle, squatting there cooking, about the flies on her face, and Belle saying, 'I feel quite happy about it, Hemingway.'

Libido and Life Lessons

When he noticed that his libido was low while in Vienna the first time he thought it was because he was travelling – the beast out of its habitat does not feel secure enough to mate or, maybe, to perform any part of the breeding act. He reasoned that animals needed to be confident of their safety. But we are not purely animals. And sometimes he had become randy while travelling. Now he didn't feel randy for days and days. It continued after his return to Australia.

'Hullo,' he said, 'is this some sort of suicide?' Was this why his grandfather committed suicide? Which came first, the loss of interest in life or the loss of libido?

His fantasy life became dulled. He was able to have sex, but without much drive. Another explanation was that he was 'growing up' and putting behind him random sexuality. Was this the way an adult genital male should be at forty? All the books said that turning forty should not affect the libido. Were the books lying?

He found too that he desired to *feel desire* as much as he wanted to have sex; to feel the full juices of desire, to be restless with appetite would please him now.

He could recall the visitations of desire for Belle. The desire strong enough to make him get up from his bed into a car and to drive in the middle of the night to see her.

He understood why Faust in the Gounod opera wanted the return of desire as part of his contract with the devil.

Or was he in fact better off without it?

He wondered that if it were absent long enough would it fade as a known part of his person – would the feel of it be beyond imaginative recall, even?

That might be all right.

But that to be able to savour it, but not to have it – not that – was the state he was in now.

It was, he would now have to explain to Belle, that he could still visually recognize sensuality or sexual attractiveness but it seemed disconnected from the hormonal physical reaction in him. The line was down.

It then occurred to him that it might be related to his hepatitis attack.

His liver specialist was bemused by the question. 'Yes, but I am a *liver* specialist.'

The doctor pondered it. 'It is possible that the liver which controls the flow of oestrogen into the body and out of the body could be affected by hepatitis. Maybe an over-supply of oestrogen.'

His meeting with Belle, the self-proclaimed slut of all times, confirmed that his libido was ailing. Her allure no longer called to him across great distances, and desire for her no longer fell upon him like a fully armed woman jumping from a tree.

'What is up with you?' she said, after they'd finished a rather underpowered love-making.

'I'm not full on,' he said.

'I can tell that.'

'I'm suffering from an over-supply of oestrogen. From my hepatitis.'

'You're turning into a woman?'

'No, not quite.'

'You were erect but you lacked a certain follow-through, a certain zing.'

'Maybe it's turning forty. Maybe the books lie. It's cruel.'

'Oh, come on – if it's from your hepatitis it'll pass. But tell me, what is being forty "like"?'

He told Belle what being forty is 'like.'

*

You finally accept that you cannot drink a cup of hot take-away coffee and drive a car at the same time.

*

You doubt that you will ever go to a 'party' again. Parties cease to be events of unlimited possibility.

*

You realize that you have spent forty years raising the child within you.

*

You find your ex-wife dying of cancer, that another friend has a noticeable lump on his face but you do not refer to it.

*

You read your CV with a comfortable curiosity to find out 'what you are really'. You run through your credentials and life experiences to remind yourself that you have 'fully lived'. You find yourself sitting in a bar reading your passport, reminding yourself of the world you've seen, about which you seem to recall so little.

You have a feeling that it's too late to bother a psychiatrist with your problems, too late to reconstruct yourself, that you have now to *live it out*. And you have a feeling that a psychiatrist wouldn't think it worth wasting time on you – too little life left to live usefully.

You have an urge to close up your life for a year and go to the seaside and re-read all the important books of your life; feeling that maybe you didn't read them properly when younger or that you would 'get more from them' now. Or that you have forgotten too much of them.

You find that expressions like 'doing what you like' and 'being nice to yourself' are traps which answer nothing very much. Respite can only follow the volatility of human interaction, stress and friction are part of life, and anxiety a fairly predictable background to a dangerous and uncertain world.

*

The excesses of life are too easily achieved, are not heroic, and yield less and less. You realize that the better pleasures are 'managed', structured, carefully sculptured from a won life.

*

The past becomes closer, as you yourself have a history. Being forty gives you an understanding of what 'forty years' is in time, how close that is. Something that happened say fifty years before you were born becomes dramatically closer.

*

You see sleep as 'part of life', not time wasted or something you 'do too much of'. You learn to enjoy sleep. You see your dreams as an interesting part of living.

*

You realize the huge distance between written descriptions of biographical detail and the density of conflict and despair which lies in the minutes and hours of those biographical descriptions. That success is always disputed, qualified by self-doubt and challenged by the ever-changing hierarchy of following generations. The formal moments and rewards of success usually come after the desire for those formal moments and rewards have passed.

*

You have days where the repetition of nail-cutting, hair-cutting, teeth-cleaning, arse-wiping, and the ever-present deterioration of self and the material world about you, tires you beyond belief.

*

You still sometimes hope for a dramatic opening in your life, for your life to alter course after meeting someone, after receiving a letter. You sometimes wish to feel the dramatic upheaval, renovation and certainty of blind conversion.

*

You realize that you've never really got your life together. That there are parts of your life always in disarray, things not properly completed, living arrangements which could be improved, life practices which could be improved. You feel at times that you need to delimit your life so as to live a more reduced life more perfectly.

*

You notice that fragments of past night dreams, fragments of travel, inconsequential fragments of past relationships, child-hood, begin to intrude or drift across your consciousness with no discernible pattern or meaning, perhaps with an intimation of insanity, derangement.

*

You realize that you have been 'homeless' most of your life, living in other people's houses, in camps, in motels, in hotels. You have camped in life.

*

With regret you realize that no person with a system of

knowledge is going to release you from intellectual dilemma. No book will now come along to alter seriously your life. You feel that you have a fair grasp of the current limitations of knowledge and reason, and the necessary compromising uses of faith. You recognize that your personal, unstable formulations are held without much confidence to stave off the sands of chaotic reality, that a refinement might take their place but you also fear that the rational shoring might one day give way entirely. You are daily made aware of how little reason and knowledge altered the course of affairs.

*

After coming to terms with the imperfect self it is then necessary to come to terms with the imperfect world, to calculate how much of the imperfection of self and the world you have to accommodate without restlessness, without engaging in ineffective efforts to change, efforts which are more protest and despair than hoped for interventions. What parts to find unacceptable, to bewail, to retaliate against. How much evil to live with. How much mess. To calculate the 'unchangeable'.

*

As well as the demands of being a loving person, from which you constantly fall short, you have to live with recrudescence of love for lovers lost, who come alive unannounced in your mind, dreams. Call to you. You find you cry over spilt love.

*

You learn that most things require a proper time for their performance for the thing to be savoured, to be performed with gratification. Including shopping.

*

You strive to keep all conversations exploratory and all positions negotiable and to avoid people who push conversation into competitiveness, or make you insecure or over-defensive, or cause you to perform poorly intellectually. Some people jam your mind and lower its quality of performance. Some people raise this performance.

*

You realize that nothing is really forgotten or lost to the mind, simply that access to the memory bank became erratic.

*

You read reports and letters written many years before and realize that you'd known much that you no longer consciously know. You hope that it is working for you in your chain of reasoning which stretched back twenty-five years.

*

You wonder if omens are unconsciously formed patterns made from myriad inputs and then erupting as signals, warnings, cautions, guidelines, messages – self-planted, self-addressed, but given this form for urgent dramatic revelation.

*

You are unable to determine whether you have led the richest of lives or the most miserable and deformed of lives.

'Well,' Belle said, 'is that all? Is that all you've learned?'

'What is sad,' he said, 'is that I've learned some of these things more than once.'

'I think I'll wait until I have to learn some of those lessons,' she said.

'Oh, they come along in time, when they are no longer of much use.'

GERALD MURNANE

The Only Adam

It was the afternoon of the thunderstorm when A. finally decided to fall in love with Nola Pomeroy or try to shag her or do something special with her in some out-of-the-way place.

The clouds began piling up late in the morning. Storms in summer usually came from the south west, where the ocean lay. But this one appeared from an unlikely quarter. A. watched it almost from its beginnings through the north windows of the school. Its black bulk was bearing down on Sedgewick North from the plains far inland.

After lunch the sky over the school showed nothing but bulging clouds that tore away continually and drifted like smoke on turbulent currents. A. had just seen the first of the lightning when Mr Farrant told the seventh grade that their film strip on Major Mitchell was ready in the cloakroom and asked them what they were waiting for. They filed out through the door. Mr Farrant called after them: 'You, A., turn the projector and read the text and send the wrigglers and gigglers back to me.'

The cloakroom was so dark that A. could not see who had gone into the lovers' corner. But the darkness made the pictures more sharp and clear than any he had seen before. He showed the map of south-eastern Australia with a wide blankness over nearly all of Victoria. He went on turning the knob. Mitchell's dotted line left the Murray River and thrust southwards. A.'s audience was unusually quiet and solemn. He supposed they were waiting for the first heavy drops of rain on the iron roof.

A. read aloud from the screen. Mitchell was so impressed by the rich and pleasant land that he named it *Australia Felix*, which meant Australia the Blessed. A. looked hard at a picture of level country with grass knee-high and huge gums grouped like trees in a botanical garden. It was hard to believe that such a landscape was part of his own State. Yet in the next frame Mitchell's dots had reached deep down into western Victoria. A. might even have said they were heading for his own district if he could have been sure where Sedgewick North should have been on the featureless map.

Still no one tried to joke or howl him down. There was not even a sound from the lovers' corner. A. wondered whether his own grade had at last found some history that took their fancy. Perhaps, like him, they were amazed to see an explorer approaching their own district – a famous man from their history course bearing down on their dairy farms and gravel roads.

The rain started. And a boy came up behind A. with some news that might have explained why everyone seemed quiet and thoughtful. It was not only the eighth graders who were privileged to shag after school. One of the couples in the cloakroom at that moment had gone into the bush somewhere and tried it only the night before. A. hadn't caught their names for the noise of the rain on the roof. But he would find out soon enough because they were going to take up shagging every afternoon. And some of their friends might be joining them.

The storm was on top of them. The thunder and rain were so loud that A. gave up reading the captions. The scenes from Mitchell's journey passed over the screen without comment. The explorer had gone deep into *Australia Felix*, but there was still no mark on the map to show how near he might have been to any place that A. knew. The boy could only look at the land on the screen and wonder what he himself could discover to compare with it.

But he had to think, too, about the couple who had taken up shagging. The senior boys had always insisted that no one in A.'s grade was old enough to do it properly. A. had to admire the two, whoever they were, for sneaking off on their own to become pioneers. No doubt they had discovered a place where none of the older shaggers could disturb them or offer them advice. A. thought that all couples – lovers and shaggers – ought to do their own exploring and establish themselves in cosy nests all around the district. If he could have reserved Pomeroys' scrub for himself he would have enjoyed thinking of Sedgewick North as a network of concealed trails leading to hide-outs for enterprising couples.

The prolonged roaring of the rain died away. A. wound the film strip until it showed the familiar insignia of the Education Department of Victoria on a field of murky grey. No one booed as they usually did to complain that their film had ended. In fact, A. heard no sound from the darkness behind him. He thought what a fool he would seem if all the others had crept quietly away to plan their shagging in all the best landscapes of the district while he was still staring at what was left of the film strip.

But at least Nola Pomeroy was still in her usual place near the projector. A. glanced back and saw her looking as though she hadn't taken her eyes off the screen.

In the last half-hour before home-time the sky began to clear over the inland. There was even a shaft of sunlight pointing down at some lucky district near the horizon. Mr Farrant told A.'s grade to open their readers at the extract, 'On Pyramid Hill, Victoria, 1836', from *Three Expeditions into the Interior of Eastern Australia* by Thomas Livingstone Mitchell.

The pupils read by turns, and A. fidgeted while some farmer's son from Sedgewick North stumbled down the long rolling sentences that led to vistas of plains. Then it was Nola Pomeroy's turn. She was given the passage that A. had been hoping to read himself. But she was a good reader and, being a girl, she delivered her words with an earnestness that would have seemed ridiculous coming from a boy.

> We had at length discovered a country for the immediate reception of civilized man, and fit to become the abode of one of the great nations of the earth. Unencumbered with too much wood, yet possessing enough for all purposes, with an exuberant soil under a temperate climate, bounded by the seacoast and mighty rivers, and watered abundantly by streams from mighty mountains, this highly interesting region lay before me with all its features new and untouched as they fell from the hands of the Creator. Of this Eden it seemed that I was the only Adam; and indeed, it was a sort of paradise to me.

A. kept himself from looking across at Nola. He watched

instead the plains of *Australia Felix* projected onto the map of Victoria like an image from some memorable film strip. He watched himself reach a hand towards the waving grasses and scattered trees. But then a shadow fell on the map, and meaningless patches of light and darkness mottled his own skin. His outstretched arm had come between the source of light and the image he was after. And Nola herself might have been still behind him in the darkness.

* *

In the last week of the school year even the rowdiest pupils were quieter and more decorous. Each morning before classes, the room was locked and the blinds were pulled down while Mr Farrant wrote up their final tests on the board. In the afternoon, while their teacher marked their test-books at his table, the upper grades filed into the infant school on the other side of the folding doors and practised for their Christmas Tree. Mrs Farrant played the piano, the upper grades sang the carols, and a select few of the younger children went through the actions of their nativity scene. Lolling against the infant-room walls under loops of coloured paper chains, A. and his friends sensed that the year was approaching some sort of climax.

They knew, of course, that the Christmas Tree was nothing much. It took place on the evening of the very last school day. The folding doors were pushed back and the desks stacked in corners. The parents and children faced each other across an empty space with the man-sized pine branch in its painted oil drum at the centre. The presents, one for each child, were heaped under the tree. The men of the School Committee, who had paid for the presents, sat on chairs beside Mr Farrant and referred to him as the Master of Ceremonies.

A. and his friends endured the carols, the nativity scene, the speeches, and finally the handing out of presents, all for the sake of the quarter-hour at the end. Then, while the parents had their tea and cakes around the tree, the older boys slipped outside into the dark and scattered. They ran and blundered and stumbled through the school garden, swinging their fists at anyone blocking their way, and made for mysterious hiding places. And even while the slower ones were still running, the howling began.

A. had first heard it years before, when he was much too small to join in. The big fellows had howled at every Christmas Tree since, and A. had tried it with them as soon as he entered the upper grades. He had known better than to ask what the rules were – he would have been told brusquely by the howlers that there were no rules. But he had learned, over the years, what a howler had to do.

You had to hide as far from the others as possible so that no one saw you when you let out your howls. You need not actually howl, but you must not make human sounds – and certainly not words. You tried to howl (or yelp or roar or crow) in turn with the others. This was hard to manage in the darkness, but if you were patient and listened carefully you heard a remarkable effect – a long, almost rhythmic sequence of strange cries from near and far, with a place reserved for your own special call-sign.

A. was always glad just to find a corner for himself and to take part in the howling, but there were some who achieved much more. Some boys moved between one howl and another. They rather spoilt things if they stumbled noisily or showed themselves. But if they shifted their places unnoticed, you had a pleasant shock when their turn came. A howl that you had last heard from the end of the school-ground might ring out from behind a bush only a few paces away. Or a howl that you expected to come from nearby would reach you faintly from as far away as the pine plantation and leave you wondering how the bastard, whoever he was, had travelled such a distance between his howls.

Even the best howling sessions lasted only a few minutes. Then the school doors would open. The light from inside would spill out over the square of asphalt by the flagpole. Parents would come out to claim their younger children from the group of loiterers listening to the howling. The nearest of the howlers would creep in from the darkness and mingle with the family groups. Down past the pony paddock the farthest howlers soon noticed the gaps in the sequence and gave one last wild cry each and came quietly back. But A., whose parents were always the first to leave any gathering, had always climbed into the back of his father's utility still hearing one or two faint calls from the most daring of the howlers.

During each howling session A. tried to fix in his mind the strangest of the cries and the whereabouts, so far as he could judge, of the furthest howlers. He enjoyed the howling itself, but he looked forward to a far greater pleasure. He planned to question the others afterwards and to establish the exact routes followed by certain howlers across the dark schoolgrounds. If he could have learned enough, he would have drawn a detailed map showing the territory that each boy had seemed to claim when he stood in some unlikely spot and uttered his peculiar cry.

But A. had never been able to learn much more after howling than the little he knew from having been a howler himself. In bright daylight, with the same old paddocks around them, boys seemed reluctant to talk about the howling. They even seemed to dislike A.'s using glibly the word 'howling' as though they and he had taken part in some annual ceremony. They seemed to want to pretend that a few tough bastards had run out into the dark to show off and a few others had followed them – and that was all.

A. invited Nola Pomeroy to the howling. He knew she could take no part in it. Not even the toughest eighth-grader would have led a girl away into the dark while her parents were just inside the school building. And no girl would have wanted to behave like a mad dog while she was dressed up for the Christmas Tree. What A. had in mind was for Nola to stand quietly outside on the asphalt and keep her eyes open.

Afterwards she might tell him the directions that the other boys had taken when they rushed off into the darkness. Days after the howling she might sit with him over his map of the schoolgrounds and the pine plantation and the nearest paddocks, marking with dotted lines the beginnings of the routes of all the howlers she had spied on. He would add some of his own observations from the hectic few minutes when he had blundered among the shapes and shadows she could not have seen. She might correct him occasionally, because she had been better placed to appreciate the whole event. But when they could not agree on a certain point they might well have to draw alternative diagrams.

On the night itself Nola walked a few paces away from the schoolroom porch and stood with her back to the windows. The first of the howlers were already leaping the lavender bushes and dodging between the dahlia beds on their way to claim their stations in the darkness. But A. moved slowly and deliberately away from the brightness of the schoolroom. He wanted to be sure that Nola observed him setting off into the obscure landscape of the howlers. If she had wondered sometimes why he had never got around to taking her into a pocket of roadside bush after school, she might now realize that he had much stranger places in mind.

He turned for a moment, and the sight of her alone against the brightness of the school windows made him pause. All year she had stood with him in the cloakroom and watched journeys of explorers in the patterns of shadows from film strips. Now there was darkness over Sedgewick North and as much as they could imagine of the rest of Australia, and Nola had placed herself in front of the brightest light for miles. The shadow she made reached far across the schoolgrounds. It merged into the unlit territory where the howlers were already following mysterious routes to their separate bases.

A. was less anxious to run out among the howlers. He moved further away from the school building, but not to search for any hiding-place among the unfamiliar shapes of shrubs and fences. He paused at what seemed the boundary of the aura from the lighted window-panes. He wanted the girl behind him to make some movement or some sign that would suddenly alter the pattern of shadows around him. He wondered how much she might do to the scenery with just a gesture.

He looked back again. She was walking away; she was no longer between him and the light. And then the first howls were sounding, and he realized he had stood and wavered when he should have been running out into the dark to find his howling place.

It was too late for exploring. He dropped to the ground where he was. He wriggled and squirmed a little against the dry grass, thinking he might mark out with his body a place like a hare's that someone would stumble on and wonder about in the long, dreary days of the summer holidays.

The most notable of the howls that year could have come from anywhere. Once, it sounded so close that A. himself could have been held responsible. At other times it seemed to come from a place too far away for any boy to have reached. Someone was making the frantic bellow of a bull trying to get through a fence to a cow on heat. It was only the simple noise of an animal wanting no other landscape than the place where his female waited to be sniffed at and mounted. Yet out in the darkness it seemed to A., occasionally, something more.

BEVERLEY FARMER

Melpo

When I married Magda, Jimmy is thinking, all our family danced. We roasted kids and lambs in our whitewashed oven outside. We drank ouzo and new wine by the demijohn. The whole village was there. My mother had cooked everything. Cheese pies the size of cartwheels, meatballs, *pilafia* . . . In spring she picked nettles and dandelions and stewed them with rice, for Lent. In autumn she brewed thick jams from our apples and figs and windfall apricots. Tubs of yoghurt and cured cheese sat wrapped all day in blankets by our stove. On feast days an aged hen seethed, tawny and plump, in the pot. Until the Germans came, and then the Civil War.

The day I married Magda, my mother led the line of dancers holding the handkerchief, making her leaps and turns barefoot on the earth of our yard, by the light of kerosene lamps.

When our family planted out tobacco seedlings in the dry fields a long cart-ride from the village, we started at daybreak and rested in the heat of the afternoon under the oak trees at the spring. We ate hard bread, and cheese and olives, and drank spring water. Once when I was small I picked up a tortoise where it lumbered among pale clods of earth. It hissed, spurting hot urine on my hands. I dropped it, then picked it up again. *Mi, Dimitraki!* my old aunts shrieked in their black scarves. Melpo! *E*, Melpo! But my mother lay there with earthen feet, in shade as cold and thick as the spring water, fast asleep. My mother. Melpo . . .

'Now your mother wants to meet me,' Kerry is saying. 'Why now?'

Kerry looks taut, as if angry, Jimmy thinks; but she is only disconcerted. Flecked with brown, her pale face is blushing. A green glow off the water, wavering up, lights her bronze hair.

'Darling, she didn't say.'

'Well, why do you think she does?'

'She said so.'

'Yes, but why?'

'She didn't say.'

Jimmy, balancing his rod on the warm concrete of the pier, lies back, his head in Kerry's lap, his heavy eyes closed against the falling sun, the swathed still sea.

'You know she wouldn't hear of it before.'

'She asked me your name again and said, "Dimitri, you sure you want to marry this woman? Really marry, in our church?" '

'And what did you say?'

'Kerry.'

'Oh yes.'

'And yes, Mama, really marry.'

'What have you told her about me?'

'Nothing much. Red hair, I said. Australian, not Greek. Divorced, with one son called Ben. A teacher of maths at the same school where I teach Greek and –'

'Did you say anything about the baby?'

'No. Not yet.'

'Well, I'm not showing yet.'

'No.' He hesitates. 'Eleni and Voula have not told her either. I asked them.'

'They *know*?'

'Well, yes. I told *them*, they're my sisters. They said they'd guessed, anyway.'

'Oh, come on.'

'Yes. When they met you at the dance. They like to think they can always tell. They are pleased. A daddy at forty-five, they keep saying. Better late than never. They like you. How about after school on Thursday? Is that all right? Nothing formal. Just in and out.'

'All right.'

'You're blushing.'

'I'm nervous.'

'Try out your Greek on her.'

'I hope you're joking.'

'Me? I never joke.'

'You said she speaks English!'

'She does. She even makes us look words up for her. She hardly ever speaks Greek now, strangely enough. But very broken English. Nothing like mine. Mine is not bad, after only twenty years here. Would you not agree?'

'For a quiet life, why not?'

Shafts of sunlight are throbbing through the water as outspread fingers do, in fan-shapes.

'She wants to meet you now,' he sighs, 'because she is dying.'

'Oh! You've told her!'

'She wanted to know. I think she knew, anyway. Don't be shocked when you see her. She is wasting away, and her mind wanders. I wish you could have known her when she was young. Her life has been – *martyrio*. *Martyrio*, you know?'

'Martyrdom?'

'Yes. Martyrdom.'

'Because of the War?'

'Oh, yes, the War. Many things. The War was the worst. I was only about eight then. My sisters were too little to help. Our baby brother was sick. We were evacuated from our village. My father was a prisoner. Can you imagine it? His mother, my Yiayia Eleni, minded the little ones. I sold cigarettes, razor blades, *koulouria* – those rolls like quoits with sesame? – on the streets all day. My mother did cleaning, sewing, washing for rich women, to feed us all. But we were starving.'

'Can you remember so far back?'

'Of course. Everything. One night I remember my mother was mending by the kerosene lamp in the warehouse we were living in, in Thessaloniki. My grandmother put her hand on her shoulder.

' "Melpo," she said. "It is time you thought of yourself."

'My mother lifted her red eyes but said nothing.

' "You are young. Your whole life is ahead of you. And what about your children?"

' "Mama," my mother answered. "Don't say this."

' "It is what I would do. He is my own son, my only son. But it is what you will have to do sooner or later. He will manage somehow, he is a man. Think of yourself as a widow,

Melpo. The War will go on for years. You are still beautiful. There are good men who will help you. It is not a sin. You have no money, no home, no food. I mean what I am saying."

' "No. Your son believes in me and I have always deserved it. I always will."

'Yiayia shook her scarved head and said nothing more. Her eyelids were wet. My mother went on sewing. My baby brother cried out and I rocked and hushed him back to sleep. When I looked back, my mother was still and sagging over her work, so Yiayia took it away and laid her down to sleep and pulled the flour sack over her. She saw me watching, and hugged me.

' "*Aman, paidaki mou*," she wailed, but quietly. "You must be the man of the family now."

' "I know, Yiayia," I said. "I am already." '

He lies still. Kerry bends over and kisses his brown forehead. 'I'm nervous,' she says again. Her long soft breasts nudge his ears. He feels her shiver. The gold spokes of sun have gone out of the water, leaving it black.

'Don't be.'

'Have we known each other long enough? Can we be sure? Long enough to get married?'

'Well, let me see. How long is it?'

'Ten months. No, eleven.'

'Is it eleven months?' He smiles. 'That sounds enough.'

'What will your mother think?'

'That we should wait. But I don't want to. You don't, do you?'

'No. She might like me, you never know.'

'Yes. Don't be too hard on her, will you, if she is rude? And by the way, better don't wear pants.'

'Pardon?'

'Pants. Trousers? Overalls? "Womans should wear only dresses." '

'Oh God!'

'It is her old age.'

'I don't have a dress. Or a skirt. I don't *own* one.'

'Oh. Well, never mind. Don't look like that. No, listen.' He sits up, agitated. 'Forget I said it. She can hardly see. Glaucoma.'

'What flowers does she like?'
'Oh, anything.'
'Roses?'
'Yes. Fine.'
'Oh God! I hope we come through this!'
'Darling, of course we will.'
'Do you love me?'
'Yes, of course. *Kouragio!*'

She grins back at him, pushing her fingers through the shaggy grey curls at his temples. Shadow lies all over the bay and the far city. High above, a gull hangs and sways, silent, its red legs folded, still deeply sunlit.

*

Eleni and Voula, exchanging looks, have served Kerry iced water, a dish of tough green figs in syrup, a glass of Marsala, then Turkish coffee. They have exclaimed over her roses and argued amiably about vases. Flustered, Kerry waits, avoiding Jimmy's eyes. She feels gruff and uncouth, awkward. A bell rings three times in another room. '*Pane*, Dimitri,' Eleni hisses. Jimmy bounds away. Kerry grins blindly at the sisters.

When he comes back and leads her to his mother's room, hot behind brown blinds and stinking of disinfectant, she misses the old woman at first among the jumbled laces and tapestries, the grey and golden faces under glass: a skull on a lace pillow, mottled, and tufted with white down. Only her thick eyes move, red-rimmed, loose in their pleated lids.

'Dimitri?' The voice a hoarse chirrup. 'This is Keri?'

'Kerry, yes. I'm glad to meet you, Mrs Yannakopoulou.'

'Good. Thank you for the roses.' Rumpled already, they sag in dim porcelain, mirrored. '*Keri* is candle in our language. *Keri* is wox.'

'Wax, Mama.'

'Yairs. Wox for candle. Dimitri, *agori mou*, put the lamp, I carn see Keri. Now leave us alone. We tok woman to woman.'

The door closes. Yellow folds of her cheeks move. She is slowly smiling.

'*Katse*, Keri, siddown.' Kerry sits in the cane armchair by the bed. 'My daughters they tell me about you.'

'They're very nice.'

'Yairs. They like you. They say good thinks about you. She hev a good heart, this *filenada* of Dzimmy, they say. She love him too much. She good mother for her little boy. Where your husband is, Keri?'

'My ex-husband. In Queensland, as far as I know. We aren't in touch.'

'Why he leave you? He hev another womans?'

'I don't know. He's been gone years.'

'You doan know?'

'No, Mrs Yannakopoulou.'

'You were very yunk.'

'Twenty-two. My son is nine.'

'How old you say?'

'Nine. *Ennea*.'

'Ach! You speak Greek!'

'I'm learning.'

'Yairs. Is very hard lenguage. How old you are, Keri?'

'Thirty.'

'Thirty. Yairs. You too old to learn Greek.'

'Oh, I'll manage. *Echo kouragio*.'

'*Kouragio*! Ah bravo.' A giggle shakes the bedcovers. 'Good. You will need *thet*, if you love Dimitri. He is quiet man. Mysterious. Always he joke. You will need to be stronk. You are, yairs. Not *oraia*, that doesun mutter. How you say?'

'*Oraia*? Beautiful. I know I'm not.'

'Better not. You not uckly. Too *oraia* no good. They fall in love with they own faces. They mek the men jealoust.' A smile bares the wires around her loose eyeteeth. 'Lonk time now Dimitri tellink me: this woman, this Keri, Mama, I want you to meet her. Keri? I say. Her name Kyriaki? No, he say, she Australian woman, she not Greek. Not Greek, Dimitri? I doan want to meet her. But he keep saying please, Mama. Orright, I say. If you thinkink to merry her, orright. Because now I hev not lonk time to live.'

'Oh, Mrs Yannakopoulou –'

'Orright. Is not secret. Everybody know.' Her hand clamps Kerry's arm. 'And before I go on my lonk, my eternity trip, I want to see my boy heppy. That is all I want now. My boy to be heppy.'

'Yes, well –'

'You are also mother. You hev a mother heart. You want what is best for your boy. You do anythink for him?'

'Yes, but –'

'You good woman. Good-heart woman. You hev *kouragio*. So mek me one favour. For *my* boy.'

'What?'

'Tell Dimitri you woan merry him. You love him. Orright. I understend love. Love him. Look after him. Live with him, orright. *Aman*. Doan merry him.'

Kerry pulls her arm away. The lamp casts a wet light on the ravelled cheeks and throat.

'So I'm not good enough.'

'You *good*. I doan say thet. But divorce woman. Not for Dimitri, no. Not for merry.'

'But he's divorced!'

'Doesun mutter. Is different. She *putana*, thet woman. He love her too much, but she go with our neighbour, our enemy. Is shame for all our family. We come to Australia for new life. Is not Dimitri fault.'

'Yes, I know. He told me.'

'Hwat he tell you?'

'It was twenty *years* ago.'

'His heart *break*. Some children they find them one night together in the pear orchard: Magda with our enemy. They mother tell me. Dimitri was away. When Magda come home, I tok to her, I tell her I know, all the village know. I cry for my poor son. He will kill you, I say. She cry, she scream. She say she waitink baby. I say we want no *bastardo* in our family. I pack all her *proika*. I say, go and never come back. When he come home, *I* tell Dimitri.'

The scaled eyes close, wet-rimmed. Kerry sighs.

'He told me about it. My divorce wasn't my fault either. And I don't play around.'

'For Dimitri next time should be only *parthena*. Veergin.'

'Isn't that up to Dimitri?'

'Is up to *you* now. You know thet, Keri. You can say no. Say *wait*.'

'And then what?'

'I know Greek girls of good femilies –'

'No. You tried that before. He told me. He wasn't interested, was he? Why arrange a marriage these days? I love Jimmy. We want to get married fairly soon. I'm going to have a baby. Jimmy's baby.'

'Hwat? You waitink baby?'

'Yes.'

'Hwen?'

'August.'

'August. I understend now.'

'So you see –'

'You should be *shame!*'

'Ashamed of a baby? Why, what's wrong with it? We aren't living in the Dark Ages. Jimmy's very happy. He likes kids. Ben adores him. He'll be a good father.'

'I understend now why he want to merry you. *Apo filotimo!* For honour. Because you trick him.'

'No. That isn't true.'

'You know hwat womans can do if they doan want baby. You know.'

'I *do* want the baby. So does he. You have no right –'

'I hev the right of mother. The right of mother who will die soon! My only livink son! Doan break my heart!'

Kerry, her face hot, pats the writhing yellow hands and stands up.

'I'd better go, Mrs Yannakopoulou. I'm sorry.'

'Wait! Listen to me: I hev money. Yes, I hev. They doan know nothink. Inside the bed.' She claws at the mattress. 'Gold pounds! Hwere they are? Take them. Hev the baby. Leave Dimitri alone. Hwere they are?'

'No, thanks.' Kerry pulls a wry face. 'I'm sorry about all this. And I was hoping you'd like me.'

The old woman is moaning. Her eyes and mouth clamp shut, and she starts shaking. Kerry shuts the door softly on the dense lamplight and goes on tiptoe to the kitchen. It is full of shrill chatter. Saucepans hiss, bouncing their lids, gushing sunlit steam. All over the table sprawl glowing red and green peppers ready to be stuffed. Jimmy, Eleni, Voula, and three children, all suddenly silent, stare with identical eyes like dates; stare up in alarm.

'Someone better go to her. Quickly.'

The sisters hurry off.

'Darling, what's wrong? What happened?'

'Ask your mother. Can you take me home?'

'Of course. Just let's wait till she –'

'It's all right, I'll get a tram. Will you come round later, though, please?'

'Yes, of course. Unless she –'

'Look, if it's all off, fair enough. But you're not to punish me. I *wasn't* hard on her.'

'Oh Kerry, punish? Why would it be all off?'

The children are gazing open-mouthed.

'She'll tell you.'

'You tell me.'

Kerry shakes her head, reddening.

'You are punishing *me*! Why are you angry?'

'Oh, later!'

The bell rings three times. Jimmy pounds down the passage.

'Mama?' His voice breaks. 'Mama?'

'Leave me alone, all of you. And you, go with your *putana*. Leave me alone.' She struggles to turn to the shadowed wall. *'To fos. Kleis' to fos.'*

He turns off the lamp and ushers his sisters out, though they linger, he knows, whispering behind the door.

'She had to go home.'

'Good!'

'Min klais, Mamaka.' He smooths her sodden hair. 'No, Don't cry. Don't cry. No. No.'

'Give me a tablet. No, this ones. Water.' He slips his arm behind her knobbled back as she gulps, flinching. 'Ach. *Pikro einai.* Bitter.'

'Tell me what happened.'

But she is silent. He picks up the photograph on her dresser. It is one of the last photographs of his father. His father is sitting in the doorway, feeding Eleni's two little daughters spoonfuls of bread and milk. They coaxed him in baby talk for *paparitsa*. It was his *paparitsa*, not theirs. It was all he could eat by then. A white hen is tiptoeing past them.

Wheat was heaped in the long room that year, a great trickling tawny mountain; the barn was too full already of barley and sesame. The best harvest since the War, his father said. Bravo, Dimitri. None of them has seen the hen yet. In the light at the door they are like three shadow puppets on a screen. He alone looks frayed, dim, melting in the air. His death is near. He regrets, Dimitri thinks, that I have had no children. No grandchild of my sowing, no grandson to bear his name. Still, he is smiling.

In the photograph the bread and milk bowl is white. In fact it was butter yellow and, catching the light, glowed in his father's hands like a harvest moon.

'Mama?' he says softly.

'*Nai.*'

'Tell me what happened.'

'She can tell you.'

'*Ela. Pes mou.*'

'This Keri. She hev not the right name. She not wox. Wox? She stone. Iron.'

'Why?'

'You want *her*? Hwat for? She not yunk. Not *oraia*. Not Greek. Not rich. For *proika* she hev hwat? A boy. A big boy. She zmok.'

'No.' He grins. 'She doesn't.'

'Australian womans they all zmok. Puff poof. Puff poof.'

'Kerry doesn't.'

'Dimitraki, listen to me. I know you like I know my hand. You my son. You doan love Keri.' She hesitates, then dares: 'Not like you love Magda.'

'Leave Magda out of it.'

'Thet time I save you.'

'Magda is gone. I was too young then. Forget Magda. I love Kerry now.'

'She waitink baby.'

'Yes.'

'Why you doan tok? You should be tell me this, not Keri. Is too big shock.' She sighs. 'If is your baby.'

'It is.'

'How you know? She maybe trick you. Australian womans –'

'Mama, I know.'

'*How* you know? Divorce woman!'

'Mama, I love Kerry. I trust Kerry. I need Kerry. All right?'

'*Thet* is how?' He is silent. 'You engry?'

'No.'

'Yes. You engry with me.'

'No. You will see in August if it is or not.'

'*Aman*, Dimitri,' she moans.

'Enough, Mama, now.'

'Orright, enough. Enough. Merry her, then. I am too tired for fight. Do hwat you want. But you wronk, you know?'

He waits.

'I hope so she hev a boy. For the name, your Baba name. Is good for his name to live. August, *aman*! You think I livink thet long, to see your little boy?'

'Mama, you will.' He squeezes her hand. 'My little girl, maybe. My little Melpo.'

''*Ochi*. If is girl, I doan want the name Melpo.'

'Kerry does.'

'Tell Keri if is girl, she must not call her Melpo.'

'You tell her. Next time she comes.'

'I *never* see her again.'

'Ah, Mamaka.'

'No. Sometime you askink *too* much.'

'You know,' he sighs, 'that if I have a girl, I will call her Melpo.'

'I doan want you to!'

'You do so.'

'*Aman*, Dimitri *mou*. Put me *rodostamo*.'

He tips red rosewater into his palm and sits stroking it over her cheeks and forehead and whimpering throat, the thin loose spotted skin of her forearms.

'Her heart is stone.'

'No. She is strong. Like you, she has had to be.'

'She will control your life, you want thet?'

'I *think* I can get used to it.'

'Well. I done my best. I hope so you woan be sorry, you know?'

'Thank you, Mama.'

He bends and kisses her ruffled cheek. Her eyes close.

'*Ela pio konta*,' she whispers. 'Closer. I have gold pounds inside the bed. Your Aunt Sophia's. Ach, if I had them in the War! The baby died from hunger. Take them, *paidi mou*. Doan tell the girls. Take them for your baby.'

'*Aman*, Mama. You and your gold pounds. You gave them to Magda. You drove her away. And I forgave you, Remember?'

'For your good. For honour.'

But only after years, Mama, he thinks. Bitter years.

'Sleep,' he says.

'I carn. I pain too much. Go and tell Eleni to come. Bring a clean sheet, tell her. When she goes, come back. Sit with me.'

'Can I do anything?'

'Nothink. Maybe Keri waitink you?'

'She will understand.'

'No. Go to her. When I was yunk, I was stronk. My God. Remember? And *oraia* also.'

'I know. There was not a woman like you in all Makedonia. You had a spirit like fire.'

'Hold my hend, Dimitri.'

One day when you are not tired, Mama, he thinks, I must ask you: do you remember the storm, that last summer in the village, before the War when I was five? You sat on the porch in this cane armchair suckling Eleni. The rain was a grey wall. Hens shot past us slithering in the brown mud. The clouds were slashed by lightning and by spokes of sunlight. Afterwards I led the horse out, fighting to hold his head down, but he tore at the grapevine, splashing rain in clusters on us all. White-eyed, his dark silver hide shivering, he munched vine leaves. I was angry. You laughed so much, Eleni lost your nipple, and kicked and wailed. Then I laughed too.

Remember how we stood in the river thigh-deep, slipping on bronze rocks. You taught me to catch little fish in my hands. We threaded them on the green stalks of water plants.

A Man In The Laundrette

She never wants to disturb him but she has to sometimes, as this room in which he studies and writes and reads is the only way in and out of his apartment. Now that he has got up to make coffee in the kitchen, though, she can put on her boots and coat and rummage in the wardrobe for the glossy black garbage bag where they keep their dirty clothes, and not be disturbing him. 'I'll only be an hour or two,' she says quickly when he comes back in. She holds up the bag to show why.

'Are you sure?' His eyebrows lift. 'It must be my turn by now.' They were scrupulous about such matters when she first moved in.

'I'm sure. I must get out more. Meet the people.' She shrugs at his stare. 'I want to see what I can of life in the States, after all.'

'Not to be with me.'

She smiles. 'Of course to be with you. You know that.'

'I thought you had a story you wanted to finish.'

'I had. It's finished. You know you don't have time to go, and I like going.'

He stands there unsmiling, holding the two mugs. 'I made you a coffee,' he says.

'Thanks.' She perches on the bed and drinks little scalding sips while, turned in his chair, he stares out at the sky.

His window is above the street and on brighter afternoons than this it catches the whole heavy sun as it goes down. He always works in front of the window but facing the wall, a dark profile.

He says, 'Look how dark it's getting.'

'It's just clouds,' she says. 'It's only a little after three.'

'Still. Why today? Saturday.'

'Why not? That's your last shirt.'

'It's mostly my clothes, I suppose.' It always is. She washes hers in the bathroom basin and hangs them on the pipes. He has never said that this bothers him; but then she has never asked. He shrugs. 'You don't know your way round too well. That's all.'

'I do! Enough for the laundrette.'

'Well. Okay. You've got Fred's number?'

She nods. Fred, who lives on the floor above, has the only telephone in the building and is sick of having to fetch his neighbours to take calls. She rang Fred's number once. She gets up without finishing her coffee.

'Okay. Take care.' He settles at the table with his back turned to her and to the door and to his bed in which she sleeps at night even now, lying with the arm that shades her eyes chilled and stiff, sallowed by the lamp, while he works late. Sighing, he switches this lamp on now and holds his coffee up to it in both hands, watching the steam fray.

Quietly she shuts the door.

The apartment houses have lamps on already under their green awnings. They are old three-storey brick mansions, red ivy shawling them. Old elms all the way along his street are golden leaved and full of quick squirrels: the air is bright with leaves falling. The few clumps that were left this morning of the first snow of the season have all dripped away now. As she comes down the stoop a cold wind throws leaves over her, drops of rain as sharp as snow prickle her face. The wind shuffles her and her clumsy bag around the corner, under the viaduct, down block after weedy block of the patched bare roadway. The laundrette seems further away than it should be. Has she lost her way? No, there it is at last on the next corner: DK's Bar and Laundrette. With a shudder, slamming the glass door behind her, she seals herself in the warm steam and rumble, and looks round.

There are more people here than ever before. Saturday would be a busy day, she should have known that. Everywhere solemn grey-haired black couples are sitting in silence side by side, their hands folded. Four small black girls with pigtails and ribbons erect on their furrowed scalps give her gap-toothed smiles. A scowling fat white woman is the only other white. All the washers are going. Worse, the coins in her pocket turn out not to be quarters but Australian coins, useless. All she has in US currency is a couple of dollar notes. There is a hatch for change with a buzzer in one wall, opening, she remembers, into a back room of the bar; but no one answers it when she presses the buzzer. Too shy to ask anyone there for the change, she hurries out to ask in DK's Bar instead. In the dark room into which she falters, wind-whipped, her own head meets her afloat among lamps in mirrors. Eyes in smoky booths turn and stare. She waits, fingering her dollar notes, but no one goes behind the bar. She creeps out again. The wind shoves her into the laundrette.

This time she keeps on pressing and pressing the buzzer until a voice bawls, 'Aw, *shit*,' and the hatch thuds open on the usual surly old Irishman in his grey hat.

'Hul*lo*!' Her voice sounds too bright. 'I thought you weren't *here*!' She hands him her two dollars.

'Always here.' He flicks his cigarette. 'Big fight's on cable.' A roar from the TV set and he jerks away, slapping down her eight quarters, slamming the hatch.

She is in luck. A washer has just been emptied and no one else is claiming it. Red-faced, she tips her clothes in. Once she has got the washer churning she sits on a chair nearby with her garbage bag, fumbling in it for her writing pad and pen. She always writes in the laundrette.

She never wants to disturb him, she scrawls on a new page, *but she has to sometimes, as this room in which he studies and writes and reads is the only way in and out of his apartment.*

A side door opens for a moment on to the layered smoke of the bar. A young black man, hefty in a padded jacket, lurches out almost on top of her and stands swaying. His stained white jeans come closer each time to her bent head. She edges away.

Now that he has got up to make coffee in the kitchen, though, she can put on her boots and coat and rummage in the wardrobe for the glossy black garbage bag where they keep their dirty clothes, and not be disturbing him.

'Pretty handwriting,' purrs a voice in her ear. When she stares up, he smiles. Under his moustache he has front teeth missing, and one eyetooth is a furred brown stump. 'What's *that* say?' A pale fingernail taps her pad.

'Uh, nothing.'

'*Show* me.' He flaps the pad over. Its cover is a photograph of the white-hooded Opera House. 'Sydney, Australia,' he spells out. 'You from Australia?'

'Yes.'

'Stayin' long?'

'Just visiting.'

'I *said* are you stayin' *long*?'

'No.'

'Don' like the U-nited States.'

She shrugs. 'It's time I went home.'

'Home to Australia. Well now. My teacher were from Australia, my music teacher. She were a nice Australian lady. She got me into the Yale School of Music.' He waits.

'That's good.' She gives him a brief smile, hunching over her writing pad.

'I'll only be an hour or two,' she says quickly when he comes back in. She holds up the bag to show why.

'Are you sure?' His eyebrows lift. 'It must be my turn by now.'

'What you writin'?'

'A story.'

'Story, huh? I write songs. I'm a musician. I was four years at the Yale School of Music. That's *good*, is it?' He thrusts his face close to hers and she smells rotting teeth and fumes of something – bourbon, perhaps, or rum. So that's what it is: he is drunk. He has a bunched brown paper bag with a bottle in it, which he unscrews with difficulty and wags at her. 'Have some.' She shakes her head. Shrugging, he throws his head back to swallow, chokes and splutters on the floor. He wipes his lips on the back of his hand, glaring round. Everyone is carefully not looking. One small black girl snorts and they all fall into giggles. He bows to them.

'I work in a piana bar, you listenin', hey *you*, I ain' talkin' to myself.' She looks up. 'That's *bet*ter. My mother and father own it so you wanna hear me sing I get you in for free. Hey, you wanna hear me sing or don't you?' She nods. 'All *right*.' What he sings in a slow, hoarse tremolo sounds like a spiritual, though the few words she picks up make no sense. The black girls writhe. The couples sitting in front of the dryers exchange an unwilling smile and shake of the head.

'You like that, huh?' She nods. 'She *like* that. Now I sing you all another little number I wrote, I write all my own numbers and I call this little number Calypso Blues.' Then he sings more, as far as she can tell, of the same song.

They were scrupulous about such matters when she first moved in.

'I'm sure. I must get out more. Meet the people.' She shrugs at his stare. 'I want to see what I can of life in the States, after all.'

'Like that one? My mother and father – *hey* – they real rich peoples, ain' just the piana bar, they got three houses. Trucks. Boats too. I don' go along with that shit. Ownin' things, makin' money, that's all shit. What you say your name was? Hey, *you*. You hear me talkin' to you?'

'Uh, Anne,' she lies, her head bowed.

'Pretty.' He leans over to finger her hair. 'Long yeller hair. Real . . . pretty.'

'Don't.'

' "I want to see what I can of life in the States after" – after *what*?'

'*All*.' She crams the pad into her garbage bag.

'You sha' or somethin'?'

'What?'

'You sha'? You deaf or somethin'? You *shacked*?'

'Oh! Shacked? Shacked – yes, I am. Yes.' She keeps glancing at the door. The first few times that it was her turn to do the laundry he came along anyway after a while, smiling self-consciously, whispering, 'I missed you.' But not today, she knows. She stares at somebody's clothes flapping and soaring in a dryer. She could take hers home wet, though they would be heavy: but then this man might follow her home.

'So where you live?'

'Never mind,' she mutters.

'What's that?'

'I don't *know*. Oh, down the road.'

'Well, you can tell me.'

'No, I'd – I don't *know* its name.'

'I just wanna talk to you – *Anne*. I just wanna be friends.

You don' wanna be friends, that what you sayin'? You think I got somethin' nasty in my mind, well, I think *you* do.' He snorts. 'My lady she a white lady like you an' let me tell *you* you ain' nothin' alongside of her. *You* ain' *nothin'*.'

She stares down. He prods her arm. 'Don't,' she says.

'Don' what?'

'Just don't.'

'Hear me, bitch?'

'Don't talk to me like that.'

'Oh, don' talk to you like that? I wanna talk to you, I talk to you how I like, don't you order *me* roun' tell me how I can talk to you.' He jabs his fist at her shoulder then holds it against her ear. 'Go on, look out the door. Expectin' somebody?'

'My friend's coming.'

'Huh. She expectin' her *friend*.' The couples look back gravely. 'My brothers they all gangsters,' he shouts, 'an' one word from me gets anybody I *want* killed. We gonna kill them *all*.' He is sweaty and shaking now. 'We gonna kill them and dig them up and kill them all *over* again. Trouble with you, Miss Australia, you don' like the black peoples, that's trouble with you. Well we gonna kill you *all*.' He drinks and gasps, licking his lips.

The door opens. She jumps up. With a whoop the wind pushes in two Puerto Rican couples with garbage bags. Leaves and papers come rattling over the floor to her feet. One of the Puerto Ricans buzzes and knocks at the hatch for change, but no one opens it; in the end they pool what quarters they find in their pockets, start their washers and sit in a quiet row on a table. Her machine has stopped now. There is a dryer free. She throws the tangled clothes in, twists two quarters in the slot and sits hunched on another chair to wait.

He has lost her. He spits into the corner, staggering, wiping his sweat with a sleeve, then begs a cigarette from the sullen white woman, who turns scornfully away without a word. 'Bitch,' he growls: a jet of spit just misses her boot. One of the Puerto Ricans offers him an open pack. Mumbling, he picks one, gets it lit, splutters it out and squats shakily to pick it up out of his splash of spit. He sucks smoke in, sighs it out. Staring round, he finds her again and stumbles over. 'Where you get to?' He coughs smoke in her face. His bottle is empty: not a drop comes out when he tips it up over his mouth. 'God*dam*,' he wails, and lets it drop on the floor where it smashes. 'Goddam mothers, you all givin' me *shit*!'

'No one doin' that,' mutters a wrinkled black man.

He has swaggered up close, his fly almost touching her forehead. '*Don't*,' she says despairingly.

'Don't, don't. Why not? I like you, Miss Australia.' He gives a wide grin. 'Gotta go next door for a minute. Wanna come? No? Okay. Don' nobody bother her now. Don't nobody interfere. She *my* lady.'

He stumbles to the side door and opens it on a darkness slashed with red mirrors. Once the door shuts the black couples slump and sigh. One old woman hustles the little black girls out on to the street. An old man leans forward and says, 'He your friend, miss?'

'No! I've never seen him before.'

The old man and his wife roll their eyes, their faces netting with anxious wrinkles. 'You better watch out,' he says.

'What if he follows me home?'

They nod. 'He a load of trouble, that boy. Oh, his poor mother.'

'Maybe he'll stay in there and won't come back?' she says.

'Best thing is you call a cab, go on home. They got a pay phone here.'

'Oh, *where*?'

'In the bar.'

'*Where!*'

The side door slams open, then shut, and they all sit back guiltily. She huddles, not looking round. Her clothes float down in the dryer, so she opens it and stoops into the hot dark barrel to pick them out, tangled still and clinging to each other. Suddenly he is bending over her, his hands braced on the wall above the dryer, his belly thrust hard against her back. She twists angrily out from under him, clutching hot shirts.

'Now stop that! That's enough!'

'Not for me it ain', not yet.'

'Leave me alone!'

'I wanna talk. Wanna talk to you.'

'No! Go away!' She crams the clothes into her garbage bag.

'Hey, you not well, man,' mumbles the old black. 'Better go on home now. Go on home.'

'Who you, man, you gonna tell *me* what to do?' He throws a wide punch and falls to the floor. With a shriek of rage and terror the old woman runs to the side door and pounds on it. It slaps open, just missing her, and two white men tumble in.

'Okay,' one grunts. 'What's trouble here?'

'Where you *been*? You supposed to keep *order*!' she wails, and the old man hushes her. The young man is on his knees, shaking his frizzy head with both his hands.

With gestures of horrified embarrassment to everyone she sees watching her, she swings the glass door open on to the dim street. A man has followed her: one of the two Puerto Ricans. 'Is okay. I see you safe home,' he says, and slings her bag over his shoulder.

'Oh, thank you! But your wife's still in there.'

'My brother is there.' He takes her arm, almost dragging her away.

'He was so drunk,' she says. 'What made him act like that. I mean, why me?'

His fine black hair flaps in the wind. 'You didn't handle him right,' he says.

'What's *right*?'

'You dunno. Everybody see that. Just whatever you did, you got the guy mad, you know?'

They are far enough away to risk looking back. He is out on the road, his body arched, yelling at three white men: the old Irishman in the hat has joined the other two and they are barring his way at the door of the laundrette. There is something of forebearance, even of compunction, in their stance. 'They'll leave him alone, won't they?' she asks.

He nods. 'Looks like they know him.'

He has seen her all the way to the corner before she can persuade him, thanking him fervently, that she can look after herself from here on. He stands guard in the wind, his white face uneasily smiling whenever she turns to grin and wave him on. The wind thrashes her along their street. In the west the clouds are fraying, letting a glint of light through, but the streetlamps are coming on already with a milky fluttering, bluish-white, among the gold tossings of the elms.

A squirrel on their fence fixes one black resentful eye on her: it whirls and stands erect, its hands folded and its muzzle twitching, until abruptly it darts away, stops once to look back, and the silver spray of its tail follows it up an elm.

The lamp is on in his window – none of the windows in these streets has curtains – and he is still in front of it, a shadow. She fumbles with her key. Rushing in, she disturbs him.

'Am I late? Sorry! There was this terrible man in the laundrette.' Panting, she leans against the dim wall to tell him the story. Halfway through she sees that his face is stiff and grey.

'You're thinking I brought it on myself.'

'Didn't you?'

'By going out, you mean? By not wanting to be rude?' He stares. 'No, you wouldn't.'

'What did I do that was wrong?'

'A man can always tell if a woman fancies him.'

'Infallibly?' He shrugs. 'I led him on, is that what you mean?'

'Didn't you?'

'Why would I?'

'You can't seem to help it.'

'Why do you think that?'

'I've seen you in action.'

'*When?*'

'Whenever you talk to a man, it's there.'

'This is sick,' she says. He shakes his head. 'Well, *what's* there?' But he turns back without a word to the lamplit papers on his table.

Shivering, she folds his shirts on the wooden settle in the passage, hangs up his trousers, pairs his socks. Her few things she drops into her suitcase, open on the floor of the wardrobe; she has never properly unpacked. Now she never will. There is no light in this passage, at one end of which is his hood of yellow lamplight and at the other the twin yellow bubbles of hers, wastefully left on while she was out. The tall windows behind her lamps are nailed shut. A crack in one glitters like a blade. Wasps dying of the cold have nested in the shaggy corners. In the panes, as in those of his window, only a greyness like still water is left of the day.

But set at eye level in the wall of the passage where she is standing with her garbage bag is a strip of window overgrown with ivy, one small casement of which she creeps up at night from his bed to prise open, and he later to close: and here a slant of sun strikes. Leaves all the colours of fire flicker and tap the glass.

'Look. You'd think it was stained glass, wouldn't you? Look,' she is suddenly saying aloud. 'I'll never forget this window.'

He could be a statue or the shadow of one, a hard edge to the lamplight. He gives no sign of having heard.

Wasps are slithering, whining over her window panes. One comes bumbling in hesitant orbits round her head. It has yellow legs and rasps across her papers jerking its long ringed belly. She slaps it with a newspaper and sweeps it on to the floor, afraid to touch it in case a dead wasp can still sting, if you touch the sting. Then she sits down at the table under the lamps with her writing pad and pen and scrawls on, though her hand, she sees, is shaking.

'Not to be with me.'

She smiles. 'Of course to be with you. You know that.'

'I thought you had a story you wanted to finish.'

'I had. It's finished.'

HELEN GARNER

The Life of Art

My friend and I went walking the dog in the cemetery. It was a Melbourne autumn: mild breezes, soft air, gentle sun. The dog trotted in front of us between the graves. I had a pair of scissors in my pocket in case we came across a rose bush on a forgotten tomb.

'I don't like roses,' said my friend. 'I despise them for having thorns.'

The dog entered a patch of ivy and posed there. We pranced past the Elvis Presley memorial.

'What would you like to have written on your grave,' said my friend, 'as a tribute?'

I though for a long time. Then I said, *'Owner of two hundred pairs of boots.'*

When we had recovered, my friend pointed out a head-stone which said, *She lived only for others.* 'Poor thing,' said my friend. 'On *my* grave I want you to write, *She lived only for herself.'*

We went stumbling along the overgrown paths.

*

My friend and I had known each other for twenty years, but we had never lived in the same house. She came back from Europe at the perfect moment to take over a room in the house I rented. It became empty because the man – but that's another story.

*

My friend has certain beliefs which I have always secretly categorised as *batty*. Sometimes I have thought, 'My friend is what used to be called "a dizzy dame".' My friend believes in reincarnation: not that this in itself is unacceptable to me. Sometimes she would write me long letters from wherever she was in the world, letters in her lovely, graceful, sweeping hand, full of tales from one or other of her precious lives, tales to explain her psychological makeup and behaviour in her present incarnation. My eye would fly along the lines, sped by embarrassment.

*

My friend is a painter.

*

When I first met my friend she was engaged. She was wearing an antique sapphire ring and Italian boots. Next time I saw her, in Myers, her hand was bare. I never asked. We were students then. We went dancing in a club in South Yarra. The boys in the band were students too. We fancied them, but at twenty-two we felt ourselves to be older women, already fading, almost predatory. We read *The Roman Spring of Mrs Stone*. This was in 1965; before feminism.

*

My friend came off the plane with her suitcase. 'Have you ever noticed,' she said, 'how Australian men, even in their forties, dress like small boys? They wear shorts and thongs and little stripy T-shirts.'

*

A cat was asleep under a bush in our back yard each morning when we opened the door. We took him in. My friend and I fought over whose lap he would lie in while we watched TV.

*

My friend is tone deaf. But she once sang *'Blue Moon'*, verses and chorus, in a talking, tuneless voice in the back of a car going up the Punt Road hill and down again and over the river, travelling north; and she did not care.

*

My friend lived as a student in a house near the university. Her bed was right under the window in the front room downstairs. One afternoon her father came to visit. He tapped on the door. When no one answered he looked through the window. What he saw caused him to stagger back into the fence. It was a kind of heart attack, my friend said.

*

My friend went walking in the afternoons near our house. She came out of lanes behind armfuls of greenery. She found vases in my dusty cupboards. The arrangements she made with the leaves were stylish and generous-handed.

*

Before either of us married, I went to my friend's house to help her paint the bathroom. The paint was orange, and so was the cotton dress I was wearing. She laughed because all she could see of me when I stood in the bathroom were my limbs and my head. Later, when it got dark, we sat at her kitchen table and she rolled a joint. It was the first dope I had ever seen or smoked. I was afraid that a detective might look through the kitchen window. I could not understand why my friend did not pull the curtain across. We walked up to Genevieve in the warm night and ate two bowls of spaghetti. It seemed to me that I could feel every strand.

*

My friend's father died when she was in a distant country.
'So now,' she said to me, 'I know what grief is.'
'What is it?' I said.
'Sometimes,' said my friend, 'it is what you expect. And sometimes it is nothing more than bad temper.'
When my friend's father died, his affairs were not in order and he had no money.

*

My friend was the first person I ever saw break the taboo against wearing striped and floral patterns together. She stood on the steps of the Shrine of Remembrance and held a black umbrella over her head. This was in the 1960s.

*

My friend came back from Europe and found a job. On the days when she was not painting theatre sets for money she went to her cold and dirty studio in the city and painted for the other thing, whatever that is. She wore cheap shoes and pinned her hair into a roll on her neck.

*

My friend babysat, as a student, for a well-known woman in her forties who worked at night.

'What is she like?' I said.

'She took me upstairs,' said my friend, 'and showed me her bedroom. It was full of flowers. We stood at the door looking in. She said, "Sex is not a problem for me." '

*

When the person . . . the man whose room my friend had taken came to dinner, my friend and he would talk for hours after everyone else had left the table about different modes of perception and understanding. My friend spoke slowly, in long, convoluted sentences and mixed metaphors, and often laughed. The man, a scientist, spoke in a light, rapid voice, but he sat still. They seemed to listen to each other.

'I don't mean a god in the Christian sense,' said my friend.

'It is egotism,' said the man, 'that makes people want their lives to have meaning beyond themselves.'

*

My friend and I worked one summer in the men's underwear department of a big store in Footscray. We wore our little cotton dresses, our blue sandals. We were happy there, selling, wrapping, running up and down the ladder, dinging the register, going to the park for lunch with the boys from the shop. *I* was happy. The youngest boy looked at us and sighed and said, 'I don't know which one of youse two I love the most.' One day my friend was serving a thin-faced woman at the specials box. There was a cry. I looked up. My friend was dashing for the door. She was sobbing. We all stood still, in attitudes of drama. The woman spread her hands. She spoke to the frozen shop at large.

'I never said a thing,' she said. 'It's got nothing to do with *me*.'

I left my customer and ran after my friend. She was half-way down the street, looking in a shop window. She had stopped crying. She began to tell me about . . . but it doesn't matter now. This was in the 1960s; before feminism.

*

My friend came home from her studio some nights in a calm bliss. 'What we need,' she said, 'are those moments of abandon, when the real stuff runs down our arm without obstruction.'

*

My friend cut lemons into chunks and dropped them into the water jug when there was no money for wine.

*

My friend came out of the surgery. I ran to take her arm but she pushed past me and bent over the gutter. I gave her my hanky. Through the open sides of the tram the summer wind blew freely. We stood up and held on to the leather straps. 'I can't sit down,' said my friend. 'He put a great bolt of gauze up me.' This was in the 1960s; before feminism. The tram rolled past the deep gardens. My friend was smiling.

*

My friend and her husband came to visit me and my husband. We heard their car and looked out the upstairs window. We could hear his voice haranguing her, and hers raised in sobs and wails. I ran down to open the door. They were standing on the mat, looking ordinary. We went to Royal Park and flew a kite that her husband had made. The nickname he had for her was one he had picked up from her father. They both loved her, of course. This was in the 1960s.

*

My friend was lonely.

*

My friend sold some of her paintings. I went to look at them in her studio before they were taken away. The smell of the oil paint was a shock to me: a smell I would have thought of as masculine. This was in the 1980s; after feminism. The paintings were big. I did not 'understand' them; but then again perhaps I did, for they made me feel like fainting, her weird plants and creatures streaming back towards a source of irresistible yellow light.

*

'When happiness comes,' said my friend, 'it's so thick and smooth and uneventful, it's like nothing at all.'

*

My friend picked up a fresh chicken at the market. 'Oh,' she said. 'Feel this.' I took it from her. Its flesh was pimpled and tender, and moved on its bones like the flesh of a very young baby.

*

I went into my friend's room while she was out. On the wall was stuck a sheet of paper on which she had written: 'Henry James to a friend in trouble: "throw yourself on the *alternative* life ... which is what I mean by the life of art, and which religiously invoked and handsomely understood, je vous le garantis, never fails the sincere invoker – sees him through everything, and reveals to him the secrets of and for doing so." '

*

I was sick. My friend served me pretty snacks at sensitive intervals. I sat up on my pillows and strummed softly the five chords I had learnt on my ukulele. My friend sat on the edge of a chair, with her bony hands folded round a cup, and talked. She uttered great streams of words. Her gaze skimmed my shoulder and vanished into the clouds outside the window. She was like a machine made to talk on and on forever. She talked about how much money she would have to spend on paint and stretchers, about the lightness, the optimism, the femaleness of her work, about what she was going to paint next, about how much tougher and more violent her pictures would have to be in order to attract proper attention from critics, about what the men in her field were doing now, about how she must find this out before she began her next lot of pictures.

'Listen,' I said. 'You don't have to think about any of that. Your work is *terrific*.'

'My work is terrific,' said my friend on a high note, 'but *I'm not*.' Her mouth fell down her chin and opened. She began to sob. 'I'm forty,' said my friend, 'and I've got *no money*.'

I played the chords G, A and C.

'I'm lonely,' said my friend. Tears were running down her cheeks. Her mouth was too low in her face. 'I want a man.'

'You could have one,' I said.

'I don't want just any man,' said my friend. 'And I don't want a boy. I want a man who's not going to think my ideas are crazy. I want a man who'll see the part of me that no one ever sees. I want a man who'll look after me and love me. I want a grown-up.'

I thought, If I could play better, I could turn what she has just said into a song.

'Women like us,' I said to my friend, 'don't have men like that. Why should *you* expect to find a man like that?'

'Why shouldn't I?' said my friend.

'Because men won't do those things for women like us. We've done something to ourselves so that men won't do it. Well – there are men who will. But we despise them.'

My friend stopped crying.

I played the ukulele. My friend drank from the cup.

What We Say

I was kneeling at the open door, with the cloth in my right hand and the glass shelf balanced on the palm of my left. She came past at a fast clip, wearing my black shoes and pretending I wasn't there. I spoke sharply to her, from my supplicant's posture.

'Death to mother. Death,' she replied, and clapped the gate to behind her.

It had once been a kind of family joke, but I lost the knack of the shelf for a moment and though it didn't break there was quite a bit of blood. After I had cleaned up and put the apron in a bucket to soak, I went to the phone and began to make arrangements.

In Sydney my friend, the old-fashioned sort of friend who works on your visit and wants you to be happy, gave me two tickets to the morning dress rehearsal of *Rigoletto*. I went with Natalie. She knew how to get there and which door to go in. 'At your age, you've never been inside the *Opera* House?' Great things and small forged through the blinding water. We hurried, we ran.

At the first interval we went outside. A man I knew said, 'I like your shirt. What would you call that colour – hyacinth?' At the second interval we stayed in our seats so we could keep up our conversation which is no more I suppose than exalted gossip but which seems, because of her oblique perceptions, a most delicate, hilarious and ephemeral tissue of mind.

At lunchtime we dashed, puffy-eyed and red-cheeked, into the kitchen of my thoughtful friend. He was standing at the stove, looking up at us over his shoulder and smiling: he likes to teach me things, he likes to see me learning.

'How was it?'

'Fabulous! We cried *buckets*!'

Another man was leaning against the window frame with his arms crossed and his hair standing on end. His skin was pale, as if he had crept out from some burrow where he had lain for a long time in a cramped and twisted position.

'You cried?' he said. 'You mean you actually shed tears?'

Look out, I thought; one of these. I was still having to blow my nose, and was ready to ride rough-shod. My friend put the spaghetti on the table and we all sat down.

'I'm starving,' said Natalie.

'What a plot,' I raved. 'So tight you couldn't stick a pin in it.'

'What was your worst moment?' said Natalie.

'Oh, when he bends over the sack to gloat, and then from off-stage comes the Duke's voice, singing his song. The way he freezes, in that bent-over posture, over the sack.'

The sack, in a sack. I had a best friend once, my intellectual companion of ten years, on paper from land to land and then in person: she was the one who first told me the story of *Rigoletto* and I will never forget the way her voice sank to a thread of horror: 'And the murderer gives him his daughter's body on the river bank, *in a sack*.' A river flows: that is its nature. Its sluggish water can work any discarded object loose from the bank and carry it further, lump it lengthwise, nudge it and roll it and shift it, bear it away and along and out of sight.

'Yes, that was bad, all right,' said Natalie, 'but mine was when he realized that his daughter was in the bedchamber with the Duke.'

We picked up our forks and began to eat. The back door opened on to a narrow concrete yard, but light was bouncing down the grey walls and the air was warm, and as I ate I thought, Why don't I live here? In the sun?

'Also,' I said, 'I *love* what it's about. About the impossibility of shielding your children from the evil of the world.'

There was a pause.

'Well, yes, it is about that,' said my tactful friend, 'but it's also about the greatest fear men have. Which is the fear of losing their daughters. Of losing them to younger men. Into the world of sex.'

We sat at the table quietly eating. Words which people use

and pretend to understand floated in silence and bumped among our heads: virgin; treasure; perfect; clean; my darling; anima; soul.

Natalie spoke in her light, courteous voice. 'If that's what it's about,' she said, 'what do you think the women in the audience were responding to?' – for in our bags were two sodden handkerchiefs.

The salad went round.

'I don't know,' said my friend. 'You tell me.'

We said nothing. We looked into our plates.

'That fear men have,' said my friend. 'Literature and art are full of it.'

My skin gave a mutinous prickle. *Your* literature.

'*Do* women have a fundamental fear?' said my friend.

Natalie and I glanced at each other and back to the tabletop.

'A fear of violation, maybe?' he said. He got up and filled the kettle. The silence was not a silence but a quietness of thinking. I knew what Natalie was thinking. She was wishing the conversation had not taken this particular turn. I was wishing the same thing. Stumped, struck dumb: failed again, failed to think and talk in that pattern they use. I had nothing to say. Nothing came to my mind that had any bearing on the matter.

Should I say 'But violation is our destiny?' Or should I say *'Nothing can be sole or whole / That has not been rent'*? But before I could open my mouth, a worst moment came to me: the letter arrives from my best friend on the road in a far country: 'He was wearing mirror sun-glasses which he did not take off, I tried to plead but I could not speak his language, he tore out handfuls of my hair, he kicked me and pushed me out of the car, I crawled to the river, I could smell the water, it was dirty but I washed myself, a farm girl found me, her family is looking after me, I think I will be all right, please answer, above all, don't tell my father, love.' I got down on my elbows in the yard and put my face into the dirt, I wept, I groaned. That night I went as usual to the lesson. *All I can do is try to make something perfect for you, for your poor body, with my clumsy and ignorant one:* I breathed and moved as the teacher showed us, and she came past me in the class and touched me on the head and said, 'This must mean a lot to you – you are doing it so beautifully.'

'Violation,' said Natalie, as if to gain time.

'It would be necessary,' I said, 'to examine all of women's writing, to see if the fear of violation is the major theme of it.'

'Some feminist theoretician somewhere has probably already done it,' said the stranger who had been surprised that *Rigoletto* could draw tears.

'Barbara Baynton, for instance,' said my friend. 'Have you read that story of hers called *The Chosen Vessel*? The woman knows the man is outside waiting for dark. She puts the brooch on the table. It's the only valuable thing she owns. She puts it there as an offering – to appease him. She wants to buy him off.'

The brooch. The mirror sunglasses. The feeble lock. The weakened wall that gives. What stops these conversations is shame, and grief.

'We don't have a tradition in the way you blokes do,' I said.

Everybody laughed, with relief.

'There must be a line of women's writing,' said Natalie, 'running from the beginning till now.'

'It's a shadow tradition,' I said. 'It's there, but nobody knows what it is.'

'We've been trained in *your* tradition,' said Natalie. 'We're honorary men.'

She was not looking at me, nor I at her.

The coffee was ready, and we drank it. Natalie went to pick up her children from school. My friend put in the plug and began to wash the dishes. The stranger tilted his chair back against the wall, and I leaned on the bench.

'What happened to your hand?' he said.

'I cut it on the glass shelf yesterday,' I said, 'when I was defrosting the fridge.'

'There's a packet of Bandaids in the fruit bowl,' said my friend from the sink.

I stripped off the old plaster and took a fresh one from the dish. But before I could yank its little ripcord and pull it out of its wrapper, the stranger got up from his chair, walked all the way round the table and across the room, and stopped in front of me. He took the Bandaid and said,

'Do you want me to put it on for you?'

I drew a breath to say *what we say:* 'Oh, it's all right, thanks – I can do it myself.'

But instead, I don't know why, I let out my independent breath, and took another. I gave him my hand.

'Do you like dressing wounds?' I said, in a smart tone to cover my surprise.

He did not answer this, but spread out my palm and had a good look at the cut. It was deep and precise, like a freshly dug trench, bloody still at the bottom, but with nasty white soggy edges where the plaster had prevented the skin from drying.

'You've made a mess of yourself, haven't you,' he said.

'Oh, it's nothing much,' I said airily. 'It only hurt while it was actually happening.'

He was not listening. He was concentrating on the thing. His fingers were pale, square and clean. He peeled off the two protective flaps and laid the sticky bandage across the cut. He pressed one side of it, and then the other, against my skin, smoothed them flat with his thumbs, and let go.

MICHAEL WILDING

The Sybarites

'I suppose what's so marvellous in fact is that you can just get out to the beach all the time,' Ian said. 'You're not trapped in a city all the time or anything.'

Andrew lay unmoving, facing Ian; he said nothing, looked blankly, the sort of blankness that might have been questioning, but there seemed nothing to question.

Helen, who lay next to him, also said nothing.

They lay in an arc, Andrew and Ian at the ends, Helen and Pat between them. Pat was between Ian and Helen. They faced towards the sea.

Not that their vision was uninterrupted. Between them and the surf stretched row upon row of sunbathers, single and in groups, all the various colours of trunks and bikinis, all the tints and bleaches of hair, and the constant tanned bodies, the constant gold sand: and the movement – people entering the water, leaving it, moving position, turning over, sitting up to talk or read or open cans of beer. In the surf, though, the figures were minute against the waves, coming in from the open sea; they were small black dots in the blue-grey mass, their beach significance lost, their gestures obscured in spray, in dazzle, lost in sudden troughs.

'It creates a democratic hedonism,' said Pat eventually, lazily from the bundle of clothes on which she was laying her head. She didn't bother to look up or to open her eyes.

They lay absorbing the sun. Ian could feel the backs of his knees beginning to burn. Helen turned her arms so that they would be browned all over, equally, regularly. The surf was the omnipresent sound, a muffling blanket on which the screams and laughs and shouts and transistor radio pops were bounced. The sand was the turned back sheet, smoother to the neck and chin. And beyond the surf, at the sea's rim, two ships edged along the horizon, two smudges of smoke marked their progress to South America, or Ant-arctica, or New Zealand. Ian had no clear idea of what the sea reached to, whether anything impeded his view of the polar wastes except the earth's curve, his sight's limitedness.

Asking, he broke the globed silence, the golden glow the other three shed around them, sherry in a fine stemmed glass on that noisy beach. The yellow sun warmed the silence to flow easily round them again. It seemed no one would speak. Then Helen slowly raised her head and throat above the level surface.

'I suppose,' she said, her voice catching an ironic rever-beration from the concave glass, 'I suppose there are lots of little islands with lots of little men growing goats and things. And apples. And seals. Digging guano as it were. They all come into Sydney for the Easter show.'

She slipped back into the liquid amber, her long blonde hair, her white bikini, her deep bronzed skin preserved in all its rich colour, an ear-ring dropped on the turned back sheet one night.

There they lay, in their arc, as if sleeping. And for all the screams and shouts, most people simply lay there, saying nothing, doing nothing, reading nothing; and idly moving. It was too hot to talk; it was too bright to read; they welcomed in the sun's rays through their open pores. Ian made patterns in the sand with his fingers, accepting the silence, holding back conversation, listening to the steady roar of the surf and the squeals and laughs it tossed into the air.

Andrew sat up and opened the Esky and handed round four cans of beer. 'It's started to get warm,' he said. And to Ian the taste was metallic from putting his lips to the edges around the opening.

'We could go and get some more,' Pat practically sug-gested, 'and put this in the freezer again when we get home.'

'Why bother?' Helen said, sitting now, leaning back, pour-ing the beer into her throat like milk from a coconut. 'Take it to a party like it is and drink somebody else's wine.'

'We could have brought a flagon,' Pat suggested.

'You can't drink hot wine,' said Andrew.

'It could have gone in the freezer.'

'Oh, my God,' said Helen; she flicked a grain of sand from

her shoulder like ash from a dinner jacket. 'Really, Pat, your hedonism *is* getting democratized. Chilled burgundy-type South Australian Bin 497 off-red plonk.'

Turning to Ian, Helen said 'Pat, for all that coiffured hair and expensive prints on the walls, has rather vulgarized tastes in pale red wines.'

'If you're talking about that one single occasion of the bottle of rosé –'

'My dear,' Helen said, holding her lower arm up and flapping the hand down at the wrist, 'how could one forget it?' Parodically.

'– it happened to be a bottle someone had left at a party and I wanted to get rid of.'

'Who wouldn't,' Helen said, 'leave it at a party?'

'Which are good wines?' Ian asked.

But Helen preferred the free spirit of criticism to the labours of documentation. 'Ask Pat,' she offered, dropping her head down to the sand again to return solely to the sun. And Pat began to list for him all the categories, but he could register neither brand names nor bins. But he listened, in the hot sun as the names poured over and around him.

'You're getting burnt,' Andrew said to Helen.

'Am I?' she said, in the same what might have been ironic tone that had become her signature. She was lying down, one eye shut, looking through the opening into her can of beer. She reluctantly put it on the sand, empty, and cradled her chin on her clasped fingers.

'Where's the oil?' he asked, aggressive in his efficiency.

'Lie still,' he said.

She wriggled with the cold shock when he poured it on her back, pulled back her shoulders suddenly which emphasized her breasts, wriggled her shoulders and the line of vertebrae. But he pushed her down on to the sand as he rubbed the oil over her and into her open pores, massaging her deeper into the beach. When he had finished her shoulders, he turned her over, and oiled her stomach, which trembled and wrinkled with little involuntary shudders. She lay back, her eyes shut and her lower arm across them, smiling.

'You can do your legs yourself,' he said, and turned to Pat, whose back he oiled more quickly, as if more proficient now into the swing of it. Then Helen oiled him and they passed the bottle to Ian who oiled himself except for his back which he couldn't reach, which Pat did for him. Their sticky bodies collected granules of sand, some of which fell off as their flesh moved in folds when they sat up or turned round.

The shark-watching plane droned out at sea.

'When it starts to circle, you get worried,' Pat said.

'We live terribly dangerously,' said Helen, her head lying on the sand, encircled by her arms, her voice light enough to lift itself out of the shifting grains.

It was Pat, who did not have Helen's contentment, who finally broke the silence again, to drag Helen from her ease there.

'What did you do with Mark at the party, kick him out of the window?' she asked her.

Helen rotated her neck; languidly; stretching it while she lay down.

'Yes,' she answered, sadly, 'he got defenestrated.'

'Who did he lock himself in the lavatory with this time, the anti-social bastard? I practically had to pee over the balcony.'

Andrew looked up at her. 'I don't quite see the force of your "practically",' he said. But pursued Mark's behaviour: 'Probably just pulling himself off, wouldn't you think?' he said, nudging Helen with his elbow that she might receive his statement.

'I doubt if he'd come at pulling anybody else off, certainly,' she conceded.

Ian listened to the recreated party, the dark room founded on the bright sand, the girls hidden in the dark edges of the room, and Mark's fingernails stamped on as he hung desperately, vainly, to the window ledge above the blank harbour. The beer, the wine, channelled rivulets amongst the grainy sand, spread deltas like hands receiving the warm sun, caressing warm bodies, moulding soft breasts, and stroking smooth declivities. He waited for a further party to be arranged, for a spontaneous decision to keep on drinking when they tired of the beach. But they lay there arranging nothing. He watched Helen, soft and undulant and flowing, and fantasized lying naked against her, and her limbs and belly and breasts warming him. The conversation slowed down again, became lazy in the continual sun. And not caring about it, they missed cues and interchanges, Pat and Helen suddenly speaking simultaneously after a long emptiness. 'It's beaut lying in the sun,' Pat said as Helen reminisced, 'It was a beaut party.'

Helen smiled at him: 'Our range is narrow but consistent. We're terribly sybaritic here.' And went off with Andrew to get some more beer from the pub.

Sybaritically they took him to drink with them one later afternoon in a pub on the harbour's edge. The sun caught the ripples on the smooth water, glistening facets shifting across the whole surface, the wind hardly felt on the hot land softly filling the sails of yachts brightly gliding past.

'Like the Opera House,' said Helen, her eyes held level at him, her legs stretched beneath the iron frame of the table, looking their longest in their fashionably faded jeans.

Gulls followed a fishing boat coming into the bay, wheeling round and swooping, squawking and wailing as they competed for the small fish or gut thrown overboard. The wash caught the sunlight.

Helen and Pat had their heads thrown back, the sun smoothing their necks and the undersides of their chins. They kept their eyes shut in the brightness. And Andrew rested back in his chair too, not so obviously sunning his under-chin, but looking blankly, emotionlessly, at the harbour's bland mouth, at the hydrofoil skimming across it in a haze of spray. And sometimes turning from it to look at Helen, to assess her, to appraise her, to ascertain that she was still there; but saying nothing.

And Ian watched the harbour, the absorbing movement across the water.

'That's a tremendous ship,' he said, as a white liner came slowly in. Pat opened her eyes, looked across without moving her head.

'The Marconi,' she said.

He was surprised. 'What, you know what they're called, how do you manage that?' Its name out of the eye's range.

She shrugged. She didn't answer. And he seemed to have stopped any chance of conversation by that, as if suggesting how incurably provincial it was to know the names, how colonially dependent on Europe. Which he had not considered, till her silence.

Tugs guided it slowly, gently into the bay's clasp. He wondered what people usually talked of, sitting in the sun of a pub garden drinking beer. He could not remember the sorts of things he'd talked of before. They could never have been significant; drowsy exchanges; desultory. Yet he felt the lack of them. Not even the insignificant dropped from their lips to agitate the hot afternoon. Not even; not at all; it was as if the insignificant would be an intrusion, triviality a diminution of the moment's rightness, fullness, a puncturing of the rested perfection. Their avoidance of the trivial, the crass, implied almost that anything spoken could only be trivial, crass; but was that anything whoever might speak it? or anything spoken by them? or all he spoke?

He was resentful that it was always Pat who would speak, and began to resent her for speaking, rather than the others for being silent: Helen who would say nothing, Andrew who merely looked at her. Resent her for a politeness that emphasized the unconcern of the others, that distracted him from watching Helen's shut eyes. He wanted to endorse their enjoyment of the bay, both to assure them of their values, and that he shared them. But he could get no assurance, no endorsement from them. They made him feel he too urgently needed to explain, to vocalize, what they could absorb pure; as if he could not appreciate the ferry steaming across to Manly, or the flying boat coming in on its descent to Rose Bay and dropping behind a promontory out of sight, without paraphrasing them into spelled-out sentences; and all the moments would be lumped into a formal paragraph, syntactically, grammatically correct. Yet he resented the implications of their silences, suspected that they were bound by an even more rigorously prescriptive grammar for the recording of their own emotions.

He tried to talk to Helen when Andrew went to buy another round. He was curious about her, about how she spent her time, the rest of her time, the sorts of parties she went to, and what she did at them, the sort of upbringing she had had, and the world she now lived in; but all he knew of her was that she sat in the sun with her head back and her eyes shut, basking.

'I suppose,' he said, 'growing up in these sort of surroundings makes you sort of more relaxed.'

'The climactic theory of climatic zones,' she offered, smiling as ever with her inevitable irony, so that he could not assess what suggestiveness she meant.

'But don't you think,' he persisted, 'that people do get a different sort of attitude to life?'

'I wouldn't know,' she said, and yawned, stretching in the sun so that her skivvy rode up over her belly, over her navel. 'I'm just a poor provincial, I've been nowhere else,' she added, to explain, not to apologize for what might have seemed curtness, a rudeness, though it could have, had she bothered, done service as apology.

He wanted to ask her about midnight swimming parties, about long days in the deserted dunes, cocktails on yachts moored in the harbour. He circled round it, reconnoitring an entry: 'I'd have thought relaxed sort of surroundings, you know, beaches and sort of pleasant places like this pub would make you more swinging.' It was so dated a word, he knew, but he did not know what would be appropriate, what their word was.

'Pleasant,' she howled, resting her feet on Andrew's vacated chair, that matched the table, slats of wood painted red, yellow, blue stripes consecutively, for gaiety, flicking the butt of her cigarette to lie with the others, and match sticks, cigarette packets and extruded silver paper, and trampled, flattened straws, spiralling blue and white, on the worn grass.

'But the harbour –'

But the harbour was lined by sand that carried like acne knots of dried seaweed, orange peel, broken glass, paper bags; and was pierced by the jetty that bore shacks for fishing bait and ice cream, hot meat pies, PEPSI HITS THE SPOT, HAMBURGERS and SAVS, buttered or battered, he could never remember.

'And everyone in his light pink with plum feature panel

two-toned Holden Special De Luxe just sitting looking at nothing and listening to 2UW and chewing meat pies.' Pure plushness the whole way through.

She became animated and beautiful; her mouth retained an ironically pursed seriousness, but her eyes were delighted. When Andrew returned with the tray of beers, she was gesturing towards other atrocities, ugly railings, lopped trees, men in bermuda shorts.

'You're getting manic again?' Andrew asked her.

But she was not rebuked so easily. 'You can always tell strines anywhere,' she said to Ian. 'Look at those two, the short back and sides, the ginger freckled legs, God knows why they all wear shorts, and that sort of look, the way they –'

'You're getting burnt,' Andrew said.

'Am I?' she asked, carelessly.

'Look at your shoulder, put something over it or move into the shade.'

She moved into the shade, saying nothing, reaching for and opening a packet of cigarettes.

'How many's that you've smoked this afternoon?'

She looked at him, her eyes black, but closed the packet again and with a tightening of her lips, put it down on the table. She was about to raise her fingers to her lips to bite her nails, but stopped, the movement half made, and reached for her beer instead.

'It is pretty skungy when you come to think about it,' said Pat. 'Damn you, Helen, now you've discomposed my afternoon.'

They sat in silence till Helen said, 'Maybe we ought to go somewhere else.'

Ian said, 'Let's do something exciting', investing it with the irony he had observed Helen use, hoping that that way then, respects having been paid to the equivoce, they might. But Andrew said 'Oh God', briefly, short equal syllables, and Pat and Helen groaned.

Ian bought another round, and they sat there watching ships and gulls passing and repassing, and the flying boat having just taken off came into view, climbing slowly above the yachts and the hydrofoil and a coastal tanker going out through the Heads. Sparrows pecked around in the litter for crumbs, and the sun, harshly taking away the beauty from the trees, took away the ugliness from the jetty and moulded everything into a warm uniformity, an apathy of acceptance.

They went back to Pat's and spent the rest of the afternoon drinking red wine and listening to Monteverdi.

'I'm not sure that he's really an afternoon composer,' said Helen.

'Come here,' Andrew called at her.

'You bastard, that's cold,' she said, as he rubbed sunburn cream on to her shoulder.

'You need someone to look after you,' he said, censoriously at the redness of her arm.

'Which reminds me, I have to phone Mark,' she said, wriggling away from the applications of his solicitude. The hanging relative.

It was a large terrace house in arty Paddington. They sat on the glassed-in balcony, catching the last of the afternoon sun. By standing on one of the couches, the top of the harbour bridge could just be seen. Ian did that, stood on one of the couches, and looked; it occupied him while Andrew and Helen sat on the other couch, and Pat phoned Mark for Helen.

'Try some of this,' said Pat, returning with a new flagon. 'There's only one way to find out which are the best and that's to drink them all.'

'Don't let Pat persuade you that you have to drink them simultaneously,' said Helen. But Andrew drew her back into their private conversation, inaudible except to them.

'But it gets you drunk quicker,' said Pat to Andrew, 'my God it does.'

So that when Mark arrived, smooth and suited from his office, they were all quite drunk.

'Have a drink, Mark,' Andrew welcomed him, polite, almost deferential, yet familiar.

'I'll have a quick one,' he conceded, 'but we can't stop. I must do some work this evening.'

The door was shut. There was no one else with him. And

then Helen said, 'Oh sorry, you haven't met; this is Ian, Mark.'

They shook hands and Ian blushed, because he had not realized that Helen was married; and because, perhaps, he felt that his fantasies could be read.

Afterwards, when Mark and Helen had gone, he could not understand how he could have missed her wedding ring; yet thinking about it, he wondered if indeed she wore one, or, indeed, if she were married; he wondered if his uncertainty were just lack of realism, because he did not want her to be married; whatever its cause, it was still uncertainty, and he wanted, but did not dare, to ask Pat and Andrew if, in truth, she was married. But he said nothing, and Pat and Andrew drove him back to his flat, and as he fumbled at the lock, swept away together down the tree-lined street.

One evening they all went out for dinner and got very drunk. And because he was drunker than usual, and they all were, and because, more at ease after settling in, he was less inhibited, Ian enjoyed himself entertaining Helen, telling her anecdotes and jokes, listening to her stories of jumping into fountains, of throwing Mark's shaving gear out of the window of their flat, of chucking at important dinner parties. His jokes got both simpler and more explicitly sexual – ones he hadn't begun the evening with but were all that remained; and her anecdotes wilder and more personally embarrassing – showing a naïve spontaneity that he found endearing. Pat also contributed, and Andrew looked on with a sort of beneficent calm; he did not seem aggressively possessive of Helen, nor resentful of Ian's monopolizing her, and Ian wondered if Andrew had broken with her, if he had ever begun with her; broken with any attempt to get her; or maybe transferred to Pat, whom after all he had driven off with that night.

And when they had at last finished eating, Helen proposed doing something exciting, like a pub crawl or a spontaneous fountain jumping circuit; but it was too late to get to a pub and find out where the party was, so she said 'Let's go back to the flat and grog on', and they all piled into Pat's car and drove back to the flat.

Helen poured them drinks in the kitchen. They went into the living room to greet Mark, who was sipping whisky and studying a brief or something like that. He was polite, yet made it clear he was working, and would be resentful of disturbance or noise, so they went out into the kitchen and slopped more drink into their glasses and Helen said, 'I know, we can go on the roof, it's a beaut evening.'

They got into the lift and as they rose Andrew asked, 'Wasn't this the lift Mark was stuck in screwing Marie-Louise?'

'It must have been fiendishly uncomfortable,' chortled Pat, 'she's not exactly dainty.'

'But cushioned,' said Andrew.

'The pneumatic bag,' agreed Pat. And the lift stopped and Helen got out first and they walked up about half a dozen steps to the roof which was locked.

'Haven't you got the key?' Andrew said to Helen.

She shook her head: 'They took it off us.'

'What do you mean, they took it off you?'

'Well, they changed the lock and wouldn't give us a new one.'

'Why not?' Andrew asked.

She shrugged her shoulders: 'You know, parties, things.'

They stood, blocked.

'We'll break it down,' said Andrew, and thumped his shoulder into it. 'Look out', and he went at it with a run. The boom resounded down the stair well.

He broke through in the end, the lock flange splintering the wood and breaking away. They stood on the flat roof, high above the streets, looking across the harbour with ferries crossing the dark water, their rows of lights like strings of lanterns doubled in reflection, the neon signs of blocks the other side vivid green and red and blue, mirrored and distorted in the rippling water; and the lights of houses and flats, yellow dots reaching right out to the Heads; and the huge girders of the bridge, floodlit, bright against the black sky. But it was the ferries, tracking backwards and forwards, and the occasional single blue light of a police launch, patrolling amongst anchored cargo ships, that wove the enchantment. Ian didn't resist the word. He suddenly loved the place at night, its stillness, its lights, its easy beauty.

Helen left them standing by the burst door and walked to the flat roof's unparapeted edge. She looked across at the harbour, and Ian felt his stomach shiver with terror at the eight-storey drop she stood beside. She sat down at the edge, dangling her legs over. He couldn't bear to look, he turned towards the bridge, swallowing against his nausea.

'Jeez, Helen, do you have to?' said Pat.

'I like it here,' she said, simply. And Andrew walked across to join her. They both sat there, their lower legs over the roof's edge, their bodies close together, talking quietly, inaudible to the two by the door, intimately, urgently, their thighs touching, his arm behind her against her back. The ferries tracked backwards and forwards, and a train clattered across the bridge, a dull tunnelling rumble.

Ian drained his glass and he and Pat squatted beside each other at the doorway, equidistant in safety from the roof's every edge. They watched Helen tip the dregs of her glass over the void, carelessly, casually, ceremonially, ritually, desperately, they could not tell, they could not hear. Pat grimaced at him and he grinned. It was as if he should have put his arm around her, out of a sort of politeness. He wondered if it would make Andrew and Helen any more at ease if he did; but they seemed to have forgotten them. And Pat anyway knew, must have known, that he was not attracted to her, that neither he nor she wanted to dissimulate; and he only hoped that she did not know that he wanted no one but Helen. To put his arm round Pat might securely have hidden his grotesque hope; but he could not do it. And, his stomach sick with vertigo and loss, he watched Helen and Andrew perched there, wondering what would be said should they fall, looking up occasionally at the lights of a passing aircraft, at the clear patterns of the stars.

Then later, they went down to the flat, joining Mark who was eating oysters and listening to Vivaldi. When the record ended, he did not replace it, so they all, except Helen, went, and dropped off Ian at his flat.

Yet his hope was renewed. They would take him to the pubs where everyone drank, they would tour the fountains that would drench their light summer clothes, they would find way-out parties they would grog on all night at, that would lead to dawn swimming, naked in the harbour menaced by sharks and vice squad prowlers. 'We'll show you,' they said, 'instant Sydney.' But not Andrew. He dropped out, had a couple of drinks over lunch with them and then left. Ian's suprise was subdued by his delight, and Helen and Pat and he sat happily all afternoon grogging on, relaxed, happy, waiting in odd pubs till the downtown crowd would be in the Newcastle about five.

Crushed in there, with all downtown wedged immovably against each other, he could not tell if it was Helen he was rubbing against or Pat, or anybody else. And the heat, from so many bodies on a hot day, was becoming oppressive. But he got beers for all of them, fighting his way, in a way he was getting used to, through to the bar, and the next round Helen bought schooners, to save having to struggle through so often. The heat made you thirsty and you drank more readily. And there was the continual noise of talking and laughing and shouting, noise and noise and noise, and backs pushing against breasts, crushing lungs, pinning arms. People came up to Helen and Pat and both and greeted them, kissed them on cheeks or necks or lips, sadly, ironically, or bitterly, and were introduced to Ian, some of them, and went on, on their way through the seething company. He was wondering whether to reach his arm round Helen and whether she would object or whether Pat might feel omitted, and yet with Andrew absent it was the time he had so long hoped for, when Mark pushed his way through to them, not conspicuous because of his suit because lots of drinkers wore suits, but because of his manner, his distaste, his determination contrasting with the beery apathy and contentment of almost all, except the frenetic barmaids, and he thrust through to the bar and ordered another round of schooners, observing with an unquestioning assurance what they were drinking, and then joined them.

'God knows how you stand it,' he said.

And Ian gulped down the last of his last beer to take the new glass, gulping it because for all that it sprayed coolly over the heat, the taste was becoming nauseous. And Pat said, 'Jeez, I wouldn't mind a spot of air.' So they struggled through, led by Mark, out of a doorway and on to the pavement that sloped steeply down towards the main road (and round to the Quay which they could almost glimpse), and Ian nearly fell, his shoes slipping on the unexpected incline. And all in all the cool air proved the end. Pat went a ghastly white and groaned to herself, and Helen smiled with a ridiculous fixed grin and Ian sat on the pavement because he felt dizzy and was afraid to slip again, and abandoned his half-drunk glass on a window ledge.

'So much for instant Sydney,' said Helen. 'We should have eaten something before we got here.' And, as if in horror at her words, turned to the gutter and vomited two, three, four times.

'Oh jeez,' Pat groaned to herself.

Mark drove Helen away from them. And Pat took Ian to the flat he had just moved into. She pulled up and stalled the car, and then switched off the ignition.

'Well,' she said, 'Helen's changed since she married, she used to be able to go on all night.'

And he felt inwardly sick again, that Pat's concentration on driving had cleared her head and made her able to contemplate going on all night.

They sat there, by the flat's entrance, and he knew he should ask her in; but he couldn't; he was too drunk and not drunk enough; he couldn't face it, not now, not with her. So they waited a while there, still, and she said, 'Well, we're neighbours now practically. You'll be able just to drop in and have a beer any old time. It's no distance to walk.' She gave a satisfied sigh. 'There's always some grog around and there's usually something going on. We'll arrange a *party*.'

He sat there in the front of the car with her. 'That'd be beaut,' he said; cautiously trying out for the first time the idioms that now he felt he had caught.

The Man of Slow Feeling

After the accident he lay for weeks in the still white ward. They fed him intravenously but scarcely expected him to live. Yet he did live, and when at last they removed the bandages from his eyes, it was found he could see. They controlled what he could see carefully, keeping the room dimmed, the blinds down, at first; but gradually increased his exposure to light, to the world around. Slowly his speech came back. He blocked for some time on words he could not remember, could no longer enunciate; but gradually his vocabulary returned. But he had lost sensation, it seemed. He could not smell the flowers Maria brought into the small private ward. And when she gave him the velvety globed petals to touch, he could not feel them. All foods were the same to him. The grapes she mechanically bought, he could only see. They had neither touch nor taste for him. If he shut his eyes and returned to darkness again, he did not know what he was eating. Yet he was not totally without sensation – it was not as if he were weightless or bodiless. He was conscious of lying in bed day after day, his body lying along the bed – perhaps because the constant pressure reached through to his numbed nerves. But the touch of Maria's fingers on his cheeks, the kiss of her lips against his, he could not feel, nor mouth the taste of her.

And yet as he lay alone in that small white room odd sensations came to him, brushed him with their dying wings. As if, lying there with only his thoughts and imaginings, he could conjure back the taste of grapes, the soft touch of Maria's hand, the searching pressure of her kiss. They surprised him, these sensations; often they would make him wake from a light sleep as if a delightful dream had achieved an actuality: but when he awoke he was always totally alone, and remembered nothing of any dream. It was often, as he

321

lay there, as if someone had actually touched him, or forced grapes against his palate, and he would want to cry out at the unexpectedness of it. If imagination, it could only have been triggered by the workings of his subconscious. He mentioned it to the nurses, and they said that it could be that he was getting his sensations back. He did not argue with them, pointing out that there were no correlatives to the sensations, no objects provoking them. It was like a man feeling pain in a foot already amputated: a foot he would not be getting back. The sensations were the ghosts of feelings he had once had, nerve memories of a lost past.

Released from hospital, Maria took him back to the house in the country. They made love that first night, but he could not feel her full breasts, her smooth skin, and making love to her was totally without sensation for him. Its only pleasures were voyeuristic and nostalgic: his eyes and ears allowed him to remember past times – like seeing a sexual encounter at the cinema. The thought came to him that the best way to get anything from sex now was to cover the walls and ceilings with mirrors, so that at least he could have a full visual satisfaction to replace his missing senses. But he said nothing to Maria. He said nothing, but he knew she realized that for him it was now quite hopeless.

He was woken in the night by a dream of intercourse, the excitement of fondling a body, the huge relief of orgasm. He lay awake, the vividness of it reminding him bitterly of what was now lost to him.

The early days back in the house he found disorienting. Within the white walls confining the ward experience had been limited for him; he saw little, encountered little; the disturbing nerve memories were few. But released, now they swelled to a riot, as if exposure to the open world had revived dormant, dying memories for their final throes. Released, his body was a continual flux of various sensations, of smell, of taste, of touch; yet still with no sensations from his experiences. He could walk beside the dung heap at the field's corner, ready to manure the land, and though he inhaled deeply hoping its pungency would break through his numbness, he could experience nothing. When Maria was not looking, he reached his hand into the dung: he felt nothing. A visual repugnance, but no physical sensation, no recoil of nausea.

Yet at tea suddenly the full pungency of the foul dung swept across to him, his hand unfeelingly holding a meringue was swamped in the heavy foul stickiness of the dung. He left the table, walked across to the window that looked out onto the wide lawns. There was nothing outside to provoke his sensations; and if there had been, how could his touch have been affected from outside? His touch and smell had not, as he'd momentarily hoped, returned. Maria asked what was the matter, but he said nothing. He went to the bathroom, but oddly did not feel nausea. He expected to, biting that momentarily dung drenched meringue. But his stomach recorded no sensations. His intellect's interpretation had misled him; his mind was interpreting a nausea he would have felt, in his past life, an existence no longer his.

Yet in bed as he reached out to fondle, hopelessly, Maria who made love with him now more eagerly, more readily, more desperately, uselessly, pointlessly than ever before, his stomach was gripped by a sudden retching nausea, and he had to rush to the bathroom to vomit.

'My poor dear,' said Maria, 'oh my poor dear.'

He wondered whether he should rest again, to recover the placidity he had known in the hospital. But to rest in bed, although he could read or hear music, meant his life was so reduced. At least to walk round the fields or into the village gave him stimulation for those senses that remained.

But activity seemed disturbing. And provoked a riot of these sense memories, these million twitching amputated feet.

Then, one day, he realized his senses were not dead.

It was a compound realization, not a sudden epiphany. In the morning he had driven the car and, going too fast over the humpbacked bridge that crossed the canal, had provoked a scream from Maria. He had asked in alarm what was the matter.

'Nothing,' she said, 'it's just that it took the bottom out of my stomach, going over the bridge like that.'

'I'm sorry,' he said, 'I didn't realize I was going that fast. I can't feel that sort of thing now.'

Indeed he had forgotten, till she reminded him, that the sensation existed.

They made love at noon, not because he could experience anything, but because in his dreams and in his waking nerve memories, he so often re-experienced the ecstasy in actuality denied him. He perhaps half hoped to recapture the experience. But never did.

Maria got up to cook lunch, absurdly spending great labour on foods he could not taste, perhaps hoping to lure his taste from its grave. She rushed from the kitchen to his bed when he gave a sudden cry. But he was laughing when she reached the bedroom.

'Sorry,' he said. 'It's just that like you said, your stomach dropped out going over the bridge, and that must have reminded me of it. It just happened this minute, lying here.'

She touched his brow with her cool hand, whose coolness and presence he could not feel. He brushed her away, irritated by her solicitude. As he ate his lunch, he brooded over his cry of alarm. And later, buying cigarettes in the village shop, for the nervous habit he realized that had always caused him to smoke, not the taste, he came on the truth as his body was suffused with the sudden aliveness of intercourse, the convulsive ecstasy of orgasm.

'Are you all right, sir?' the shopkeeper asked.

'I'm fine, fine,' he said. 'It's, it's' (it's nothing he was about to say mechanically, but it was ecstasy); 'it's quite all right,' he said.

Walking back, he was elated at realizing sensation was not denied him, but delayed. He looked at his watch and predicted he would taste his lunch at four o'clock. And sitting on the stile at the field corner, he did. In excitement he ran, his meal finished, to tell Maria, to tell her ecstatically that the accident had not robbed him of sensation, but dulled and slowed its passage along his nerves. When he tripped on a log and grazed his knee without any feeling, he knew, ambivalently, that in three hours the pain would be registered: he waited in excitement for confirmation of his prediction, in anxiety about the pain it would bring.

* * *

But his knowledge was a doubtful advantage. The confusions

of senses before had been disturbing, but not worrying. It was the prediction now that tore him with anxiety. Cutting his finger while sharpening a pencil, he waited tense for the delayed pain; and even though cutting his finger was the slightest of hurts, it filled three hours of anxiety. He worked out with Maria that the well-timed cooking of food could appetize his tasteless smell-less later meal; but few meals could produce rich smells three hours before serving. He could not do anything the slightest nauseating, like cleaning drains or gutting chickens, for fear of the context in which his senses would later register and produce in their further three hours the possibility of his vomiting. Defecation became nightmarish, could ruin any ill-timed meal, or intercourse. And ill-timed intercourse would ruin any casual urination. He toyed with the idea of keeping a log book, so that by consulting what happened three hours back, he knew what he was about to feel. He experimented one morning, and in a sort of way it worked. For he spent so long noting down each detail in his book, he had little time to experience anything. He realized how full a life is of sensations, as hopelessly he tried to record them all.

He developed a device, instead, consisting primarily of a small tape-recorder which he carried always with him. He spoke a constant commentary into it of his sensate actions and, through earphones, his commentary would be played back to him after a three hours delay, to warn him of what he was about to feel. The initial three hours, as he paced the fields, were comparatively simple, though he worried at the limitations it would impose on his life and experience, having to comment on it in its entirety, each trivial stumble, each slight contact. But after three hours had passed, and his bruised slow nerves were transmitting his sensations, the playback came in. And he found he could not both record his current activities in a constant flow, and hear a constant commentary on his three-hours-back activities, momentarily prior to his sensations of those past ones. He braced himself for the predicted sensation that his recorded voice warned him of, and in doing so forgot to maintain his current commentary for his three hours hence instruction. And maintaining his commentary, he forgot to act on the playback and lost the value of its warnings. And returning again to it, intent on gaining from its predictions, he began to follow its record as instructions, and when he caught the word 'stumble' from his disembodied voice, he stumbled in obedience, forgetting to hold himself still for the sensation of stumbling. And what, anyway, warned of a stumble, was he to do? Sit passively for the experience to flow through him and pass? What he had recorded as advice seemed peremptory instruction, terse orders that his nerves responded to independent of his volition. The playback possessed an awful authority, as if the voice were no longer his, and the announced experiences (which he had never felt) foreign to him: and at each random whim of the voice, distorted parodically from his own, his sensations would have inevitably to respond. And he the mere frame, the theatre for the puppet strings to be hung and tugged in.

He could never coordinate commentary and playback: the one perpetually blocked the other, as he tried to hear one thing and say another. And he would confuse them and having spoken a sensation into the microphone before him would immediately prepare to experience it, forgetting the delay that had to come. His sensations became as random to him as before in that maze of playback and commentary and memory. And when he did accidentally, reflectively, re-enact the activity his playback warned him to prepare for, then he had to record another warning of that activity for his three hours later sensation: and it was as if he were to be trapped in a perpetual round to the same single repeated stumble.

He abandoned notebooks and tape-recorders. He sat at the window awaiting his sensations. Sex became a nightmare for him, its insensate action and empty voyeurism bringing only the cerebral excitement of a girlie magazine, its consequence a wet dream, the tension of waiting for which (sometimes with an urgent hope, sometimes with the resistant wished-against tension) would agonize him – keep him sleepless or, in the mornings, unable to read or move. And the continual anxiety affected his whole sexual activity, made him ejaculate too soon, or not at all; and he had to wait his three hours for his failures to reach him, knowing his failure, reminded of it cruelly three hours after his cerebral realization.

He could not sleep. Any activity three hours before sleep, would awaken him, bumping into a door, drinking wine, switching off a record player. The sensations would arouse his tense consciousness. He tried to control against this, spending the three hours before sleep in total stillness and peace, but the tension of this created its own anxiety, produced psychosomatic pains: of which he would be unaware until they woke him.

He thought back with a sort of longing to his hospital bed, when without stimulation he had experienced only the slightest of sensations. But in those bare walls of the bare room, he might almost have been in a tomb. If life were only bearable without sensation, what was the life worth that he could bear?

* * *

Maria came back from town one day to find him dead in the white, still bathroom. He had cut his arteries in a bath in the Roman way, the hot water, now rich-vermilioned, to reduce the pain of dying. Though, she told herself, he would not have felt anything anyway, he had no sensation.

But three hours afterwards, what might he have felt?

PETER CAREY

American Dreams

No one can, to this day, remember what it was we did to offend him. Dyer the butcher remembers a day when he gave him the wrong meat and another day when he served some-one else first by mistake. Often when Dyer gets drunk he recalls this day and curses himself for his foolishness. But no one seriously believes that it was Dyer who offended him.

But one of us did something. We slighted him terribly in some way, this small meek man with the rimless glasses and neat suit who used to smile so nicely at us all. We thought, I suppose, he was a bit of a fool and sometimes he was so quiet and grey that we ignored him, or forgot that he was there at all.

When I was a boy I often stole apples from the trees at his house up in Mason's Lane. He often saw me. No, that's not correct. Let me say I often sensed that he saw me. I sensed him peering out from behind the lace curtains of his house. And I was not the only one. Many of us came to take his apples, alone and in groups, and it is possible that he chose to exact payment for all these apples in his own peculiar way.

Yet I am sure it wasn't the apples.

What has happened is that we all, all eight hundred of us, have come to remember small transgressions against Mr Gleason who once lived amongst us.

My father, who has never borne malice against a single living creature, still believes that Gleason meant to do us well, that he loved the town more than any of us. My father says we have treated the town badly in our minds. We have used it, this little valley, as nothing more than a stopping place. Somewhere on the way to somewhere else. Even those of us who have been here many years have never taken the town seriously. Oh yes, the place is pretty. The hills are green and the woods thick. The stream is full of fish. But it is not where we would rather be.

For years we have watched the films at the Roxy and dreamed, if not of America, then at least of our capital city. For our own town, my father says, we have nothing but contempt. We have treated it badly, like a whore. We have cut down the giant shady trees in the main street to make doors for the school house and seats for the football pavilion. We have left big holes all over the countryside from which we have taken brown coal and given back nothing.

The commercial travellers who buy fish and chips at George the Greek's care for us more than we do, because we all have dreams of the big city, of wealth, of modern houses, of big motor cars: American dreams, my father has called them.

Although my father ran a petrol station he was also an inventor. He sat in his office all day drawing strange pieces of equipment on the back of delivery dockets. Every spare piece of paper in the house was covered with these little drawings and my mother would always be very careful about throwing away any piece of paper no matter how small. She would look on both sides of any piece of paper very carefully and always preserved any that had so much as a pencil mark.

I think it was because of this that my father felt that he understood Gleason. He never said as much, but he inferred that he understood Gleason because he, too, was concerned with similar problems. My father was working on plans for a giant gravel crusher, but occasionally he would become distracted and become interested in something else.

There was, for instance, the time when Dyer the butcher bought a new bicycle with gears, and for a while my father talked of nothing else but the gears. Often I would see him across the road squatting down beside Dyer's bicycle as if he were talking to it.

We all rode bicycles because we didn't have the money for anything better. My father did have an old Chev truck, but he rarely used it and it occurs to me now that it might have had some mechanical problem that was impossible to solve, or perhaps it was just that he was saving it, not wishing to wear it out all at once. Normally, he went everywhere on his bicycle and, when I was younger, he carried me on the cross bar, both of us dismounting to trudge up the hills that led into and out of the main street. It was a common sight in our town to see people pushing bicycles. They were as much a burden as a means of transport.

Gleason also had his bicycle and every lunchtime he pushed and pedalled it home from the shire offices to his little weatherboard house out at Mason's Lane. It was a three-mile ride and people said that he went home for lunch because he was fussy and wouldn't eat either his wife's sandwiches or the hot meal available at Mrs Lessing's cafe.

But while Gleason pedalled and pushed his bicycle to and from the shire offices everything in our town proceeded as normal. It was only when he retired that things began to go wrong.

Because it was then that Mr Gleason started supervising the building of the wall around the two-acre plot up on Bald Hill. He paid too much for this land. He bought it from Johnny Weeks, who now, I am sure, believes the whole episode was his fault, firstly for cheating Gleason, secondly for selling him the land at all. But Gleason hired some Chinese and set to work to build his wall. It was then that we knew that we'd offended him. My father rode all the way out to Bald Hill and tried to talk Mr Gleason out of his wall. He said there was no need for us to build walls. That no one wished to spy on Mr Gleason or whatever he wished to do on Bald Hill. He said no one was in the least bit interested in Mr Gleason. Mr Gleason, neat in a new sportscoat, polished his glasses and smiled vaguely at his feet. Bicycling back, my father thought that he had gone too far. Of course we had an interest in Mr Gleason. He pedalled back and asked him to attend a dance that was to be held on the next Friday, but Mr Gleason said he didn't dance.

'Oh well,' my father said, 'any time, just drop over.'

Mr Gleason went back to supervising his family of Chinese labourers on his wall.

Bald Hill towered high above the town and from my father's small filling station you could sit and watch the wall going up. It was an interesting sight. I watched it for two years, while I waited for customers who rarely came. After school and on Saturdays I had all the time in the world to watch the agonizing progress of Mr Gleason's wall. It was as painful as a clock. Sometimes I could see the Chinese labourers running at a jogtrot carrying bricks on long wooden planks. The hill was bare, and on this bareness Mr Gleason was, for some reason, building a wall.

In the beginning people thought it peculiar that someone would build such a big wall on Bald Hill. The only thing to recommend Bald Hill was the view of the town, and Mr Gleason was building a wall that denied that view. The top soil was thin and bare clay showed through in places. Nothing would ever grow there. Everyone assumed that Gleason had simply gone mad and after the initial interest they accepted his madness as they accepted his wall and as they accepted Bald Hill itself.

Occasionally someone would pull in for petrol at my father's filling station and ask about the wall and my father would shrug and I would see, once more, the strangeness of it.

'A house?' the stranger would ask. 'Up on that hill?'

'No,' my father would say, 'chap named Gleason is building a wall.'

And the strangers would want to know why, and my father would shrug and look up at Bald Hill once more. 'Damned if I know,' he'd say.

Gleason still lived in his old house at Mason's Lane. It was a plain weatherboard house with a rose garden at the front, a vegetable garden down the side, and an orchard at the back.

At night we kids would sometimes ride out to Bald Hill on our bicycles. It was an agonizing, muscle-twitching ride, the worst part of which was a steep, unmade road up which we finally pushed our bikes, our lungs rasping in the night air. When we arrived we found nothing but walls. Once we broke down some of the brickwork and another time we threw stones at the tents where the Chinese labourers slept. Thus we expressed our frustration at this inexplicable thing.

The wall must have been finished on the day before my twelfth birthday. I remember going on a picnic birthday party up to Eleven Mile Creek and we lit a fire and cooked chops at a bend in the river from where it was possible to see the walls on Bald Hill. I remember standing with a hot chop in my hand and someone saying, 'Look, they're leaving!'

We stood on the creek bed and watched the Chinese labourers walking their bicycles slowly down the hill. Some-one said they were going to build a chimney up at the mine at A.1 and certainly there is a large brick chimney there now, so I suppose they built it.

When the word spread that the walls were finished most of the town went up to look. They walked around the four walls which were as interesting as any other brick walls. They stood in front of the big wooden gates and tried to peer through, but all they could see was a small blind wall that had obviously been constructed for this special purpose. The walls themselves were ten feet high and topped with broken glass and barbed wire. When it became obvious that we were not going to discover the contents of the enclosure, we all gave up and went home.

Mr Gleason had long since stopped coming into town. His wife came instead, wheeling a pram down from Mason's Lane to Main Street and filling it with groceries and meat (they never bought vegetables, they grew their own) and wheeling it back to Mason's Lane. Sometimes you would see her standing with the pram halfway up the Gell Street hill. Just standing there, catching her breath. No one asked her about the wall. They knew she wasn't responsible for the wall and they felt sorry for her, having to bear the burden of the pram and her husband's madness. Even when she began to visit Dixon's hardware and buy plaster of paris and tins of paint and waterproofing compound, no one asked her what these things were for. She had a way of averting her eyes that indicated her terror of questions. Old Dixon carried the plas-ter of paris and the tins of paint out to her pram for her and watched her push them away. 'Poor woman,' he said, 'poor bloody woman.'

From the filling station where I sat dreaming in the sun, or from the enclosed office where I gazed mournfully at the rain, I would see, occasionally, Gleason entering or leaving his walled compound, a tiny figure way up on Bald Hill. And I'd think 'Gleason', but not much more.

Occasionally strangers drove up there to see what was going on, often egged on by locals who told them it was a Chinese temple or some other silly thing. Once a group of

Italians had a picnic outside the walls and took photographs of each other standing in front of the closed door. God knows what they thought it was.

But for five years between my twelfth and seventeenth birthdays there was nothing to interest me in Gleason's walls. Those years seem lost to me now and I can remember very little of them. I developed a crush on Susy Markin and followed her back from the swimming pool on my bicycle. I sat behind her in the pictures and wandered past her house. Then her parents moved to another town and I sat in the sun and waited for them to come back.

We became very keen on modernization. When coloured paints became available the whole town went berserk and brightly coloured houses blossomed overnight. But the paints were not of good quality and quickly faded and peeled, so that the town looked like a garden of dead flowers. Thinking of those years, the only real thing I recall is the soft hiss of bicycle tyres on the main street. When I think of it now it seems very peaceful, but I remember then that the sound induced in me a feeling of melancholy, a feeling somehow mixed with the early afternoons when the sun went down behind Bald Hill and the town felt as sad as an empty dance hall on a Sunday afternoon.

And then, during my seventeenth year, Mr Gleason died. We found out when we saw Mrs Gleason's pram parked out in front of Phonsey Joy's Funeral Parlour. It looked very sad, that pram, standing by itself in the windswept street. We came and looked at the pram and felt sad for Mrs Gleason. She hadn't had much of a life.

Phonsey Joy carried old Mr Gleason out to the cemetery by the Parwan Railway Station and Mrs Gleason rode behind in a taxi. People watched the old hearse go by and thought, 'Gleason', but not much else.

And then, less than a month after Gleason had been buried out at the lonely cemetery by the Parwan Railway Station, the Chinese labourers came back. We saw them push their bicycles up the hill. I stood with my father and Phonsey Joy and wondered what was going on.

And then I saw Mrs Gleason trudging up the hill. I nearly didn't recognize her, because she didn't have her pram. She carried a black umbrella and walked slowly up Bald Hill and it wasn't until she stopped for breath and leant forward that I recognized her.

'It's Mrs Gleason,' I said, 'with the Chinese.'

But it wasn't until the next morning that it became obvious what was happening. People lined the main street in the way they do for a big funeral but, instead of gazing towards the Grant Street corner, they all looked up at Bald Hill.

All that day and all the next we gathered to watch the destruction of the walls. We saw the Chinese labourers darting to and fro, but it wasn't until they knocked down a large section of the wall facing the town that we realized there really was something inside. It was impossible to see what it was, but there was something there. People stood and wondered and pointed out Mrs Gleason to each other as she went to and fro supervising the work.

And finally, in ones and twos, on bicycles and on foot, the whole town moved up to Bald Hill. Mr Dyer closed up his butcher shop and my father got out the old Chev truck and we finally arrived up at Bald Hill with twenty people on board. They crowded into the back tray and hung onto the running boards and my father grimly steered his way through the crowds of bicycles and parked just where the dirt track gets really steep. We trudged up this last steep track, never for a moment suspecting what we would find at the top.

It was very quiet up there. The Chinese labourers worked diligently, removing the third and fourth walls and cleaning the bricks which they stacked neatly in big piles. Mrs Gleason said nothing either. She stood in the only remaining corner of the walls and looked defiantly at the townspeople who stood open mouthed where another corner had been.

And between us and Mrs Gleason was the most incredibly beautiful thing I had ever seen in my life. For one moment I didn't recognize it. I stood open-mouthed, and breathed the surprising beauty of it. And then I realized it was our town. The buildings were two feet high and they were a little rough but very correct. I saw Mr Dyer nudge my father and whisper that Gleason had got the faded 'U' in the BUTCHER sign of his shop.

I think at that moment everyone was overcome with a feeling of simple joy. I can't remember ever having felt so uplifted and happy. It was perhaps a childish emotion but I looked up at my father and saw a smile of such warmth spread across his face that I knew he felt just as I did. Later he told me that he thought Gleason had built the model of our town just for this moment, to let us see the beauty of our own town, to make us proud of ourselves and to stop the American Dreams we were so prone to. For the rest, my father said, was not Gleason's plan and he could not have foreseen the things that happened afterwards.

I have come to think that this view of my father's is a little sentimental and also, perhaps, insulting to Gleason. I personally believe that he knew everything that would happen. One day the proof of my theory may be discovered. Certainly there are in existence some personal papers, and I firmly believe that these papers will show that Gleason knew exactly what would happen.

We had been so overcome by the model of the town that we hadn't noticed what was the most remarkable thing of all. Not only had Gleason built the houses and the shops of our town, he had also peopled it. As we tip-toed into the town we suddenly found ourselves. 'Look,' I said to Mr Dyer, 'there you are.'

And there he was, standing in front of his shop in his apron. As I bent down to examine the tiny figure I was staggered by the look on its face. The modelling was crude, the paint work was sloppy, and the face a little too white, but the expression was absolutely perfect: those pursed, quizzical lips and the eyebrows lifted high. It was Mr Dyer and no one else on earth.

And there beside Mr Dyer was my father, squatting on the footpath and gazing lovingly at Mr Dyer's bicycle's gears, his face marked with grease and hope.

And there was I, back at the filling station, leaning against a petrol pump in an American pose and talking to Brian Sparrow who was amusing me with his clownish antics.

Phonsey Joy standing beside his hearse. Mr Dixon sitting inside his hardware store. Everyone I knew was there in that tiny town. If they were not in the streets or in their backyards they were inside their houses, and it didn't take very long to discover that you could lift off the roofs and peer inside.

We tip-toed around the streets peeping into each other's windows, lifting off each other's roofs, admiring each other's gardens, and, while we did it, Mrs Gleason slipped silently away down the hill towards Mason's Lane. She spoke to nobody and nobody spoke to her.

I confess that I was the one who took the roof from Cavanagh's house. So I was the one who found Mrs Cavanagh in bed with young Craigie Evans.

I stood there for a long time, hardly knowing what I was seeing. I stared at the pair of them for a long, long time. And when I finally knew what I was seeing I felt such an incredible mixture of jealousy and guilt and wonder that I didn't know what to do with the roof.

Eventually it was Phonsey Joy who took the roof from my hands and placed it carefully back on the house, much, I imagine, as he would have placed the lid on a coffin. By then other people had seen what I had seen and the word passed around very quickly.

And then we all stood around in little groups and regarded the model town with what could only have been fear. If Gleason knew about Mrs Cavanagh and Craigie Evans (and no one else had), what other things might he know? Those who hadn't seen themselves yet in the town began to look a little nervous and were unsure of whether to look for themselves or not. We gazed silently at the roofs and felt mistrustful and guilty.

We all walked down the hill then, very quietly, the way people walk away from a funeral, listening only to the crunch of the gravel under our feet while the women had trouble with their high-heeled shoes.

The next day a special meeting of the shire council passed a motion calling on Mrs Gleason to destroy the model town on the grounds that it contravened building regulations.

It is unfortunate that this order wasn't carried out before the city newspapers found out. Before another day had gone by the government had stepped in.

The model town and its model occupants were to be

preserved. The minister for tourism came in a large black car and made a speech to us in the football pavilion. We sat on the high, tiered seats eating potato chips while he stood against the fence and talked to us. We couldn't hear him very well, but we heard enough. He called the model town a work of art and we stared at him grimly. He said it would be an invaluable tourist attraction. He said tourists would come from everywhere to see the model town. We would be famous. Our businesses would flourish. There would be work for guides and interpreters and caretakers and taxi drivers and people selling soft drinks and ice creams.

The Americans would come, he said. They would visit our town in buses and in cars and on the train. They would take photographs and bring wallets bulging with dollars. American dollars.

We looked at the minister mistrustfully, wondering if he knew about Mrs Cavanagh, and he must have seen the look because he said that certain controversial items would be removed, had already been removed. We shifted in our seats, like you do when a particularly tense part of a film has come to its climax, and then we relaxed and listened to what the minister had to say. And we all began, once more, to dream our American dreams.

We saw our big smooth cars cruising through cities with bright lights. We entered expensive night-clubs and danced till dawn. We made love to women like Kim Novak and men like Rock Hudson. We drank cocktails. We gazed lazily into refrigerators filled with food and prepared ourselves lavish midnight snacks which we ate while we watched huge television sets on which we would be able to see American movies free of charge and forever.

The minister, like someone from our American dreams, re-entered his large black car and cruised slowly from our humble sportsground, and the newspaper men arrived and swarmed over the pavilion with their cameras and note books. They took photographs of us and photographs of the models up on Bald Hill. And the next day we were all over the newspapers. The photographs of the model people side by side with photographs of the real people. And our names and ages and what we did were all printed there in black and white.

They interviewed Mrs Gleason but she said nothing of interest. She said the model town had been her husband's hobby.

We all felt good now. It was very pleasant to have your photograph in the paper. And, once more, we changed our opinion of Gleason. The shire council held another meeting and named the dirt track up Bald Hill, 'Gleason Avenue'. Then we all went home and waited for the Americans we had been promised.

It didn't take long for them to come, although at the time it seemed an eternity, and we spent six long months doing nothing more with our lives than waiting for them.

Well, they did come. And let me tell you how it has all worked out for us.

The Americans arrive every day in buses and cars and sometimes the younger ones come on the train. There is now a small airstrip out near the Parwan cemetery and they also arrive there, in small aeroplanes. Phonsey Joy drives them to the cemetery where they look at Gleason's grave and then up to Bald Hill and then down to the town. He is doing very well from it all. It is good to see someone doing well from it. Phonsey is becoming a big man in town and is on the shire council.

On Bald Hill there are half a dozen telescopes through which the Americans can spy on the town and reassure themselves that it is the same down there as it is on Bald Hill. Herb Gravney sells them ice creams and soft drinks and extra film for their cameras. Here is another who is doing well. He bought the whole model from Mrs Gleason and charges five American dollars admission. Herb is on the council now too. He's doing very well for himself. He sells them the film so they can take photographs of the house and the model people and so they can come down to the town with their special maps and hunt out the real people.

To tell the truth most of us are pretty sick of the game. They come looking for my father and ask him to stare at the gears of Dyer's bicycle. I watch my father cross the street slowly, his head hung low. He doesn't greet the Americans anymore. He doesn't ask them questions about colour television or Washington DC. He kneels on the footpath in front of Dyer's bike. They stand around him. Often they remember the model incorrectly and try to get my father to pose in the wrong way. Originally he argued with them, but now he argues no more. He does what they ask. They push him this way and that and worry about the expression on his face which is no longer what it was.

Then I know they will come to find me. I am next on the map. I am very popular for some reason. They come in search of me and my petrol pump as they have done for four years now. I do not await them eagerly because I know, before they reach me, that they will be disappointed.

'But this is not the boy.'

'Yes,' says Phonsey, 'this is him all right.' And he gets me to show them my certificate.

They examine the certificate suspiciously, feeling the paper as if it might be a clever forgery. 'No,' they declare. (Americans are so confident.) 'No,' they shake their heads, 'this is not the real boy. The real boy is younger.'

'He's older now. He used to be younger.' Phonsey looks weary when he tells them. He can afford to look weary.

The Americans peer at my face closely. 'It's a different boy.'

But finally they get their cameras out. I stand sullenly and try to look amused as I did once. Gleason saw me looking amused but I can no longer remember how it felt. I was looking at Brian Sparrow. But Brian is also tired. He finds it difficult to do his clownish antics and to the Americans his little act isn't funny. They prefer the model. I watch him sadly, sorry that he must perform for such an unsympathetic audience.

The Americans pay one dollar for the right to take our photographs. Having paid the money they are worried about being cheated. They spend their time being disappointed and I spend my time feeling guilty, that I have somehow let them down by growing older and sadder.

'Do You Love Me?'

1 The Role of the Cartographers

Perhaps a few words about the role of the Cartographers in our present society are warranted.

To begin with one must understand the nature of the yearly census, a manifestation of our desire to know, always, exactly where we stand. The census, originally a count of the population, has gradually extended until it has become a total inventory of the contents of the nation, a mammoth task which is continuing all the time – no sooner has one census been announced than work on another begins.

The results of the census play an important part in our national life and have, for many years, been the pivot point for the yearly 'Festival of the Corn' (an ancient festival, related to the wealth of the earth).

We have a passion for lists. And nowhere is this more clearly illustrated than in the Festival of the Corn which takes place in midsummer, the weather always being fine and warm. On the night of the festival, the householders move their goods and possessions, all furniture, electrical goods, clothing, rugs, kitchen utensils, bathrobes, slippers, cushions, lawnmowers, curtains, doorstops, heirlooms, cameras, and anything else that can be moved, into the street so that the census officials may the more easily check the inventory of each household.

The Festival of the Corn is, however, much more than a clerical affair. And, the day over and the night come, the householders invite each other to view their possessions which they refer to, on this night, as gifts. It is like nothing more than a wedding feast – there is much cooking, all sorts of traditional dishes, fine wines, strong liquors, music is played loudly in quiet neighbourhoods, strangers copulate with strangers, men dance together, and maidens in yellow robes distribute small barley sugar corn-cobs to young and old alike.

And in all this the role of the Cartographers is perhaps the most important, for our people crave, more than anything else, to know the extent of the nation, to know, exactly, the shape of the coastline, to hear what land may have been lost to the sea, to know what has been reclaimed and what is still in doubt. If the Cartographers' report is good the Festival of the Corn will be a good festival. If the report is bad, one can always sense, for all the dancing and drinking, a feeling of nervousness and apprehension in the revellers, a certain desperation. In the year of a bad Cartographers' report there will always be fights and, occasionally, some property will be stolen as citizens attempt to compensate themselves for their sense of loss.

Because of the importance of their job the Cartographers have become an élite – well-paid, admired, envied, and having no small opinion of themselves. It is said by some that they are over-proud, immoral, vain and foot-loose, and it is perhaps the last charge (by necessity true) that brings about the others. For the Cartographers spend their years travelling up and down the coast, along the great rivers, traversing great mountains and vast deserts. They travel in small parties of three, four, sometimes five, making their own time, working as they please, because eventually it is their own responsibility to see that their team's task is completed in time.

My father, a Cartographer himself, often told me stories about himself or his colleagues and the adventures they had in the wilderness.

There were other stories, however, that always remained in my mind and, as a child, caused me considerable anxiety. These were the stories of the nether regions and I doubt if they were known outside a very small circle of Cartographers and government officials. As a child in a house frequented by Cartographers, I often heard these tales which invariably made me cling closely to my mother's skirts.

It appears that for some time certain regions of the country had become less and less real and these regions were regarded fearfully even by the Cartographers, who prided themselves on their courage. The regions in question were invariably uninhabited, unused for agriculture or industry. There were certain sections of the Halverson Ranges, vast stretches of the Greater Desert, and long pieces of coastline which had begun to slowly disappear like the image of an improperly fixed photograph.

It was because of these nebulous areas that the Fischer-scope was introduced. The Fischerscope is not unlike radar in its principle and is able to detect the presence of any object, no matter how dematerialized or insubstantial. In this way the Cartographers were still able to map the questionable parts of the nether regions. To have returned with blanks on the maps would have created such public anxiety that no one dared think what it might do to the stability of our society. I now have reason to believe that certain areas of the country disappeared so completely that even the Fischerscope could not detect them and the Cartographers, acting under political pressure, used old maps to fake-in the missing sections. If my theory is grounded in fact, and I am sure it is, it would explain my father's cynicism about the Festival of the Corn.

2 The Archetypal Cartographer

My father was in his fifties but he had kept himself in good shape. His skin was brown and his muscles still firm. He was a tall man with a thick head of grey hair, a slightly less grey moustache and a long aquiline nose. Sitting on a horse he looked as proud and cruel as Genghis Khan. Lying on the beach clad only in bathers and sunglasses he still managed to retain his authoritative air.

Beside him I always felt as if I had betrayed him. I was slightly built, more like my mother.

It was the day before the festival and we lay on the beach, my father, my mother, my girlfriend and I. As was usual in these circumstances my father addressed all his remarks to Karen. He never considered the members of his own family worth talking to. I always had the uncomfortable feeling that he was flirting with my girlfriends and I never knew what to do about it.

People were lying in groups up and down the beach. Near

us a family of five were playing with a large beach ball.

'Look at those fools,' my father said to Karen.

'Why are they fools?' Karen asked.

'They're fools,' said my father. 'They were born fools and they'll die fools. Tomorrow they'll dance in the streets and drink too much.'

'So.' said Karen triumphantly, in the manner of one who has become privy to secret information. 'It will be a good Cartographer's report?'

My father roared with laughter.

Karen looked hurt and pouted. 'Am I a fool?'

'No,' my father said, 'you're really quite splendid.'

3 The Most Famous Festival

The festival, as it turned out, was the greatest disaster in living memory.

The Cartographers' report was excellent, the weather was fine, but somewhere something had gone wrong.

The news was confusing. The television said that, in spite of the good report, various items had been stolen very early in the night. Later there was a news flash to say that a large house had completely disappeared in Howie Street.

Later still we looked out the window to see a huge band of people carrying lighted torches. There was a lot of shouting. The same image, exactly, was on the television and a reporter was explaining that bands of vigilantes were out looking for thieves.

My father stood at the window, a martini in his hand, and watched the vigilantes set alight a house opposite.

My mother wanted to know what we should do.

'Come and watch the fools,' my father said, 'they're incredible.'

4 The ICI Incident

The next day the ICI building disappeared in front of a crowd of two thousand people. It took two hours. The crowd stood silently as the great steel and glass structure slowly faded before them.

The staff who were evacuated looked pale and shaken. The

caretaker who was amongst the last to leave looked almost translucent. In the days that followed he made some name for himself as a mystic, claiming that he had been able to see other worlds, layer upon layer, through the fabric of the here and now.

5 Behaviour when Confronted with Dematerialization

The anger of our people when confronted with acts of theft has always been legendary and was certainly highlighted by the incidents which occurred on the night of the festival.

But the fury exhibited on this famous night could not compare with the intensity of emotion displayed by those who witnessed the earliest scenes of dematerialization.

The silent crowd who watched the ICI building erupted into hysteria when they realized that it had finally gone and wasn't likely to come back.

It was like some monstrous theft for which punishment must be meted out.

They stormed into the Shell building next door and smashed desks and ripped down office partitions. Reporters who attended the scene were rarely impartial observers, but one of the cooler-headed members of the press remarked on the great number of weeping men and women who hurled typewriters from windows and scattered files through crowds of frightened office workers.

Five days later they displayed similar anger when the Shell building itself disappeared.

6 Behaviour of Those Dematerializing

The first reports of dematerializing people were not generally believed and were suppressed by the media. But these things were soon common knowledge and few families were untouched by them. Such incidents were obviously not all the same but in many victims there was a tendency to exhibit extreme aggression towards those around them. Murders and assaults committed by these unfortunates were not uncommon and in most cases they exhibited an almost unbelievable rage, as if they were the victims of a shocking betrayal.

My friend James Bray was once stopped in the street by a very beautiful woman who clawed and scratched at his face and said: 'You did this to me, you bastard, you did this to me.'

He had never seen her before but he confessed that, in some irrational way, he felt responsible and didn't defend himself. Fortunately she disappeared before she could do him much damage.

7 Some Theories that Arose at the Time

1 The world is merely a dream dreamt by God who is waking after a long sleep. When he is properly awake the world will disappear completely. When the world disappears we will disappear with it and be happy

2 The world has become sensitive to light. In the same way that prolonged use of say penicillin can suddenly result in a dangerous allergy, prolonged exposure of the world to the sun has made it sensitive to light.

The advocates of this theory could be seen bustling through the city crowds in their long, hooded black robes.

3 The fact that the world is disappearing has been caused by the sloppy work of the Cartographers and census-takers. Those who filled out their census forms incorrectly would lose those items they had neglected to describe. People overlooked in the census by impatient officials would also disappear. A strong pressure group demanded that a new census be taken quickly before matters got worse.

8 My Father's Theory

The world, according to my father, was exactly like the human body and had its own defence mechanisms with which it defended itself against anything that either threatened it or was unnecessary to it. The ICI building and the ICI company had obviously constituted some threat to the world or had simply been irrelevant. That's why it had disappeared and not because some damn fool god was waking up and rubbing his eyes.

'I don't believe in god,' my father said. 'Humanity is god. Humanity is the only god I know. If humanity doesn't need something it will disappear. People who are not loved will disappear. Everything that is not loved will disappear from the face of the earth. We only exist through the love of others and that's what it's all about.'

9 A Contradiction

'Look at those fools,' my father said, 'they wouldn't know if they were up themselves.'

10 An Unpleasant Scene

The world at this time was full of unpleasant and disturbing scenes. One that I recall vividly took place in the middle of the city on a hot, sultry Tuesday afternoon. It was about one-thirty and I was waiting for Karen by the post office when a man of forty or so ran past me. He was dematerializing rapidly. Everybody seemed to be deliberately looking the other way, which seemed to me to make him dematerialize faster. I stared at him hard, hoping that I could do something to keep him there until help arrived. I tried to love him, because I believed in my father's theory. I thought, I must love that man. But his face irritated me. It is not so easy to love a stranger and I'm ashamed to say that he had the small mouth and close-together eyes that I have always disliked in a person. I tried to love him but I'm afriad I failed.

While I watched he tried to hail taxi after taxi. But the taxi drivers were only too well aware of what was happening and had no wish to spend their time driving a passenger who, at any moment, might cease to exist. They looked the other way or put up their NOT FOR HIRE signs.

Finally he managed to waylay a taxi at some traffic lights. By this time he was so insubstantial that I could see right through him. He was beginning to shout. A terrible thin noise, but penetrating none the less. He tried to open the cab door, but the driver had already locked it. I could hear the man's voice, high and piercing: 'I want to go home.' He repeated it over and over again. 'I want to go home to my wife.'

The taxi drove off when the lights changed. There was a lull in the traffic. People had fled the corner and left it deserted and it was I alone who saw the man finally disappear.

I felt sick.

Karen arrived five minutes later and found me pale and shaken 'Are you all right?' she said.

'Do you love me?' I said.

11 The Nether Regions

My father had an irritating way of explaining things to me I already understood, refusing to stop no matter how much I said 'I know' or 'You told me before'.

Thus he expounded on the significance of the nether regions, adopting the tone of a lecturer speaking to a class of particularly backward children.

'As you know,' he said, 'the nether regions were amongst the first to disappear and this in itself is significant. These regions, I'm sure you know, are seldom visited by men and only then by people like me whose sole job is to make sure that they're still there. We had no use for these areas, these deserts, swamps, and coastlines which is why, of course, they disappeared. They were merely possessions of ours and if they had any use at all it was as symbols for our poets, writers and film-makers. They were used as symbols of alienation, lovelessness, loneliness, uselessness and so on. Do you get what I mean?'

'Yes,' I said, 'I get what you mean.'

'But do you?' My father insisted. 'But do you really, I wonder.' He examined me seriously, musing on the possibilities of my understanding him. 'How old are you?'

'Twenty,' I said.

'I knew, of course,' he said. 'Do you understand the significance of the nether regions?'

I sighed, a little too loudly and my father narrowed his eyes. Quickly I said: 'They are like everything else. They're like the cities. The cities are deserts where people are alone and lonely. They don't love one another.'

'Don't love one another,' intoned my father, also sighing. 'We no longer love one another. When we realize that we need one another we will stop disappearing. This is a lesson to us. A hard lesson, but, I hope, an effective one.'

My father continued to speak, but I watched him without listening. After a few minutes he stopped abruptly: 'Are you listening to me?' he said. I was surprised to detect real concern in his voice. He looked at me questioningly. 'I've always looked after you,' he said, 'ever since you were little.'

12 The Cartographers' Fall

I don't know when it was that I noticed that my father had become depressed. It probably happened quite gradually without either my mother or me noticing it.

Even when I did become aware of it I attributed it to a woman. My father had a number of lovers and his moods usually reflected the success or failure of these relationships.

But I know now that he had heard already of Hurst and Jamov, the first two Cartographers to disappear. The news was suppressed for several weeks and then, somehow or other, leaked to the press. Certainly the Cartographers had enemies amongst the civil servants who regarded them as over-proud and overpaid, and it was probably from one of these civil servants that the press heard the news.

When the news finally broke I understood my father's depression and felt sorry for him.

I didn't know how to help him. I wanted, badly, to make him happy. I had never ever been able to give him anything or do anything for him that he couldn't do better himself. Now I wanted to help him, to show him I understood.

I found him sitting in front of the television one night when I returned from my office and I sat quietly beside him. He seemed more kindly now and he placed his hand on my knee and patted it.

I sat there for a while, overcome with the new warmth of this relationship and then, unable to contain my emotion any more, I blurted out: 'You could change your job.'

My father stiffened and sat bolt upright. The pressure of his hand on my knee increased until I yelped with pain, and still he held on, hurting me terribly.

'You are a fool,' he said, 'you wouldn't know if you were up yourself.'

Through the pain in my leg, I felt the intensity of my father's fear.

13 Why the World Needs Cartographers

My father woke me at 3 a.m. to tell me why the world needed Cartographers. He smelled of whisky and seemed, once again, to be very gentle.

'The world needs Cartographers,' he said softly, 'because if they didn't have Cartographers the fools wouldn't know where they were. They wouldn't know if they were up themselves if they didn't have a Cartographer to tell them what's happening. The world needs Cartographers,' my father said, 'it fucking well needs Cartographers.'

14 One Final Scene

Let me describe a final scene to you: I am sitting on the sofa my father brought home when I was five years old. I am watching television. My father is sitting in a leather armchair that once belonged to his father and which has always been exclusively his. My mother is sitting in the dining alcove with her cards spread across the table, playing one more interminable game of patience.

I glance casually across at my father to see if he is doing anything more than stare into space, and notice, with a terrible shock, that he is showing the first signs of dematerializing.

'What are you staring at?' My father, in fact, has been staring at me.

'Nothing.'

'Well, don't.'

Nervously I return my eyes to the inanity of the television. I don't know what to do. Should I tell my father that he is dematerializing? If I don't tell him will he notice? I feel I should do something but I can feel, already, the anger in his voice. His anger is nothing new. But this is possibly the beginning of a tide of uncontrollable rage. If he knows he is dematerializing, he will think I don't love him. He will blame me. He will attack me. Old as he is, he is still considerably stronger than I am and he could hurt me badly. I stare determinedly at the television and feel my father's eyes on me.

I try to feel love for my father, I try very, very hard.

I attempt to remember how I felt about him when I was little, in the days when he was still occasionally tender towards me.

But it's no good.

Because I can only remember how he has hit me, hurt me, humiliated me and flirted with my girlfriends. I realize, with a flush of panic and guilt, that I don't love him. In spite of which I say: 'I love you.'

My mother looks up sharply from her cards and lets out a surprised cry.

I turn to my father. He has almost disappeared. I can see the leather of the chair through his stomach.

I don't know whether it is my unconvincing declaration of love or my mother's exclamation that makes my father laugh. For whatever reason, he begins to laugh uncontrollably: 'You bloody fools,' he gasps, 'I wish you could see the looks on your bloody silly faces.'

And then he is gone.

My mother looks across at me nervously, a card still in her hand. 'Do you love me?' she asks.

BARRY HILL

Fires on the Beach

From Lisbon they went up the coast on a slow train, stopping at a village supposed to be relatively free of tourists. For part of the way they had a view of the sea – pale, glittering – but then they lost sight of it until they got off at the beautiful little railway siding. Sunflowers grew along the platform and pastel coloured tiles adorned the ticket office, and there, through the miniature archway, was the sea again – still pale, but angry now with surf rolling in all the way from North America. After three winters in London it was a sight to behold. It was, above all, what they both wanted, and it only remained for them to get to the hotel and they would be launched, properly, on their holiday.

With barely a thought for Sally, Andrew scooped up the luggage and headed off, brusquely dismissing a porter, trusting that she would quickly follow on – which she did, the tangerine beach bag over her shoulder, impressing the porter with her abandon. Andrew laboured with the bags, sweating, already irritable, but under no circumstances would he resort to tipping. She followed on agreeably because she knew it was the only occasion he would have to carry everything at once: this year they had readily agreed on one thing – it would be best for them both to settle in one spot rather than feel compelled to see a whole new country.

The hotel was at the end of the beach. Andrew dumped the bags at the foot of the concrete steps and together they pushed open the frosted glass doors. Inside all was aluminium tubing and plastic. The people at reception were churlish – and slow. When they were finally shown to their room it turned out to be in the far wing at the end of cellular corridors, with its balcony looking inland. They waited until the boy left and threw themselves down on opposite sides of the rickety bed. The impossibility of advance booking! Yet,

Andrew insisted, like the relatively young husband that he was, what else can one do but hope that a simple plan will work? She was not blaming him, Sally said, and they went downstairs to order coffee. In the lounge they sat in airport chairs set in a rectangular well, the centre of which was occupied by an enormous fish tank. The hotel had a reputation for excellent seafood. Green light from the tank seeped evenly towards each corner of the room. There was no window to the outdoors. A waiter came to ask if they wanted Irish coffee, and then, when they turned incredulously to each other, and each was faced with the other's lime green grief, they broke into laughter and ordered beer. Mishaps united them. They would stay the few days they had paid for in advance, then they would find somewhere else. At least they had reached the sea.

They spent the mornings reading, walking, swimming, before lunching sumptuously of seafood at one of the beach cafés (the hotel restaurant was not what it was cracked up to be). After lunch they made love, which was followed by a voluptuous siesta; then, late afternoon, they emerged hand in hand on the promenade, strolled to the village square, selected a quiet spot amongst the forest of chairs and tables. Each then resumed their reading, each, in their own way, continuing the siesta which Andrew declared governed the life of the nation. He read *Books and Bookmen* because even when half asleep and on holiday he felt that one could not afford to be completely divorced from what the other publishing houses were up to. Sally read Iris Murdoch's *The Bell* because he had strongly recommended it. Of course they talked with each other as well: they still had a good deal to say to each other, especially considering they had been together for ten years (eight married, two as teenage lovers prior to that), and they did talk, quite animatedly about some things. But then the conversation would lapse and they contentedly returned to their reading, or observing the world about. Trust was still sufficient for one to be able to nudge the other and for them both to look – silently, while each assumed that the other was thinking and feeling at least roughly similar things. Together they managed to see a good deal of Asia, and most of Western Europe.

But here Andrew could not get over the locals, or rather, those villagers who did not depend for a living on selling trinkets and port wine. It was supposed to be a thriving fishing village. But there, out on the sand, were a solid proportion of the workforce. They lay on the sand between the dilapidated hulls of their boats which someone had dragged up from the water. In their black sweaters and shawls they sprawled – individually, in pairs, in cumbersome clumps, like schools of beached whales. Men, women, and children, men especially he noticed, seemed to spend the day with their heads down, faces into their black sleeves. One only saw their faces in the late afternoon, when they sat up, lit fires on the beach, and gathered in groups with their backs to the setting sun. On their way back to the hotel, Andrew could not resist going much closer to them than Sally thought necessary or polite.

He wanted to photograph them, to capture this unique feature of the shoreline, but as he approached children leapt away from the fires and pitched mussel shells at his telephoto lens. Their parents smiled: his lens would have brought up their rows of broken teeth wonderfully. 'You shouldn't,' Sally said, and he turned away from her in disgust. That cautionary tone of voice riled him as much as his own compulsion to set the most random of objects into some sort of order. He knew he took a good photograph: it was his way of making a little more sense of things. Were these the men who went off in the night fleet? Were these the same families they had seen at the daily fish auction? Sally did not show any interest in these things. And he did not want to encroach upon them unduly, there would have been something morbid in that. Yet what could be more morbid than a beach littered with the shrouded bodies of entire families? He felt intensely put out. She put his irritability down to their poor accommodation.

At last they could move out of what Andrew had come to call The Aquarium. Along the way they found a room right over their favourite café. It gave, in one direction, a view of the beach: the hulls, the bodies dormant, and of the sea which, when they went out on their balcony in the mornings, was a flat, wide silver blade all the way to the horizon, so dazzling that one almost overlooked the line of surf, that forever pounded in, running so hard that Andrew wondered whether a fisherman might occasionally be picked up from the beach and swept out. In the other direction they looked to the bluff, and the little white chapel which sat on the cliff top. It was altogether an excellent situation; they virtually looked out upon the best part of the village. Life seemed to flow beneath the awning of the café and they could have well sat there all evening, sipping their port, letting sounds signify reality.

Inevitably though, at dusk, they went down. They descended to the promenade, drawn by the smell of the sardines. For each evening, without fail, the promenade became an avenue of tiny barbecues. On the portable grills the sardines were roasted over charcoal. This was the surplus of the day's catch and the smell of the fish – pungent, so rank of the sea – was such that one felt it in the palate whether it was being devoured – white, soft fleshed beneath the crust of burnt scales – or not. For Sally they were a little too strong. But he loved them. Each evening he insisted that they sit at one of the grills and eat until the sun was out of sight. 'Something to do,' he laughed – a most peculiar remark.

Each day she was perfecting her tan: a safe time on her neat, flat tummy, bronzing perfectly triangular shoulder blades, then on her back, an open invitation to the sun, cheeks and thighs glowing with the skin's osmosis and the best quality Swiss lotion. Lying an arm's length away, at an obtuse angle, he persisted with his reading, observing, from time to time, her easy transition from almond to honey, from bees' wax to maple syrup – she would stick at it for hours, occasionally rising to inspect the dark against the lighter patches, then resuming her position like a sleepwalker. When she sat up her eyes were blank from the marathon baking. Even when he said, into her perspiring face, 'Do you want a swim?' she would say, 'No,' and flop back comatose, fearless of sunstroke. He calculated that her mind would be completely vacant again by the time he hit the water.

The dip would save him.

Day after day the weather was perfect. Very soon they were both at their physical best. She was blonder than before;

he was taut, pared down by the sun. Dressing for dinner, each admired the other as if they had only recently met – he, her delicate, low-backed frocks, she, his swank in the Indian cotton shirt. He threatened to wear her straw hat into the café, the lilac ribbon flowing. 'Don't you dare,' she protested, though she would have loved him to. It occurred to him that with someone else – God knows who though – he blooming well might have.

In the sun she could feel her body loosening from the London winters. She had decided that they should never stay away from real summers for that length of time again. The sun eased one into deeper mutualities. Lying nearby, he found it hard to credit that a village could be as white, and as quiet as this one. The hour before noon was utterly hollow. If it had not been for the heaving of the sea, he might have thought they were on an outcrop of coral, coral dried dreadfully by the sun, then left uninhabited for decades.

Sometimes she stretched and said, 'Oh, oh, I could live here forever.'

In the evening he vomited. Feverish, he lay on the bed in their charming room, shaking, cold, squirming with the contractions of the diarrhoea. She was very concerned and brought him numerous hot and cold drinks from the café below. He moaned about the cost. She reprimanded him for stinginess. In the course of the evening he began to improve. He sat up in bed with refreshments, wearing sunglasses against the glare of the bed lamp. She laughed, and then he did put on the floppy straw hat. She forgave him his irritability, and, acknowledging that sunstroke was a bugger and that he was really putting up with it quite well, said, 'You'll just have to be more careful.' Whereupon he threw the hat at her like a saucer. Next day he was properly better.

Agreeably – for she was, above all, an agreeable woman, seldom meaning to offend, a woman who had grown into the position of being a young wife with considerable ease – agreeably she was prepared to shorten their morning sessions in the sun. It was simply a matter of lunching earlier and siestaing with the resignation of the locals. So in the mornings she continued to turn her windowless face to the sun, while he read until they went in – with more time ahead of them to eat, and make love. She seemed, too, to be replete with the sexual attention he was, on holiday, able to pay her. Afterwards she slept with that animal indifference which would have gratified most husbands. But Andrew was not so sure, or rather, he could not bear to lie beside her on such shallow assumptions. Before she woke, when he could not sleep at all, he crept out of the room, down to the streets, walking through the deserted lanes of the village, taking the narrow ones as far as its outskirts, returning via the wider ones which ended at the sea, the lanes which seemed to telescope the sea and sky to a prism. He would return replenished in time to hear her splashing in the shower, in time for a quiet cigarette on the balcony while she dressed. 'Are you ready, dear?' he said, 'Of course,' and catapulted his cigarette towards the sea. And later, during dinner, he had occasion to go back to the room alone. He looked into his London contact book, into the diary, the snakes and ladders of weeks and months. They had been in the village for eight days. A week to go.

On the cliff top, beyond the chapel, there was a bullfighting arena. It was a modest affair, and they discovered that in Portugal they did not kill the bulls. It was worth a visit. Of course Sally was still dubious. She loathed cruelty of any sort, and cattle, even bulls, were to her close cousins of the horses she had loved so dearly as a girl. Andrew persisted: it would be nothing like they had seen in Spain, not at all like they had been subjected to on Madrid television, where, eating in cheap cafés, they had the day's bullfights replayed like the football – all while they tried to enjoy the hot sausages. No, it would be nothing like that, he laughed. They should go up to the arena while it was under the full moon and watch the gentle art of Portuguese bullfighting.

And it was a highlight – of sorts – for him. It was a handsome, high-tiered arena, and they sat in good, middle-priced seats while the bulls came and went under the arc lights, the moon adding to the occasion. Young bulls, it seemed, that came down the race in fits and jerks of vigour, promising good entertainment. Sally sat tightly beside him, still anticipating the worst, shivering in her light dress. Their seat caught the wind from the sea. He put his arm about her and thought of the Roman women at the Colosseum, how they were open and wet at the sight of blood. Sally said, 'They're not going to, are they?' and hid her face in his neck. 'Of course not. How many times do I have to tell you.' He had snapped again. He tried to compensate with an extra hug. She pulled away. The bull continued to charge about, the gaily dressed young men in hot pursuit, then in rapid retreat when the bull turned and they had to tumble over the rail, their laughter revealing that the escape from the thundering hooves was just a little too easy, a little too safe. It was a very antique, courtly affair, with nothing any longer at risk. At one stage a bull dared to stand completely still in the arena, brazenly benign – moonstruck. And even when he was jabbed and poked, the run that he made towards the toreadors was desultory. It was as if the courtship of bulls had gone on for too long for everybody's good. The little arena stood on a splendid cliff top, only a dash from the raging sea, yet everything happening in it was tame: all events seemed to be held in abeyance.

Yet it was not until the following day that Sally said, finally, what he knew to be preoccupying her, what she had been grooming herself to say, what she always brought them around to on holidays, when she considered they had reached a certain state of mind. She had the knack of waiting for the peaceful moment. They were eating breakfast on the balcony. He was poised over his eggs. The surf had not yet sprung up. She spoke with eyes wide – blue with the morning.

'Andy, are we going to make a baby – one day?'

She spoke with such loving, unavoidable sweetness.

'Yes, of course, yes.'

'Are we really?' She was looking up under his gaze.

'Yes,' he said, smiling, and drawing the word out. He could be immensely patient, soft. He could say just about anything to forestall the next question.

He explained that clearly it partly depended on the reshuffle in the marketing division, whether it happened or not. Then they had to decide whether he was willing to be posted abroad, and whether they really wanted to start a family in the UK, or wait until they might be well set up in the US. He went on to reassure her that she was not really starting late (she was twenty-seven): loads of women had perfectly healthy children well into their thirties, the risks, statistically, empirically, factually speaking, were not that great, not really.

Sally heard him out before asking, 'Don't you wish we had a love child?'

'Can I just finish my breakfast before we go on?'

'Bugger.'

'Sal, please don't spoil the morning. What difference does it make if we wait another eighteen months, another two years even? Why should we rush into it now and spoil all the other options?'

'Options. Options.'

'Sal . . .' he said. He finished off the hard, cold egg. He swirled his cheeks full of coffee, discarded the toast. This was giving her plenty of time to be reasonable and now he was going to stand up. He was on the way to the beach, since she was not going to be sensible. He threw down the napkin as she said, 'I know, I know that. I'm being silly,' and he smiled, thinking that the pale blue of the morning was back between them, when she added, 'I know that we've got a whole lifetime ahead of us.'

Together they went down to the beach and lay on the sand. The sun was ruthless. He was forced to let drop his small volume of verse and shut his eyes. The heat, biting his back as if it were shell grit, drove away the light and seemed to wedge solid shadow at the back of his eyes. There was little point in looking up at things. He was indifferent to everything. He longed for something to happen – anything.

Something did. The next day there was what might be called an incident.

It was towards the end of the morning and they had been reading, nodding off, even swimming together, in a fairly amicable way, his seizure of the previous day having insinuated itself, somehow, elsewhere – perhaps into the hulls of the forsaken boats, into the bodies of the fishermen, into the azure sky. He had, at any rate, settled for a morning's decent reading, from time to time lifting his head to look out to sea. The breeze off the water was immensely refreshing. He kept taking lungfuls of it, quite unaware of how much he would need them.

There were people in the water – splashing in the shore break rather than swimming, throwing their arms up and down in tune with the surf, shrieking when the water billowed over their heads: simpletons at play, the epilepsy of the faint-hearted and incompetent. Andrew had always been an able, much praised swimmer. His eyes swept beyond the shore breaks towards the line of proper waves, those which reared into glassy walls before rushing down their invisible race to the beach. Beyond that line a man was swimming, and absent-mindedly, with half a thought to joining him, Andrew was looking. The man was waving.

God only knew who to.

But he kept waving.

Andrew returned to his book.

Sally sat up and said: 'I think that man out there is in trouble.'

'Hell, I think you're right.'

It was ridiculous, the way one had no choice about such things. Andrew ran down the sand at a graceful trot, as if he might have been running up the beach for an ice cream rather than down to the surf which he waded through with quick high knees, pushing himself through and under the early waves, before striking out in the heavy water. When he took his first strokes he felt his heart beating. All of a sudden he wondered whether he was fit enough to pull it off.

A good fifty yards dash it was to the drowning man. Between the waves he dipped and disappeared from Andrew's view. Once reached, he was gurgling, and calling out in Portuguese. As soon as he drew close enough, he heaved and scratched in an effort to sit on Andrew's head.

'Turn around,' Andrew said.

The man lunged.

Andrew punched the man firmly in the ear. Then, very quickly, he turned him about, and lassoed the man's chest with his right arm, rolling the thrashing body on to his hip. That was the way you did it. Now you side-stroked, if you could, back through the foam, doing your level best to keep the patient's face in the air. The man was still yelling in Portuguese.

'Save your bloody breath, will you,' Andrew tightened his grip.

A breaker swamped them.

'Keep still, you mad wog.'

The next wave was a high roller which did not break but gave them a spurt towards the beach. Andrew began to do his side-stroke like a champion. The man stiffened, but lay still. They made progress.

In fact they made such rapid progress that they were in chest-deep water before Andrew realized; he was side-stroking determinedly when the Portuguese broke loose and stood up, waving and calling to the bathers in the shore break. Within seconds they were surrounded by people. Men, women and children, the children coming up to pull on the belt of the man's bathers, touch his arm, walk in his wake, gathered around to hear the man's story of a life almost lost, and, presumably, regained. It was impossible for Andrew to tell as all this took place in Portuguese, and, before he could say anything, the man had left the water and was holding court on the sand.

'Did you see that? Did you bloody well see that?' Andrew flopped beside Sally.

'You can still swim,' she said, admiringly.

'No, no – did you see that chap just walk off like that, like a bloody peacock?'

'He's happy to be alive,' she said.

'He didn't even say thanks!' Andrew spluttered.

'Perhaps he doesn't speak English.'

'You must be joking . . . look at him. Anybody would think he'd pulled me out.'

Sally laughed.

'What the hell is so funny?'

'Come on, come and lie down and get your breath.'

'Look, if someone hadn't gone to get that rat he would have swallowed the Bay of Biscay.'

'See, you're making poetry out of it already. Sit down, Andy, for God's sake.'

He did, eventually, lie flat out beside her, waiting for his chest to stop thumping. He had his face in the crook of an arm, could feel his eyeballs, of all things, pulsing with fury at the man's cockstrutting exit along the beach. He lay there for a long time in a rage. Rage at his outburst. Rage at his pettiness, and a seething pulsating rage at her equanimity, her calm, her dogged refusal to acknowledge that he had put himself at risk. Yes, that was it – her absolute insistence on taking for granted everything he did, would do.

Three days to go.

He professed, unashamedly, a weariness with the village. The need to exercise on an open stretch. While she slept he would explore the coast the other side of the cliff, look at the chapel, perhaps take a few photographs from the cable car. 'We could do all that together,' she said. 'I want to go for a hard run,' he replied, and, fortunately, she did not take offence. After all, they had been married long enough for that sort of thing to be said without threat of desertion.

At 1.30 in the afternoon he trundled into the air on the cable car. The cabin was filled with cream trousered, middle-aged men, and young mothers, their children so excited by the ride that their ice-creams melted over the edge of their cones, running unlicked to their fingers. One woman seemed to be unescorted, a pretty creature in a green silk scarf. She was French, most likely. He could feel her in pursuit of his eye. But as was a married man's unwitting wont, Andrew spent his time in the sky looking elsewhere; he looked back and down to the village, observing the patterns in the bleached hives, the dark clumps on the beach, the expanse of sand beyond the village, a coastline which the midday sun had drained of colour. Andrew let it all slide back beneath him as the cabin crawled in the air. He did not look at the woman until they reached the top.

Passengers went off in the direction of the little chapel, to the look-out point, or inland towards the bull-fighting arena. The French woman went towards the only hotel on the cliff top, a large, pine verandah affair which occupied dry ground beneath some bedraggled palms. Andrew thought he might have a drink there on the way back.

He went to the edge of the cliff.

A path went steeply down to the beach. It was a long, very exposed beach, and it was deserted, wonderfully deserted. As soon as he reached it he ran. He took off his shirt as he began to run. He ran to the first headland. The next. The beach was still deserted. He ran on and on. With the surf beating its way in beside him, raging, he ran until he had to stop, bend, drop into the soft, powdery sand before him. And there he rested, splayed upon the warmth. And then, so quickly, urgently did his loins burrow into the sand, the sea heaving and rising from its depths to meet him, that he pulled back and sat up.

He ran straight into the sea.

It was icy, so different from the water at the village beach. And the surf was stronger. Waves beat him back. He attacked again, head down, legs as pistons, lunging beneath the assault of white. Finally his feet left bottom. Soon he was swimming in the skimming troughs of large waves, making progress, striking out with his real strength, jubilant in the knowledge that he would ride the waves all the way back to her, that he would land to tell her that he had to go, that he had gone, gone long ago, that they had been together long enough, too long, that not even solid, sound things should have to last forever.

Beyond the break he paused. He trod water. It was sensible to deliver the news gently. It was sensible to transmit this still, pellucid water. Treading water: the sea beneath his feet emerald, the water around him as pure as the sky.

He floated on his back – whistled, spurted, breathed deeply as he floated. A world up-turned. Sun beat upon the silver rivulets on his chest and loins as he lolled – a firm, fine piece of free floating timber.

He would tell her nothing but the truth.

Truth lives in water. He duck-dived. Came to the surface with a howl. Roaring, swimming like a sea lion, he forgot her then completely. Already he had accomplished the deed.

After a time he looked back towards the beach. An amusing surprise: he was a mile, at least, off shore. The surf tow had swept him, silently, effortlessly, a good way out. He would have a pleasant job of it getting back in, bridging the chasm between himself and the dry land. But he set out, more or less at once, still roaring within himself – swimming with strong, steady strokes, making simple clean work of the task, exhilarated, in a way, by the mild risk which had been so immediately granted him. He put his face down and pressed forward with pleasure.

He was carried further out.

He had, of course, a great deal of worthwhile experience in the sea. He knew that it was often pointless, once one was caught in a decent sweep, to struggle against the flow. Best to go with it until it petered out somewhere further off shore, then swim in to the nearest land. That was the sensible thing to do if one was in real difficulty, and if one wasn't there was no harm in testing the strength of the current before giving up.

So he swam seriously, concentrating on a regular rhythm, pulling evenly with each arm, touching each thigh with his thumb, the better to ensure that accuracy of his bearing. He had lined up a dune just down from the chapel – that was how far along the beach the current had taken him – and he was heading for that. But when he paused to look up he was already in line with the cross. And when he stopped the next time, it was clear that he had made no progress towards the shore but was being carried around the cliff to the village beach.

'Ahoy,' he thought. 'A free ride home.'

He could see the cable car inching its way up the rock face. A perfect profile, one that fishermen must have each dawn. He felt immensely privileged.

He let himself drift.

Such deep, crystal water, the sun pouring into the halls of light below him. His feet circled in the upper reaches of cathedrals.

He trod water. It was cold, but he kept his arms moving as well.

Only a matter of exercising patience and commonsense.

Around the point he went. He was, in steady succession, in line with the cable car, the ticket office for the cable car, the village square, the three hotels south of the square, the body of the village, dumb white in the glare, the tents of the fair, the long rectangle, parallel with the shore, of the fishing market, which was, he could see, shut tight and deserted of the people who manned the boats. Boats, in fact, were anchored off the point, in the direction of which he appeared

to be travelling. If he continued in the way that he was going
– drifting was a much easier business than he had thought –
he would actually come to those boats and be able to climb
aboard and dry himself in the sun. If he drifted as far as those
boats he would be able to lie on their salty decks until sunset,
then set off with the fleet for the evening's work, returning at
dawn with a good supply of mackerel which could be eaten at
breakfast. If he drifted as far as the boats he would at least be
able to get warm again.

He thrashed about with his arms. Swam a while with the
current.

Then, well before reaching the boats, he stopped. No, he
had not stopped so much as eddied to a perpetual pause in
roughly the same vicinity – he could tell from the stationary
landmarks. Directly opposite the outskirts of the village his
current seemed to have exhausted itself against an outgoing
drift from the beach. He splashed, shouted, waved towards
the shore, then rolled on his back once more. His own Sar-
gasso. He floated and thought.

If he put all his efforts into swimming in against the current
from here, he ran a risk of being too exhausted by the time he
reached the breakers. If he set out for the boats he risked the
complications of another cross current. Whereas if he stayed,
the tide, surely, would turn. He would get in pretty much
under its own steam. It was only a matter of keeping warm.
And hoping to Christ against sharks.

> Ship ahoy, sailor boy
> Don't you get too springy
> The admiral's daughter
> Lays down by the water,
> She wants to ride your dinghy

Towards the cable car he projected his voice. It drowned in
the spray of the first breakers. Defiantly, he performed
several duck dives and thought: 'Yes, this is keeping calm. I
am being fairly brave.'

He could see the shore so well. Lit by the late afternoon
sun, it was as clearly defined as a stage set. The stripes on
the umbrellas in the village square stood up pink and yellow,
the awnings of the cafés had already been rolled down for the

370

evening, people bicycled and walked along the promenade in uniform fits and starts, and, for some inexplicable reason, a light went on in a second storey, then went off again, as if signalling a boat on the horizon. And he could see the people still on the beach, the bathers standing, looking, to all intents and purposes, towards him, one of them, God knew how, actually engaged in conversation with one of the fishermen. Andrew waved.

The fisherman stood up from his hunched position on the sand. He joined another – their black figures leaning together. Others joined them, who gathered near one of the beached hulls. They crouched, as if in conference, and then he saw, between them, the dart of orange. The flame of the fire lit their feet. And not long afterwards he could smell, yes, he could smell the tang of burning skin, as the flavour of the sardines settled on the still water right under his nose.

Every detail of life was going on without him.

Where was she?

The day ended.

In the dark, in the cold dark that fell on him so quickly, he could see everything happening on the beach. Beyond the fires, lights went on. Rooms above every café were lit. Waiters bustled beneath the awnings. The well-dressed emerged on the promenade. He fancied he could see the couple who had sat with them the night before, the turn of the man's shoulder. The wife's gesture. It was not so far away in there after all. He could see everything going on – regardless.

What was she doing?

As he waited for the tide to turn he consoled himself in the cold dark that he was not thinking of her in ways which were in any way pathetic. He kept his body moving. He did not romanticize. His mind did not fill with images of her beauty, he did not yearn for her warmth at his back at night; not even then, in the cold dark, did he yearn for that, the marital addiction. Nor did he pause to think of her constancy, the gentleness of her womanhood which had budded since knowing her. No, what he thought of was her getting ready for dinner.

She was in their room. She had showered. She had put on the cotton frock and was luxuriating before the mirror, dabs of Ma Griffe already at her throat as she hummed to herself, because, yes, for once, he was late, he was the one that would keep them from dinner, make them late to the table. She was humming because just for once he had nothing to be irritable about. She sang with girlish relief.

Andrew's burst of laughter left him breathless.

Then, out in the dark water, the tide turned. His legs felt the shift of the current. Press in now – or never.

In the cold inkiness he swam breast stroke, biding his time, watching carefully for the first line of breakers. The waves would come upon him suddenly. He had to watch for the quick fluorescence of the surf, listen for the roar of the first valley he would slide into. He took it easily, sure now that when he went down into the first trough that he would be loose enough to roll with the swirl of the bottom, firm enough with his chest barrel full of air to come up again with the next toss, with the sea's endlessly renewable force. It was simply a matter of going with its incessant, inexorable energy.

He rolled.

There is no such thing as a simple reversal of forces. He went a distance along the bottom.

Up from the first wave, he could again see the shore: lights in the village, the square bustling, and the sand, when he reached it, bone dry. Even as he lay there – grey-fleshed, chilled, breath rasping back to normal, he could see the fishermen up ahead of him, each one of them huddled about their fires. They were settled, well and truly, about their fires. And later, as he made his way up the beach to her, he was taking very deep breaths – and still no one was noticing him.

BARBARA BROOKS

Summer in Sydney

The time. When you're not working, the days stretch and float. Swimming in the mornings, reading in the afternoons, going out to restaurants at night. Getting up late and reading the paper. What day is it, and what do I have to do? People come and go, from London, Tennant Creek, Brisbane. Postcards and letters slide under the door.

Summer heat passes over quickly, wilting the garden but leaving some corners of the house untouched. At the beginning of summer it rained a lot.

The unemployed could go on beach crawls, all summer. But couldn't afford the trimmings. We sit around all morning eating croissants and watermelon in gentrified poverty, and go to Bronte at two in the afternoon. By then the sun has gone. There's a storm, hailstones drop out of a green sky. We put ice down each other's backs and shelter under the eaves of the dressing shed. The water is a kind of oily grey with a strip of sunlight along the horizon. All summer long the water is cold; the currents flow in from out in the Pacific, where the French exploded their bomb.

In Europe, it's the new ice age, not to be confused with the new cold war. In Scotland, a man is found with his lips frozen to his car; he was blowing into the doorlocks to thaw them. Peter's plane froze to the ground in Manchester for three days at 27 below. Here in the southern hemisphere this doesn't make sense, but we have already agreed that staying sane fifty per cent of the time is a good average. Down at Bronte on Friday afternoon, we take his jetlag for an airing; it floats in green water, along with a faint slick of suntan oil and the soft touch of well being, or is it cold water? We eat pies and hot dogs and the sun turns us pink and happy.

A postcard from Italy: We're in smog-clouded Venice, but Marian thinks it's Vienna (we must go to the opera). This is the rapid transit method of seeing Europe, concerned with: railway timetables, hot showers, art galleries, cheap restaurants, what day of the week is it and where do we go to keep warm? Culture comes by osmosis; we drift across Europe as the clouds gather – smog, snow, fear? A limited nuclear war for America, he said as we sat at the dinner table, could mean total devastation for Europe. Another glass of wine? What's the rage in Paris and London? Cocaine, herpes, the economic malaise; two million in anti-nuclear marches.

> In the supermarket of Europe
> what exotica they buy,
> the travellers, like the Cruise missiles,
> flying high.

We make love, joined at mouth, breast, genitals. I like to think of a circle, bodies looped and joined, continuity I guess. It comes in waves, like water. Afterwards our bodies are at rest, solid, still, still joined together, while our minds drift on the silver cord that ties them to us, and everything is quiet. Then somebody knocks on the door, and we get up and go downstairs.

We swim at Camp Cove on Saturday evening. There's a man on the beach with a metal detector, picking up the débris of affluence – ringpulls from cans, mostly, and the odd gold watch. I bought it for the kids, he says, they never use it but it's paid for itself. The lighthouse is flashing on South Head, and the fishermen are out with the mosquitoes; down below green water turns white around the rocks. We look across to Manly highrise, and back to the city. It's so quiet here, but the city is full of friction. I can close my eyes any night and see a dirt road lined with gum trees, any one of the roads I have driven or been driven along. When you came in through the heads for the first time, what did you think? Back in your past, you talk about the badlands: gold and uranium in the bluffs and buttes, Indian villages on top of them. MX missiles in the tunnels underground. There's a cannon on the cliffs along here, aimed at a paling fence. We grew up in a temporary lull, a period of relative calm and affluence.

Coming back to this country, coming back to your past, the first thing you notice is the size of the sky. Huge, open, clear as a bell, full of a hard metallic light. The country unrolls under the wing of the plane for hours and the travellers shift in their seats, preparing to arrive. Emptied out onto the tarmac in the heat, they waver, then head for the terminal. The duty-free whisky falls out of the SIA bag and breaks on the terminal floor. Watching faces separate out; coming home. Hanging on the fringes of things, backs to the mountains, everyone lives near the sea, waiting to make a getaway when the tide, or history, turns. That empty beach we took with us as our emotional refuge has gone; L. J. Hooker or the Japanese? On the east coast it's sunrise over the water through the palm trees, on the west coast it's sunset; and this summer, the blacks come to Canberra to argue their land claims. Red rocks, heat and dust, uranium mines and tailings dams; white perspex domes sending messages back to . . . Do you want to be the centre of attention? Pine Gap puts us on the map.

The tourists lie on beaches in the Deep North; nothing has entered their dreams except the smell of coconut oil and the taste of warm salt water. The B52s touch down in Darwin and fly over North Queensland on their training runs. Brown bodies roll over all the way down the east coast and the sound of planes is drowned out by hundreds of transistors playing rock music. The DJ says, it's the Clash! the B52s!

The moon is a fish that swims underwater in the daytime. A highly intelligent silver jewfish, swimming from one side of the sky to the other. What is the moon? Something that goes down, in the dark, and is forgotten. In the morning there will be blue hills round the rim.

We are just mooning around this summer, swimming through the weather like fish.

377

In Brisbane, it's 35 degrees in the shade, and we're flat on our backs. We lie around all day, and get up for the action at 5 in the afternoon. We sit on the veranda and make desultory conversation. Muggy, isn't it? Feels like a storm. We watch the storm pass, listen to rain on the iron roof, try to tell the difference between the sound of toads and frogs. Do you know that smell that comes from the backyard after rain? This is the edge of the storm, somewhere there are high winds, and as usual the power goes off. We sit on the veranda while it gets dark. The electricity workers have a rolling strike against anti-union legislation. Should have gone to the drive-in, Lloyd says, and goes out to the fridge for a beer. We eat fish and chips, drink beer, light mosquito coils, turn the radio on and off. Lloyd goes inside to read the paper by kerosene lamp. We crack nuts by torchlight, sitting on the back steps, and boil the kettle on the Primus. The lights are back on in the morning and so is the heat. The grass is two inches longer. At 5 in the afternoon it's cool enough to start the mower. Dozens of little grasshoppers decamp from long wet grass.

'The last I heard of Julie she was in an ashram, I thought she looked OK. I can't talk to her about it; it's one of those circular things where everything is explained by a belief that can't be explained. She says it's not the way for everyone, but it is for her.' There are posters at the Oxford Street bus stops saying 'He sees God', and the graffiti underneath says, but only when he's drunk, or, and he smokes Marlboro. 'I will consider anything – acupuncture, yoga, herbal tea – but it must have a rational basis.' Rationality is only half of it; there is nothing to be counted on as a prop. 'I said, you know there is nothing to believe in that justifies the mind suspending its questions, but even so you are always slipping up.' We came out of the church after the wedding, someone was playing the flute. There were white moths around the cabbages in the market gardens, and flies around our faces. We were thinking about love.

The way change happens, it's more like a slow sliding than anything you can put your finger on.

Peter is driving through the hot flat country of western New South Wales in an old Holden with a blanket over the seat and uncertain brakes. Heading for Adelaide, Washington, London and the political life again. We were sitting in the pub looking at brochures on Tahiti. What's happening in Australia? It's hard to find out in summer, seasonal adjustment. The other night, when the heat got worse than the mosquitoes, we went out to sit in the garden; and a voice from the dark on the other side of the table said, summer is a good time for a coup, no one would come back from the beach for anything. The first day of the trip your mind keeps racing, but after that the thoughts begin to untangle.

On the wall of the Casablanca Furniture Factory, over the road from the pub, someone has written: The workers united will never be defeated, and some intellectual has changed it to 'would'. The TAA posters along Moore Park Road have a woman in a bikini on a beach with the caption: Worker's compensation. Ripped off all year, and fucked on holiday. Everyone is reading a novel called *History*.

'I have this feeling that everything is irrelevant, and I'm falling apart at the seams. Don't know if it's objective historical circumstance, some life crisis, lack of sleep or the weather. I wish it would pass, it's disturbingly convincing to experience.' It does, and you're off to the bush with friends, kids, bottles of white wine, to lie on air mattresses in the dam and wait for the cool change. You could always go bush and you might find out you were right; summer is a good time of year. Later, surrounded by books and papers, empty coffee cups: 'It's beginning to make sense'.

There are the floating mornings, and the times at the end of the day when the light changes and the cicadas start, and someone has a radio on, very quietly, so that the sound fades in and out; outside of this sometimes things fail to connect. Sometimes it helps if you stop reading the papers, but even that is a kind of addiction, and it depends what you do for a living. Five days on Stradbroke and you find yourself after the morning swim waiting for the *Courier Mail*; after a few weeks I guess you'd stop worrying, a mind full of salt and blue glaze.

Jane is in the kitchen, insulting us the way only an astrologer can, tracing the planets over our heads. She's written a song about the economic cycle and sings us the chorus: it goes boom depression boom depression boom boom BOOM.

It's the middle of the night in Annandale, dogs barking, someone trying to start a car. We are lying in bed in a weatherboard house, like frozen moments in the yellow room. You are talking about conspiracy theories (What really happened in 1975?) and while I listen I can hear beyond you what the body and the heart say, the old harmony, mystery, short-circuiting logic; there are these moments when you put out your hand and nothing is said but everything is there. In the morning the room seems familiar, there are noises like a tin roof creaking in the heat. You wake up and ask, did you have any dreams? Then you go downstairs and bring the papers, oranges, cups of tea. I am standing at the window, but nothing outside has any significance; I am still interior, and the shape of the room protects me. Did you know this window has a flaw in it, like water?

Do you remember, when you were a child, watching dust moving in the bits of sun that came into a dark room? I used to think about atoms and electrons, stars and moons, other worlds. There always seems to be another door opening. Often, it seems, we go through it alone.

At the State Emergency Service, they have pamphlets: what to do in case of nuclear attack. Don goes to classes at the SES, but all he can tell me is that when it's about to happen we should head for the hills. We are standing in Woolworths at the time, I notice philodendrons, parlour palms, weeping figs, ferns, a spider plant in a teapot on special. I can hear a rumbling, but it's only the trains underneath us in Town Hall Station.

Apart from the new ice age, and the new cold war, there's the

New Age. Down the road in Darlinghurst there's the Satprak-ash Meditation Centre, where they say, don't just do some-thing, sit there. When the mind stops its questions, this is Nirvana. Is this worth serious consideration? This was the summer the orange people moved in, or out; the bagwash is orange, terracotta and red, and the colours are all down Oxford Street, the vegetarian restaurant, the boutique, the orange vegetable trucks, the building teams. Bhagwan is in trouble again, the Rolls is bogged in the Oregon mud. This was the summer Billy Graham asked us to forgive Richard Nixon because he didn't know what he was doing, and several people renounced Christianity in its more obvious forms. There's the Natural Healing and Personal Develop-ment Centre and a galaxy of delights for mind and body, colour therapy, yoga, massage with exotic oils, psycho-therapy for the mind subject to pressure. It's possible that even here there will be therapy sessions where you can articulate your fears about nuclear war and 'come to terms' with them. Meanwhile you might be cut off the dole. You can buy tapes of dolphins and whales, pay to change your post-ure, major in Zen, donate money to save the rainforests. Over the road there are books that will change your life. Is this part of the process of evolutionary change, or just a momentary confusion? This is the street of Middle Class Fantasies. It's just near the bus stop, and St Vincent de Paul is over the road. It's the street of All Australian boys, party drugs, gay bars and coffee houses. There isn't a decent super-market for miles. Something is wrong but you're not quite sure what. Sometimes it occurs to us, like a kind of bad dream, that we live in the shadow of war and can't do anything about it. 'So you think you can tell/Heaven from hell/Blue skies from pain . . .' Are we being conned again?

Tomorrow will be full of possibilities. You can ring up work and say you're sick, drink *café latte* at the Roma, cut off your jeans, take the kids to the park.

Down in George Street, the story is the sound of cash regis-ters, the relatively innocent rustling of paper and money, as the crowds come and go, looking for something to justify the occasion. Money leaps out of your purse like a fish every time you open it, this time of year. Christmas is the silly season; office parties, flights home, cases of mangoes, hams and turkeys. It's late night shopping, the Thursday before Christmas week, Myers' windows full of animated fairy tales, just like the newspapers; somewhere above all this the moon slides through a sky the colour of deep water.

And so you say, this is the political life, faint light at the end of the tunnel, and what can I say I have accomplished? There are moments when I think how happy I am, in a car going down the hill to the beach, then the muffler falls off and everything changes. 'We don't live in isolation; the relationships between people can be just or unjust, on the smallest scale or the largest.'

While we are down at the beach that afternoon, in Brisbane it's several degrees hotter, he's working in the sun all day, and when he comes in something happens; something stops functioning for a moment and an inconsistency spreads through the veins and the muscles. Something shifts; it happens quickly and is out of control. Does it make any sense? It's been a hard life, someone without money has to make his body and his strength his capital, working from early in the morning till late at night, seven days a week at times. Some people act on the world, with others you can see they could be crushed. But the heart goes on. What do we know about the heart? When we were twenty we thought the answer was to love someone and make them happy; stuck with love and rebellion for several years we wondered why it didn't work the way we expected. One, we were women, trying to change. Two, we were gullible. Three, we had no context that made any sense – not that you can ask for one.

Inside the train, there are small sleeping compartments. The nightlights are faintly blue, and the sheets on the bunks are starched and ironed. The train goes into a mountain and comes out on the other side and we have crossed a border; we wouldn't have known, that feeling of being stretched tight between different things comes and goes, at random it seems. The landscape passes: still water, rain, paddocks with cows, and houses with lighted windows, empty platforms on country stations, then factories and railway yards. Coming into the city late at night, we've lost the moon, it was somewhere over to the left just before.

At Palm Beach at 6 in the evening there are people playing football, flying kites, rolling around on the sand in an inner tube. We wonder if they're Christians; very few people hang around in large groups looking lively these days. They don't come from Darlinghurst. But we're tourists ourselves. The water is warm, and there's very little undertow, but there's a slight drift north. Half an hour ago when we went into the water the swimmers were south of us, now they're right in front. In another hour or so they might all disappear behind Barrenjoey into the mouth of Broken Bay, shouting and laughing, while we have moved over to the Pittwater side of the peninsula, and are eating chips and drinking beer, watching the windsurfers and the sun going down behind West Head. This is the life.

This was the summer of early rain, when the roof leaked in two places after the storm. The paper dropped on the doorstop every morning and it all went on, Poland, Ronald Reagan, the nuclear buildup, the blackouts. Everywhere we went someone was listening to the cricket. So what's the story? What's the deal? There were stories, political thrillers with speculative endings, love stories with whatever is a happy ending now – they decided to live together, or separately, he left, she became a feminist, they agreed who would have the kids. There was a revolution, a coup, a large amount of US aid, a 'free election'. This is just what happened; the plots are all different now. Forget the moon; those little lights in the sky were Air America, shuttling money between here and Hong Kong.

Some of this is already in the head. There were times when the mind drifted, weightless, in certain moments, the slanting light in the afternoons, the long blue evenings. We had a good time, mostly, then we packed it in and went back to work. The pages fill with names and 'facts' and the pile of newsprint grows in the corner; there is no one thing that will tell you, but we wait for something still under the surface that meets inbetween the words. When we touch each other we imagine that we are part of something, but still whole on our own. Do you feel my history, and its tricks, when you run your hand over my skin? Sometimes we don't understand, sometimes we do but it's not quite possible to speak or act directly out of it. 'It may not be as clear as you wanted, but it's there.' Say it: this is what we are, this is what is going on.

JOAN LONDON

New Year

They are in the middle of a heatwave. All across the city people are doing unusual things. Walking into fountains, sleeping on the beach, holding conversations under a sprinkler . . . 'It's the heat': don't the Arabs have a wind, Rowena is trying to think of the name of it, a desert wind, so hot that a man is excused for killing his wife while it is blowing?

Harry and Rowena are having dinner with the Hutchisons. This is not unusual, since they live in the Hutchisons' house and share most meals with them: but it's New Year's Eve and here they are on the terrace, legs looped over chairs, opening their second bottle of wine. Festive yet resigned, like workers choosing to drink together after a hard day. The Hutchisons have chosen to stay home with Harry and Rowena tonight. This is what is unusual.

This is what Rowena thinks, stirring Harry's chicken stock in the kitchen. The kitchen is a glassed-in veranda three steps up from the terrace. Tonight it is a little box lit up with heat. Grease glistens in beads behind the stove. Oily fingers seem to have smeared everything, handles, cookery books, jars of herbs. Vine leaves over the terrace drape around the windows, limp and still, dropped hands.

The chicken stock is for pilau, Harry's speciality. Later Rowena, who doesn't have a speciality, will make a fruit salad. It's their turn to cook tonight.

Although Rowena likes watching stock, it's slow rich bubble, she knows it does not really need stirring. She is really listening out for her baby Tom. If she can get to him quickly when he wakes – he wakes a great deal – she might be able to settle him back to sleep. Meanwhile she gives a few busy taps to the saucepan with the side of the spoon.

'The person who really needs a drink', Hutch calls out, 'is Rowena'.

Lately Rowena has suspected a consensus in the house about her, about maternal over-commitment. Her case has been discussed, heads shaken . . . coming down the kitchen steps now as this person is not quite real to her. She feels a fruitless swinging to her arms, she is breasting dark air. She sits down quickly.

'This is very civilized,' Hutch is saying. He has just taken off his T-shirt and he stretches out, rubbing the fan of black hair that spouts up over his waistband.

'Hardly civilized,' Harry says, 'taking off your clothes.' He has a way of drawing out the Australian accent that makes everything he says sound measured and judicious.

'Let's face it,' Harry says, 'we're a hedonist culture. On a night like this we ought to take off the lot.' His hand hovers for a moment over the front stud of his jeans.

'D'you hear what your husband's proposing?' Hutch turns to Rowena. She has no answer. She never has an answer for Hutch.

'Diane has more of the hedonist spirit,' says Harry. Diane is wearing a sarong hitched up and looped around her neck like a miniature toga.

'Oh for heaven's sake,' says Diane, rearranging her legs. 'It's *hot*.'

'Or is she just going with the *au naturel* flow of our household?' Hutch says to Harry.

'I'll drink to that,' says Harry. Across the table his torso is white amongst the shadows of the terrace. Winter white. Like her own hands around her glass. It had stopped being winter when they first arrived here from the beach house. They had stood beside their car in the mild city air, pale, in coats, as if they had come a long way . . .

'What are you looking at?' Harry's voice is low across the table.

'My hands.'

'What's *wrong* with your hands?' Harry mutters. But a steady droning is rising from the house. Their eyes lift and meet. Tom.

'Already?' Diane says. 'He's incredible.'

'He fell asleep early,' Rowena says on her way back up the steps. 'It's the heat . . .' But who would understand the logic and rhythm of Tom's day? Who would want to? She takes her glass with her.

'How about some music,' Hutch is saying.

'It's your *turn*,' Diane says.

2

In that house music was kept going like a tribal fire. Whoever came home first went straight to the living room and put on music. The speakers were lugged up and down the hall on long cords, following the action. When they left again Rowena let the music die. There were many arrivals and departures. The Hutchisons were both studying part time. They belonged to societies, separately, they went to films and rock concerts. Harry often went with them.

In the weekends they were careful to keep the sound well stoked. Music nudged away each moment, bit at the fringes of thought. Open the bedroom door and you swam wordless into it. The first nights they were here Rowena went walking. Up the empty street. Turn the corner. Drawn curtains at the end of driveways silhouetted with shrubs. Silence. Block after block of it. The beat of the music met her again on the home stretch. Their house looked party bright. She sat on the front steps and leaned her head against a column. It seemed to have caught a pulse inside it. She watched the light behind the roofs of the houses across the road. She didn't know where else to go.

Now as Tom sucks, his head seems to pump back and forward against her, in time. Their room is another piece of the verandah, a partitioned cavern. Curtainless, it is dark all day, shadowed by the house next door, but at night the neighbours' bathroom light beacons through the louvres and everything, the cartons from the beach house stacked around the walls, Harry's shirt dangling from the door frame, the roundness of Tom's head, is outlined in this dull radiance.

Last night, lying like this on the mattress, she had said to Harry: 'How much longer are we going to stay here?'

Harry had just shut his book, put out the light and turned over: there was a sense of purpose about everything he did these days, even to going to sleep. He turned onto his back and unfolded one finger, two, as if they had been waiting to spring open.

'We're still paying off the bookshop.' He had to whisper. Behind the wall next to them were the Hutchisons, also in bed. 'We could never afford to live like this so close to the city.' End of point two: he closed his hand into a fist over their sheet.

'I could live in a tiny flat,' Rowena said. Whispering was provisional, it was like taking off your shoes and tiptoeing around each other. 'I could live in a room. If we were alone.'

'We're always alone,' Harry said.

Tom sucks and, elbow up, she sips her wine.

3

The light is on under the vines of the terrace but nobody is there. Moths bang against the light bulb and fall among the glasses on the table. Somebody has watered the ferns and they rustle and drip around the steps. Intermission. This happens sometimes. Everybody will suddenly desert on private missions, to read the newspaper, make a phone call, slump across a bed . . . The light is on in the kitchen too. Harry is cooking.

He looks up as Rowena comes up the steps, his chin lifted, eyes gathered together to hold in the tears. But it will do for a greeting, it is so familiar. Onions. He turns back to his chopping board. Steam rises, oil sizzles ready, his strokes are neat and sure. Harry cooks with a sense of ceremony. Step by step, a beautiful patient logic towards a known destination: no panicky improvisations, no peering at the recipe wishing it would tell you more.

He is singing, a beat behind and lower than the larger voice that fills the room beyond them.

> *Still crazy,*
> *Still crazy,*
> *After all these years . . .*

Harry singing, onions frying: Rowena stands for a moment in the doorway. He has always sung, to car radios, in supermarkets and restaurants, easily, knowing the words, 'Yester-day', 'O Sole Mio', 'You Are So Beautiful', as if in tune with a fellow experience.

'Want some help?'

He never says he does.

The Hutchisons' house is old, one day they are going to knock it down. Meanwhile they have hung mounted posters of things like sneakers and Coca Cola bottles on the stucco walls. Leads and aerials loop between picture railings. The mantel pieces are cluttered with jokey plunder: KEEP LEFT and NO SMOKING signs, a Chinese demon kite, a Snoopy mug half full of small change. But the rooms remain dark and sedate; tonight each is a cell of hot still air. The two visions of the house don't match, they are overlaid like illusionist sheets, demand something of you ... a trick of wit, Rowena feels, and she would see it as a style.

The front door is open, the steps of the porch are still warm. Rowena lights a cigarette. She has taken up smoking again.

'Are these for real?' she had asked Hutch, pointing at the NO SMOKING signs.

'Why else would they be there?' Hutch said.

Why else did Rowena, finding an old packet of cigarettes in Harry's winter jacket, take one out and smoke it? The air before her lifted and shook. She took another one. This time it tasted more real, the house seemed to retreat behind the fraying coil of smoke. She bought her own packet. She enjoyed the crackle as she opened it, the neat decision of the cylinders stacked as close as bullets. She took to carrying a packet in the pouch pocket of her overalls. At odd moments, outside the house, she smoked them.

Just as she lights up now, Hutch breaks through the dark-ness at the side of the house, pulling a hose. In the other hand he carries his glass of wine. He doesn't seem to see her, but if she wasn't there would he stroll across the lawn like this, taking sips as he plants the sprinkler near her and turns on the tap? He suddenly sinks beside her.

'Very contemplative,' he says.'You're always very contem-plative Rowena.'

The sprinkler's arms have corralled them against the porch. Water patters at their feet. Hutch is always setting up these little moments with her and she always comes away feeling she has failed a test.

'The madonna,' Hutch says. 'I take it that's what you want to be.'

His voice has dropped, his blond head is bowed towards her. Rowena hunches her shoulders. She will not look at him.

'Dinner,' she says, waving her arm vaguely, getting up. 'Must help Harry.' Her voice is husky, out of practice. She throws her cigarette into the garden and then remembers it is his garden and makes a little useless dive mid-air. She closes her eyes for a moment on her way back up the hall. She should have stamped the butt out at his feet, raised her eyebrows, stalked off . . . Why? Because he would have liked that? In this house value is given to performance.

Just as Harry places the big platter of yellow rice on the terrace table, Tom wakes. A loud outraged howl this time.

'Oh God,' Diane says. 'How do you bear it?'

Harry serves, and Rowena hands out plates.

'Maybe I'm just not the type,' Diane goes on. She picks up her fork with her narrow freckled hand, looks around the table. She often has this moment of animation when a plate of food is put in front of her, Rowena has noticed. 'Why do people *do* this to themselves, d'you think?'

'Because they don't know what they're letting themselves in for,' Harry says.

Hutch stands up, turning and turning at the corkscrew embedded in the bottle between his legs. They all watch, wait for the triumphant Pop! 'Tight one,' Hutch says, chasing sweat across his forehead in a kind of salute.

Tom's cry is urgent. Rowena drains her glass, reaches over and takes a forkful of pilau from the platter. She won't be back for a while.

'All I know is,' Diane says, turning to her plate, 'nobody could ever make me miss my meal.'

'Go on,' Harry says to Rowena. 'We'll leave you some.'

4

One night Harry came home very late to the beach house. It was so black outside you could imagine that he might never find them again, the frail house could disappear into a shifting fold of the dunes . . . He would have phoned, if of course there was a phone . . . it was becoming bloody impossible . . . he swayed slightly above her and Tom in the bed. He'd been drinking with Hutch and his wife, he'd been thinking . . . The Hutchisons said, come and live with them, they're interested in sharing . . . No, the Hutchisons have no children. But a child shouldn't make any difference, they said.

Harry seemed to have forgotten that he used to say that too.

There are photos – here, kept close beside the bed – of the time that they first brought Tom home to the beach house. In this bright darkness the black and white leap out at you as if in moonlight. They are good photos of Rowena because she has at last stopped looking at the camera. She is smiling, she can't stop smiling, looking at Tom in her arms. Her hair, which reaches to her elbows, is now tucked back out of the way. She's wearing overalls, but you can see that her breasts are enormous. In the background a ti-tree brushes against asbestos. That's the beach house.

The photos of Harry with Tom are slightly out of focus. Rowena took them. There was no one else around to take them all together, *en famille*. The blurring gives the impression of a high wind. Harry is bending over Tom in his pram as if he's sheltering him. He is frowning in a comic-father way. The ti-tree appears to be in violent action, caught up in a storm. But you can see that the cigarette Harry holds behind him is still alight.

The bathroom of the beach house was separate, a quick dash from the back door. When one of them wanted a shower the other had to be there to feed the chip heater. The heater roared, the pipes shuddered, draughts rushed in through the warped door. Spiders rocked their cradles of dead blowflies in amongst the steam.

Bent over the heater one morning she thought she heard Harry groan.

'What's the matter?'

He stood still. He was wearing her shower cap. Water ran on and on, clung to the tip of his nose, the panels of black hair on his shoulders, his chest, above his penis, swirled about his feet. He looked straight ahead, through water.

He didn't go to the shop that morning. He went to bed. He stayed there for nine days. It wouldn't matter, nobody came anyway, he said. (Second-hand books! Out there! You must be crazy, everyone had said when he set up the shop.) He slept for twelve hours at a time.

Tom cried and cried. She walked him up and down the verandah, around the peripheries of the house. It might be after midday before she could get dressed. When he slept she lay on the couch with him in the crook of her arm, like a book.

Sand crept in under the doors. Mice scrabbled, but she could not bear to set the traps. Every living creature reminded her of Tom. The fridge went empty. From time to time she found herself before the open kitchen cupboard eating nuts and raisins fist after fist. She trod carefully past Harry's door. It seemed to take her whole being just to keep Tom alive.

When Harry was awake she sat on the end of the gritty bed, feeding Tom.

'Do something different!' Harry said, sitting up, smoking, watching her with glittering eyes. 'Is this all you ever do? Surprise me! Surprise me sometimes why don't you.'

(He didn't remember saying any of this, later on.)

A storm passed quickly on the beach front. You saw it coming, a mist wiping out the horizon ruled across the windows, whiteness on whiteness, while somewhere a blind flapped, louvres rattled, trees grew furtive. The voice outside took over, the house was hollowed into darkness, din, like a loss of consciousness: five minutes and it was over, a bird sang, the radio spoke again.

Harry got a job with the Government. In the mornings the car steamed as he encouraged Tom to wave bye-bye. It would be well after dark by the time he got back from the city. He made friends with someone called Hutchison, his age, but a senior administrator in the department. He stopped taking a packed lunch. He gave up smoking.

In the late afternoon the wind dropped and Rowena and Tom went walking. Down the carefully curved roads, some still gravel, named 'Pleasant Drive' or 'Linden Way'. It was all allotments, waiting to become numbered houses in a suburb; flowers grew among scrub and hillocks, tough, close-clustered, with a medicinal perfume that scented the dunes. When she picked them she could feel the shadow of clouds moving across the sunlight on her bent back.

At this hour retired couples came out like moths and walked arm in arm towards the glow settling over the sea. The rattle of the pram echoed behind them. They turned to smile at her from their end of the road.

The beach itself was unspectacular, edged with seaweed and miniature limestone cliffs. The winter sea was milk-turquoise, a great bowl in sluggish motion.

The sun glares low over the horizon, shows its power, the sea is a silver reflection, the road gleams, dances with struck flint, Rowena has to half shut her eyes. The wind presses against her, against her eyes and mouth so that she is smiling, blinded over the pram, and yes, she is happy, in some way about as happy as she can be.

The wine has spread through her.

Tom's head is slumped back like a drunk's, around it the dim bedroom, the house, the music, the lit heads on the terrace spin out in a circle.

5

It is as hot outside as in.

'*Good* evening!' Hutch calls out as Rowena stands blinking on the steps. 'I was just volunteering to go and wake you up.' He pulls out a chair for her with his foot.

'There's plenty left,' Harry says, waving his hand over the table. It doesn't look appetizing. Amongst the spilled glasses, the plates scattered with grains of rice and chicken bones, moths are dragging in circles, grounded in pools of amber oil.

'Aren't you hot in those overalls?' Diane asks. Her legs are spread, she is fanning herself with a sandal.

'Take 'em off,' shouts Harry.

Their faces under the light look yellowish and greasy. Their eyes have almost disappeared.

'Wine,' Harry says, searching for a glass for her. 'Wonderful wine.' His mouth is faintly rimmed with black.

'Eases the pressure of family life,' says Hutch.

Rowena starts collecting plates.

'Just relax,' Hutch says.

'Moths,' Rowena says. She sees Tom's head lolling, a dark spot on their bed where she has left him.

Rowena is making fruit salad. Watermelon, rock melon, grapes, peaches, passionfruit, mangos, plums: she has taken them out of their stained brown paper bags and lined them up on the bench. Whether to make it minimal and chic, just the melon and grapes say, or to throw in everything . . . Rowena has an idea, she has seen a picture somewhere, the watermelon carved like a bowl, the fruits spilling out of it . . .

The big knife has made her bold, slicing through cheeks of pink flesh . . . it comes away from the rinds with a sucking sound . . . take it all off . . . and then chop, chop into children's blocks, pink, all shades of pink, orange, tawny . . . The music throbs, Rowena chops, she is hot, she has never felt so hot. The kitchen is so crowded, its bin is overflowing, the benches are covered with plates, scraps, fruit . . . she had to work on a chopping board balanced on a chair, crouching, so that the buckles of her overalls bite into her, she can hardly move or breathe . . .

It is so simple. It works with the speed of a good idea. To unbuckle. Unpeel. To step out of the overalls, kick at them, and feel that trusty roughness, thigh against thigh. She gathers up rinds, pips, peel, and dumps them in the sink. Why stop there? Already she is moving easily, the T-shirt slips easily up her spine, cooling it, releasing her head. It's as if a breeze is suddenly blowing all over her body. She's in a hurry now. A glass splinters outside and there's laughter. *Wait*. Her breasts come loping out of their milk-stiffened cups, she could almost fear for them as she bends over her knife . . . the final touches . . . pants, you need two hands and they're over

your knees, binding them, but – you just step out of them . . .
She's wading in her own clothes, hands plunged up to the
wrists in fruit, mixing it, the passionfruit sprays out as she
squeezes its upturned pouch . . . She washes her hands.

Here is Rowena, descending a staircase, her bowl held out
before her, while somewhere over towards the city there is a
rude outbreak of car horns. New Year. She is only aware of
the whiteness beneath her, this company of globes and tri-
angles, trusting them with her own grave progress.

And the faces looking up at her are frozen, their mouths
are frozen open as if they cannot open wide enough for the
laughter, they are stamping their feet, clutching their chairs
with laughter, like uncles who have had one of their own
tricks played on them. Tears run down Harry's face. Hutch
claps.

Something white flies by and catches on the vines. Clothing? Actions bring results . . . but she is beginning to feel a
drop, a fatal fading of interest. She has already been
delivered of one miracle. She is tired. She places the watermelon bowl on the table in front of Harry.

'Here you are,' she says.

KATE GRENVILLE

Slow Dissolve

My name's gone from the label by the bell. Now there's just a neatly typed C. Stone. I wonder how she likes it on her own. I can hear her coming down the inside stairs. A nice smile now.

– Caroline!
– Mirrie!
– Nice to see you!
– It's been so long!

I feel that my smile shows too many teeth. So does hers. We stare at each other's mouths for a moment.

– I kept meaning . . .
– Nearly phoned you . . .
– Absolutely flat out . . .
– Tried to call you . . .

And here we are. There was nothing to say when we shared this flat, and there's still nothing to say.

– Hope my things haven't been in your way.
– No, no, plenty of room.
– Good good I kept meaning.
– Cup of tea?
– Lovely thanks.

The smell of the kitchen is the same as ever. The ghosts of a thousand sausages still hang in the air. Greasy fluff clings to the leg of the stove as it always did. The gap in the lino is full of the same black crumbs.

Caroline is straight out of the pages of the glossy magazines. What London's best-dressed secretaries are wearing.

– You're looking good Caroline.
– Oh thanks but I'm a mess my hair's terrible today.

She still talks in a whine like a broken motor. Her sharp little cat-face only cracks its varnish to smile when absolutely necessary.

– That's a great dress, I say.

– Oh this old thing. Just an old thing for work.

Her eyes flicker over my collection from the jumble sales.

– You're looking good too.

Making the tea, she moves around the kitchen slowly as if drugged. There's a slow walk to the cupboard for the sugar bowl and she lifts it down slowly from the shelf. There's another slow walk back to the table with the sugar and a long consideration about where to put it. She hovers it down as cautiously as the helicopter containing the Queen. It might be dangerous to interrupt this trance but if I don't speak I'll break into a high-pitched cackle.

– Going away this summer?

– I don't really know.

She takes a teabag out of the box.

– I went away last summer.

After frowning thought she takes out another teabag.

– I went to Bermuda.

– That must have been good.

She closes the box carefully, as if small creatures are seething inside.

– It was all right.

The box is finally safe back on the shelf.

– Did you go there with someone?

– Yes, oh yes I went there with a fellow I knew here, see, he asked me to go, only we had a fight and then he came back here but I didn't want to so I stayed there.

After this she seems exhausted.

– But it must have been good being in Bermuda? Even without him?

The silence has set like old yolk.

– It was all right. Sun and . . . beaches. Beaches and . . . swimming and all that. I got a good tan.

She inspects a patch of arm.

– Gone now.

She scratches with a fingernail at the vanished tan.

– I was really brown. But it faded.

– You didn't meet anyone else?

– Well you see everyone there was like in a couple. Every man was with a woman and there weren't any free men. And it was really expensive. Eating cost a lot and even a Coke was nearly a pound.

She stares bleakly round the room.

– See, if I'd of found a man he could've taken me out to dinner and bought me drinks and that and I could've stayed at his hotel and it wouldn't have cost me hardly anything, he could've taken me out to dinner every night. I couldn't afford to eat hardly by myself, but all the men were with women, they'd brought them with them, see.

She stares at me until I nod, then goes on.

– Anyway just before I had to leave I found a man and it was all right then. He was kind of old but all right. But I only had a few days of that and then I had to go back home. But the last few days were okay it didn't cost me anything and I could move out of my hotel and all that and he could buy me dinner.

The kettle makes a stifled screaming noise and after staring at it for a moment she pours the water into the mugs. When she puts the kettle back on the stove it keens softly to itself.

– What about your boyfriend, I ask. Still seeing him?

– You mean Pete, well he and I broke up. He had a lot of money you know, quite well off really. But he was very mean with it. Never took me anywhere nice or anything.

She stirs her tea as if she plans to wear through the bottom of the mug with the spoon.

– I mean I don't expect people to spend a lot of money on me all the time or anything. But when they've got it, it seems mean I think. He had a good job and all that.

She shifts in the chair and smooths the skirt over her knees.

– And there was another girl of course. I knew about her all along, it was all right by me. But she was just out for what she could get. Clothes and fancy meals. Jewellery even. Then she just dumped him, must have got all she wanted.

She licks the spoon and holds its curve against her cheek as if warming herself.

– Makes you think doesn't it. Like you should be out for what you can get. I was with him two years, two years I spent on him.

The spoon must be cold and she flips it across the room towards the sink, where it skitters along the enamel and disappears down the back. She watches as if expecting to see it crawl back up.

– Two years. Nearly three really. And then we broke up and I'm back where I started.

Her lips pucker towards the steaming tea and for a moment she looks like an old woman with her teeth out. She sighs.

– Everything's so dear. I've got to get my hair done once a week and that's going on ten pounds right there. Then clothes, they get dearer all the time, but you've got to look nice, otherwise . . .

She glances at me but doesn't finish the sentence.

– And after two years.

She runs a hand down her shin, closely inspecting it. It's a fine shin, but the sell-by date is moving up fast and the goods will soon start to look a little shabby. With a sputter and pop she squeezes cream out of a bottle and smooths it into her hands.

– Want to get your things?

These two shabby coats, the boots that need mending, and the boxes of tired paints were hardly worth coming back for. The suitcase bulges when everything's packed in. I'm leaving her the broken pith helmet and the eiderdown that leaks feathers. She must get cold alone here at night.

The living-room is full of a faint twittering from the television, and ghostly shadows of colours move about on the screen. Caroline sits unblinking, staring at a huge mouthing face.

– I asked someone to meet me here at six, mind if I wait?

– Of course, fine.

She shifts in the chair so her body is receptively turned to me as if for a chat but her attention is now fixed on three women pointing at a wet floor.

– So what are you up to these days Mirrie, she says. Still doing your drawings?

I remind myself that the only artist she knows by name is Leonardo da Vinski.

– Yes. Paintings actually.

– And what about . . . still by yourself?

She waits for my well-practised explanation of how much

I like living on my own. Practice makes perfect, but it makes a nice change to surprise her.

– Actually there's a man I'm seeing quite a lot of.

Caroline sits forwards in her chair.

– That's wonderful, she whispers. Wonderful.

Her eyes retreat to the television. I'm afraid she might suddenly crack the varnish and start to cry.

– It may not last, of course, I say. Who can tell?

She glances at me sharply. I see she's thinking there's already trouble.

– I mean, we just get on well. That's all.

Her attention on me is so great that I can see her inspecting first my right eye, then my left, for the truth. Her eyes are devouring my face.

– But I never believe in looking into the future.

Caroline nods and I hear myself rushing on.

– Just enjoy the moment, that's what I always say.

Caroline switches the television off and turns her full attention on me. I feel myself smiling brightly.

– Known him long?

– Three months.

She nods like a housewife sniffing a dubious grapefruit.

– What's he do?

– He's a designer.

– How old is he?

– Thirty-five.

– Sounds good. Planning to get married?

– We don't see the point of marriage. We don't believe a piece of paper makes any difference.

She nods but her smile doesn't seem quite convinced.

– Anyway, I've got my work.

She glances at my clothes again.

– Wouldn't it be easier if you got married?

One of my fingernails has just been broken and I have to stop myself tearing at it.

– We just don't think it's necessary.

She glances out the window at the darkening sky.

– He been married before?

– Well yes. But it was a long time ago. And she was a bitch.

Caroline is rubbing a hand over and over the same patch of

her knee. She's stopped watching me. Somehow she's got the wrong idea of all this.

Finally, in a voice that's a pitch too high, she says:

– Well that's wonderful Mirrie, I'm sure you'll be really happy, I certainly hope it all works out for you.

She snaps on the television again and switches from channel to channel. At last the doorbell rings.

– That'll be Allan now.

She glances at her watch and I can't avoid hearing what I know she's going to say, although I hurry out of the room:

– Bit late isn't he?

I run down the stairs two at a time. When I open the door, there he'll be, my lovely man. I open the door and Allan is staring at me as if he wants to break my nose.

– You gave me the wrong fucking address.

I start to apologize and put my hand on his shoulder but he pushes past me up the stairs. Up in the living-room, Caroline has turned off the television and is standing with a welcoming hostess smile. Allan barely glances at her.

– These your things?

He's already picked up my bag and is waiting for me by the door. Caroline is smiling, and keeps smiling as Allan goes heavily down the stairs.

– He's a real strong silent type isn't he, she says and giggles. Real strong and silent.

We can hear Allan get into his car and slam the door. He starts the engine with a gnashing sound and revs up so hard the whole house seems to shake. When he gives a blast on the horn, the living-room is filled with the blare. Caroline and I stand staring at each other, listening to the noise echoing until at last it fades away.

DAVID BROOKS

John Gilbert's Dog

I

William Hovell, John Septimus Roe, Paul Edmund ('The Count') de Strzelecki, Louis de Torres, Charles Throsby, John Claus Voss, de Freycinet, Cristovao de Mendonca, Nicholas Kostas, Wommai, Lieutenant Tobias Furneaux: almost exclusively, the real history of my country has been the history of its exploration. The names of its discoverers, fêted in the court of Portugal, or lost in the Great Sandy Desert, echoed in the schools of my childhood and were taken home as projects to be researched in the encyclopaedia or, more actively, in a series of explorations long before begun in the furthest corners of the yard and soon extended to daring, morning-long ascents of the mountain that began at the end of the street. Even now, what I most remember from my early summers are the days of discovery, afternoons when the heat in the houses would drive us out to picnics in Westbourne Woods or the Cotter Reserve, or down to Lennox Crossing, now so many fathoms beneath the surface of a man-made lake. In the one it was the world of endless pine-trunks, the thick carpet of dry needles that could be scraped into ships or fortresses; in the others it was the vast forest of bullrushes with the beaten, trodden places that we made our camps, or the world of the rocks and water, the thick ti-tree that, on nights at Scout camps years later, would fill with real torches, real staves, real raiding-parties.

Later, in school holidays, it would be the dunes of Huskisson. Alone or with others, I would press further and further down the three-mile beach toward Vincentia before turning abruptly inward, grabbing for clump-grass, pulling myself up through sliding sand toward the moment when the reliable familiarity of the ocean side gave way to the

unpredictable. One day it was to find dense and impenet-
rable scrub, another a stagnant lagoon, another the yard of a
delapidated shack, another, to my great confusion, only the
back fence and chook pen of our summer landlady. Now,
decades later, when I sit down to what I sometimes think of
as realer matters, each paragraph, each set of images that
might begin a poem or a story, can become a track through
bullrushes, a path through ti-tree, a sliding climb through
clump-grass that might lead, yes, into the street I am living
on, but also, as it sometimes does, into a place I had never
imagined – as if one were to climb into the familiar ash tree in
one's own backyard, only to find that it now continued, that
its boughs joined other boughs, its leafy arcades others, until
there were systems, tree-scapes, countries that had been inconceivable before.

One kind of exploration ends, another – if the myths, the
traditions, the childhoods are strong – begins. Of history, as
of the parched, dust-covered men on exhausted horses, a
linear progression ceases and the lateral, the vertical take
over. The lines on the charts, once straight and simple, begin
to turn back on themselves, to buckle and convolute as more
and more is known, until the maps resemble less a primitive
rock painting than the surface of a brain.

II

In one of the drawings of a Dutch artist whose work I have
long admired, files of human figures are moving in opposite
directions on a staircase. If we follow either line – the one
going up, or the one going down – we find that, although the
figures never reverse direction, and although the stairway
continues to rise in front of the one set and descend before
the other, the head of each line meets its tail, the four turns in
the stairway having formed a square in which, although there
is a strictly limited number of steps, there is one flight perpetually rising, another forever going down. Both flights are
the same flight. We call this an Optical Illusion, which is our
way of denying that somewhere this place, this same set of
stairs, exists.

This denial, this shutting of the gates, is perhaps just as

well, for if it were possible that this staircase existed in space, it would have – since all ascents and descents take some period to accomplish – to exist in time also. It would then be possible that, just as the figures perpetually climb or descend, yet perpetually meet the tail of their own line, so time passes and yet never advances, and that, as it both advances and fails to advance – as it moves forward only to repeat itself – so there is alongside it a time scale that perpetually 'regresses', perpetually repeats itself, another temporal zone, moving in a direction opposite to our own.

In Canada, working on a thesis through the steaming summer, I would turn from a dull passage in some academic text, and look out from my second-storey window, and there would be the leaves of the chestnut, with the tunnels along the branches, the secret passages. Then, as sometimes even now. I would imagine myself entering, penetrating even further than before. And what if, now, today, I should do that, should go down one of the corridors, follow it through all the turnings and the bough-lanes? Would I find myself, my earlier self, the young child in his ash world, or the student in a hot Toronto summer? Would he know me? Would he understand me? Would I believe what he had to say?

Is this inconceivable? I don't think so, for surely human life itself is so to any other creature, its extravagance and its wonder so great that few of us ever get out, or wish to, from under its perplexing shadow, but instead spend all our days numb to its true dimensions, so afraid of the hugeness, the strangeness revealed by every wayward step, that we have long ceased to take such steps and in preference pass the time until our end in the drawing of closer barriers, the erection of walls, as if each new word were a wolf, each strange thought or angle of perception a barbarian on a thunderous horse, bearing down upon us, his spear already launched.

No. Nothing is inconceivable. Life itself is so unlikely that our very presence denies the privilege of denial. If our time is a thing that moves 'forward', if 'distance' is a thing that separates, if 'reality' is distinguishable from 'dream', if human consciousness is, as I sometimes suspect, a flickering circle of light about a dark, bewildered centre, these are only our terms, our language, the small salvage of the bewildered from the incomprehensible, and may, as yet, be like the myths that supposed primitives have evolved to explain their universe: that the moon is an ancient hag chasing her wayward son, that the stars are the sand flung up behind her. And who is to say that the very extravagance of the human imagination, pedestrian as it might seem to a greater eye, is not another 'reality' beckoning, as a child lures a pony with sugar, or a dog is thrown scraps from a table? An explorer's dog – John Gilbert's, say, or Watkin Tench's – gnawing at the shin-bone of a beast he's never seen before.

III

This early evening there is a cool breeze through the coral trees. I can detect the faint, almost-imperceptible scent of the jacaranda that at the end of the yard is coating the gravel with its lilac blooms, and from behind me there comes the drier earthen smell of potatoes baking. I am sipping hot tea and thinking of the beauty of objects in this cool grey light that has in it the first faint touch of darkness. It is the artist's light, the light of still life. From my balcony every shade of the leaves' green is discrete and the trees are wholly at home in their bodies, as if they, too, need the first hint of death in their senses to live truly. In my small flat, with my busyness, my debts, I would call this moment one of luxury, my balcony in its green cathedral, the smell of the potatoes baking, the birds beginning to sing – three different sounds already – and every object distinct.

A man is whistling as he zigzags up the stairs of the building opposite, and an Indian woman in a red top and bright orange sari pauses on the landing to call to someone I cannot see. She is a splash of rich colour through the leaves. Moments like these – so particular, and yet almost without identity – seem as if suspended between worlds. One could be nowhere but here, and yet here could be anywhere: in Australia, in Brazil, in California, in India. The woman standing on the stair is unaware that she is poised upon a border, that she has just stepped very nearly out of time and